To

Ingrid

They moved my Bowl

Fifth Revised, Expanded Edition, 2012
Fourth Limited Edition, 2010
Third Edition, 1994
Second Edition, 1985
First Printing, February 1982

Library of Congress Catalog Card Number: 62-90110
ISBN 978-0-9608798-2-3

Published by
D.B.C
PO Box 246, Elberta AL
United States of America

MAN'S BEST FRIEND

The one absolutely unselfish friend that man can have in this selfish world, the one that never deserts him, the one that never proves ungrateful or treacherous, is his dog.

A man's dog stands by him in prosperity and in poverty, in health and in sickness. He will sleep on the cold ground where the wintry winds blow and snow drives fiercely, if only he may be near his master's side. He will kiss the hand that has no food to offer. He guards the sleep of his pauper master as if he were a prince. When all other friends desert he remains. When riches take wings and reputation falls to pieces he is as constant in his love as the sun in its journey through the heavens.

If fortune drives the master forth an outcast in the world, friendless and homeless, the faithful dog asks no higher privilege than that of accompanying him to guard against danger, to fight against his enemies; and when the last scene of all comes, and death takes the master in its embrace and his body is laid away in the cold ground, no matter if all other friends pursue their way, there, by his grave side, will the noble dog be found, his head between his paws, his eyes sad but open in alert watchfulness, faithful and true even to death.

Senator George Graham Vest (1830-1904)

ACKNOWLEDGMENTS

A vast number of people have, knowingly or unknowingly, helped in gathering the information presented in this book. While it is impossible to list all names, their contributions are acknowledged with gratitude.

I am indebted to the many authorities on canine matters, here and abroad, who have shared their knowledge with me; to the numerous dog trainers who have worked with me on various projects; to the large number of people and groups who have given me a chance to help them with their training and to learn from their problems; and to all the correspondents, clients and friends who have consulted with me and who have encouraged me to write this book.

A special "thank you", however, goes to the ones who started it all: my dogs

> Anka von Berg, SchH II, CDX
> Asta (Waldeslust's Jetta)
> Brika von Berg, SchH III, CDX
> Catja von Berg, SchH II, CD
> Dina von Berg.

The official Seal of
WORKING DOGS OF AMERICA, INC. (WDA)

Starting with the top position, going clockwise and ending in the center, the eight major recognized working dog breeds are: Hovawart, Boxer, Bouvier des Flandres, Giant Schnauzer, Rottweiler, Doberman, Airedale, German Shepherd Dog.

A DOG WILL READILY, AND HAPPILY, COMPLY WITH ANY REASONABLE REQUEST, HE USUALLY KNOWS ALREADY HOW TO DO IT.

THE TRAINER, HOWEVER, MUST FORMULATE THE REQUEST IN A MANNER THAT IS UNDERSTOOD BY THE DOG.

DOG TRAINING IN A NUTSHELL

1. Kindness, Patience, Persistence, and Common Sense are the credentials of a good dog trainer.

2. Your voice is the most elegant, the most effective, and the always present training tool.
    Even a threat can be whispered, your dog has a very fine sense of hearing.

3. Never demand compliance if you are not in a position to enforce it (except for emergencies).
    "Down", "down", "down", "down" ..... just teaches your dog to ignore you (and you look like a fool).

4. Never repeat a command more then once, after that make him do it
                                        (provided your dog is familiar with the command).

5. Once your dog has learned a routine, use my "1-2-3-4 Rule":
    One: give the command
    Two: see what your dog does
    Three: praise, or redress/correct and then praise him, depending on his response
    Four: praise him some more.

6. There are two, and only two, orders that the dog must obey expediently, no matter what, where, when, and how. They are: "down"   and   "out"   (=release the grip / bite).

7. Use common sense when following the advice of Dog Trainers, Dog Experts and Dog Whisperers. They do not have to be licensed, and all those fancy titles, diplomas, credentials, certificates, trophies just proof that the candidate has spent enough money to acquire them. Several highly publicized and popular series on national and international TV networks, and many Internet websites, are great examples of cleverly marketing insignificant individuals as "authorities".

Follow these guidelines and you will not have to read this book or any other one.
As I see it, a good instructor knows all the shortcuts which can make your job much easier,
but you do not really need a coach.

PS: If you are looking for an introduction to Schutzhund,
you might want to start with
"Schutzhunding", page 150.

"Schutzhunding", page 150.

PREFACE TO THE FIFTH EDITION

Colonel Konrad Most, a Police Commissioner at the Royal Prussian Police Headquarters, was one of the first behaviorists to describe in detail dog training procedures, and to apply them on a large scale to the instruction of service dogs. Even today his book "Die Abrichtung des Hundes", published in 1910, is considered by many to be an authoritative source for canine training.

"Top Working Dogs", since 1982, has built on the Colonel's foundations, aligning them with advances in the fields of technology, science and psychology. Thirty years later, with its Fifth Edition, "Top Working Dogs" presents a timely update of Most's efforts, combining practice and theory, technique and terminology, experience and common sense. Numerous dog breed and training clubs throughout the world, owners of working dogs, breeders, handlers, trainers, instructors, judges, veterinarians, researchers, scientists and pacesetters have contributed to the information that we present here in useful form. You would have to pick bits and pieces from thousands of websites and hundreds of books, DVD's, seminars and lectures on the subject to find what we give you here - and you would still come up short by many miles.   Proof?   When "TWD" was in short supply, copies were sold on E-bay for several thousand dollars each (check it out, it's true !).

The 5th Edition has been completely revised and considerably expanded. New sections have been added, some chapters have been condensed, others enlarged, reorganized and updated with the latest information available. Newcomers to the sport will enjoy the chapter "Schutzhunding", and the larger print will surely please many readers.

"TWD" is truly a Training Manual, and world-wide it is still the only complete guide for the training of the various kinds of working/service dogs, competition dogs (AKC/CKC, Ring Sport to a large degree), Police dogs and Schutzhund dogs. Novices and experts, even owners of small breeds, can find valuable information here. If you are looking for a book with pretty pictures you must search elsewhere, but aside from that you and your dog will enjoy this book for many years to come.

Much of the writing and editing of "TOP WORKING DOGS" took place in Tahiti, Haiti, Turkey, Italy, France, Germany and the USA. To these countries goes a "honorable mention" for the inspiration and the support we found there.

Prof.Dr.rer.nat.Dr.phil.Dietmar Schellenberg

Excerpts from the Preface to the Forth Edition:
...... The increased interest in the Schutzhund sport worldwide, and the remarkable success of American participants, have prompted us to re-visit training techniques and methods. We have included in this Limited Forth Edition new ideas and refinements not described before. As stated in earlier editions, the use of electronic gadgets as short-cuts does not find our approval and is not covered.

Excerpts from the Preface to the Third Edition:
...... With a very large number of copies sold, only one was ever returned. Readers and reviewers rave about the book and the results obtained with its help. They tell us that TOP WORKING DOGS gives them the most complete, the most comprehensive, the most detailed, the most useful and the most easily to follow instructions. They say that TOP WORKING DOGS describes many valuable training techniques which can not be found anywhere else. And they like TOP WORKING DOGS' extensive coverage of problem recognition and resolution.

Excerpts from the Preface to the Second Edition:
...... "TOP WORKING DOGS" seems to have filled a void - judging by the demand for it, and by the positive feedback we have received. Press reviews and reader comments were complimentary, without exception.
.... Reader response played an important role in this process, and we continue to invite your comments.

Excerpts from the Preface to the First Edition:
...... Successful Schutzhund trainers are typically reluctant to share their secrets. As a result, the majority of the few books available on the subject concentrate on explaining trial routines and on the instruction of adult dogs via force training. " TOP WORKING DOGS " , the manual for the training of working dogs in tracking, obedience and protection work, is novel and unique in several ways:
- it aids the trainer in using psychological principles, by giving descriptions and explanations,
- it presents in detail the methods used by experts not usually revealed,
- it offers a multitude of approaches for the individual routines,
- it lists the problems most often encountered, and it suggests a variety of remedies,
- it focuses on the general components of working dog training which can readily be applied to specific situations,
- it stresses and explains playful instruction of the young dog.

The ultimate goal of this book is to make the man/dog relationship more meaningful, and more enjoyable, for both partners.

D. Schellenberg,   February 1982

CONTENTS

I. THE OBJECTIVE

A. WORK FOR WORKING DOGS

Since the early days of domestication about 30,000 years ago (Reference: Mietje Germonpré; Archeaological Studies at Goyet Cave / Belgium), dogs had to earn their keep. To be useful they had to be taught, and dog training, therefore, can be considered one of the oldest skills of mankind. Methods and approaches have changed, usually in tune with progress in the field of psychology, yet many of the ancient training procedures still have some application today.

Advances in science and technology curtailed tasks that dogs had handled with excellence in the past. However, there are a few areas where canines still outperform even the most sophisticated equipment, such as nose work, guarding, or protecting. "Job openings", unfortunately, are extremely rare, and today most working canines are owned by dog fanciers. "Unemployed" and living on "welfare", their providers usually forget that in addition to food and care, engagement in a meaningful activity is necessary to maintain physical and mental health. Just look at our human societies, they collapse because of the very same neglect.

Owning a working dog involves a moral obligation to provide some meaningful activity for the canine. Joining the police force or starting a herd of sheep is usually out of the question, but we can train for competition or for enjoyment. The most universal program available, the one that is the foundation of all the other ones (sled dogs, water dogs, hunting dogs, herding dogs, service dogs, Search and Rescue dogs, military dogs, police dogs, etc.) is known worldwide by the name of Schutzhund ("Protection Dog"; German). Schutzhund combines tracking, obedience and protection work. Training is versatile, challenging, enjoyable, it provides physical and mental exercise for both handler and dog, and it can be done in very small groups of participants. Training locations are generally available, time requirements are reasonable, and benefits even for the average dog owner, like control, are obvious.

To meet an ever-growing demand, some breeders betray the characteristic temperament traits of working dogs, cranking out "lap dogs in Doberman suits". Many of today's behavior problems are the direct result of this irresponsible breed manipulation. There is no such thing as a "Pet Shepherd" that will not bark, growl, or even bite, when provoked.

IF SOMEONE LIKES THE LOOKS OF THE WORKING BREEDS BUT NOT THEIR WORKING TEMPERAMENT, THEN HE SHOULD BUY A STATUE.

B. SCHUTZHUND VS. ATTACK DOG

People often confuse Schutzhund with Guard / Attack Dog, but there is a crucial difference: the attack dog trainer uses the survival instinct ("fear death"), while the Schutzhund trainer relies on the prey and the pack instinct ("love life").

The attack/guard dog must regard ALL humans (except his care taker) as enemies. In training, he is being prevented from escaping and then, in the absence of his master, threatened, scared, beaten, abused until he sees no way to survive but to bite whoever and whatever gets close enough to him. The dog comes to realize that he has no friend but his master who cares for and feeds him. The dog has come to hate mankind.

What a contrast to the Schutzhund dog ! He is trained with love, not hatred. He takes his cues to be protective from the hostile BEHAVIOR, not the mere PRESENCE of a person. In a Schutzhund trial, for instance, the dog is sent about 100 yards after a fleeing "criminal". He will go straight for the villain and fight him enthusiastically but ignore the judge or close-by spectators. Right afterwards, we can leave him all by himself with a group of children or adults and he will not threaten or bother anybody.

People often give our four-legged friends much less credit than they deserve. Even the authors of a popular American Schutzhund book claim - wrongfully - that "dogs, well trained or not, simply do not possess the capacity to safely and reliably judge when and whom they should bite, and when not". Such a statement is irresponsible as well as ignorant of every bit of evidence available on the aggression/defense subject. Excluding the attack/guard dogs mentioned above, **aggression** against humans involves either mentally or physically ill animals, or dogs that were provoked, abused or improperly trained. At fault are the dog's owners/keepers, not the ability of canines to make the right decision. **Defensive behavior**, though, must not be confused with aggression. It is an appropriate and justifiable response to hostility forced upon the animal.

Dogs are smarter than people in many ways. They will, for instance, not kill each other for a prized possession. Any normal dog in private hands which was kept and/or trained in a sensible way will intuitively make a sensible decision, as far as biting is involved. The initial response might be spontaneous, but there is a natural barrier, an inhibition, before the dog inflicts any harm. For example:

a) In the Schutzhund courage test, the dog will bite the bad guy who runs toward him and threatens him with a raised stick.

b) At some other time, a happy little boy with a stick runs toward the very same dog - no problem. The dog may approach, bark for the stick, jump up, sniff, circle or even bump into the kid by accident, but since there is no hostility apparent he will not bite. His handler can easily recall him without any harm done to the child. The untrained dog, on the other hand, is facing a novel situation and has not learned to obey his master. He is less predictable, less controllable, and therefore much more dangerous. Schutzhund dogs are well behaved, happy, friendly yet alert, controllable family dogs that become an asset, and not a nuisance, or even a danger, to society.

At a fox hunt, one female hound is permitted to join the all-male pack. The dogs disappear in a hurry. The confused hunters question a farmer standing on the roadside: "Did you see a pack of dogs running past here?" "Sure did!" "Where did they go?" "Dunno, but that's the first time I ever saw a fox chasing hounds!"

II. THE PLAYERS

A. THE IDEAL HANDLER

A large number of police officers volunteering for duty with a canine unit are being rejected since working with those dogs requires an intrinsic disposition that many people do not have. However, anyone who is determined to train a dog can attain a certain proficiency. Taking an intelligent approach, investing time and effort, and soliciting the help of experts may indeed lead to outstanding results. Some people will have to work very hard, others do it effortlessly if they have that certain flair for working with animals, and for teaching. Of course, ill-tempered, reckless, cruel, impatient people, or drug and alcohol addicts, should never own a dog.

Based on personality and motivation, most handlers fit one of the following categories:

♦The true **COMPETITOR,** a sportsman, is interested in improving his performance and in comparing it with others. He works systematically and diligently, and he remains objective. The dog, his partner, receives proper attention and care. Suggestions offered to him are scrutinized and implemented if meaningful. In the long run, only talented, gifted dog handlers will remain in this category.

♦The **TROPHY HUNTER.** His primary goal is not the training by itself but the reward, the trophy, the certificate or the recognition for successful trial competition. He will accept advice only if it guarantees better trial performance.

The professional trainer may belong to this group.

♦The **FITNESS TYPE** got into dog training because he considers it to be a meaningful alternative to jogging (etc.) and he happened to have a suitable dog. He is easy-going and will casually follow up on suggestions. Competition is of lesser importance to him.

♦The **DOG LOVER** realizes that his dog enjoys training. Anthropomorphism, or relating to the dog by human standards, leads him to reject many valuable training suggestions. A considerate trainer has the best chance to work with such a person. Trial performances, nevertheless, may be marginal.

♦The **DOG BREEDER** wants to prove to the world that his bloodlines are top quality.

Because of an intimate knowledge of his animals, he can accomplish tasks that others had considered impossible. He is open to suggestions and willing to experiment with training recommendations, if they fit.

♦ The **DOG KEEPER** supports the idea of the service dog, he may even work with such an agency. For him, dog training is a means to accomplish certain tasks with the help of the dog, and he will modify the concept to suit his purpose.

♦ The **ALTRUIST**'s goals are beyond personal achievement, he is the guardian of dogdom. Insisting on true and proper motivation, and demanding unconditional reliability and serviceability, he maintains that dogs can keep their place in society only by serving mankind.

♦ The **MILLIONAIRE** typically starts out as a novice, but with an expensive, fully trained and titled dog - usually imported from overseas. He travels with his dog extensively and demands top honors everywhere because the "Advanced-Schutzhund" experts have assured him "you just need to learn to signal the dog and properly command him". Objective judges and trainers are often not welcome, on occasion they are even met with hostility.

♦ The **POLITICIAN** is a smooth-talking con-artist. He promises change, like Heaven on Earth, but delivers Hell instead. Once elected, you can not get rid of him. He pays back those whose money got him into office, for favors he appoints his "experts", and together they enforce radical ideas and miasmal concepts, routinely subjecting dogs to paralyzing, even inhumane, restraints. He is blissfully ignorant, clue-less, incompetent, reckless, unscrupulous, dishonest, selfish and greedy. He begs, borrows and steals the club's and all of the members' treasures, claims it is in your own best interest, but freely spends the money to further his own goals. You don't want a person like that in your club. Trust me.

♦ The **WARRIOR** uses his dog as a weapon, often to compensate for his (perceived) own inferiority.

Unless there is definite hope to remodel this person's thinking, he should be removed from training tactfully. Dogs owned by such persons are taught to attack on command, even when the situation does not warrant it. Since the hostility is directed toward unsuspecting people, the image of the dog sport is discredited.

Everything considered, one should be looking for these qualities in a good handler: a well balanced mixture of gentleness and firmness, patience, tolerance, empathy, adaptability, consis- tency, persistence, authority, open-mindedness, common sense, cooperation, willingness to learn and to share.

You got 'em all? Terrific!

B. SELECTION OF A SUITABLE CANINE

1. HEREDITY and ENVIRONMENT

A dog's physical and mental characteristics are determined by heredity and environment. Heredity provides the raw block from which the owner / trainer shapes the final product by manipulating the environment.

Both factors must be considered when trying to find the most promising dog for Schutzhund training. It is unreasonable, even irresponsible, to dismiss a dog just because he does not bite well on the first try-out (as suggested by the authors of a popular American Schutzhund book). To bite a human full-force is not an innate action of a normal dog but a skill that must be developed and refined, and the better trainer will end up with the better dog. Of course, it is much easier to blame the breeder, junk the dog and get another one. But can we really justify a "cash for clunkers" (USA, 2010) approach, trading in solid value for promised, but paltry, benefits? I too want to start out with the most promising candidate. But I also accept the challenge and the responsibility to develop my dog's capabilities to the fullest extend.

Here is some more food for thought: Out of the millions of young, healthy, normal working dogs in the whole world, just three or four (ok, maybe six or seven) would bite the decoy's sleeve full force without training. YOUR chance of getting one of these dogs is practically zero. If you believe the "experts" (who will not tell you their training secrets) and reject all but the perfect candidate, then you have fallen for their trap: one less rival for them to worry about.

2. DRIVES

Manipulating the heredity factor through selective breeding, man has propagated and improved upon desirable, inherent characteristics of working dogs. If we look at natural instincts, inborn/innate responses, primal urges and motivators, then certain characteristics are particularly important to the Schutzhund fancier: the pack, survival and retrieve instinct, the prey, play, defense, fighting, protection drive, courage, perseverance and hardness. The German SV (Shepherd Dog Club) for instance has adopted a rigidly controlled breeding program. Only those dogs with pronounced desirable traits are sanctioned to propagate. The outstanding specimen of the SV-German Shepherd Dogs are the envy of the world.

Talking "drives" has become fashionable lingo. You must "see that he has the right drives", "read his drive", "build drive", "get his drives going", "turn up his drive", "get him into high drive". If you don't, the "Schutzhund Experts" will declare you incompetent (Americans just love to "drive").

3. BREEDS

For training purposes, for service duty, and even for most competitions, working dogs do not have to be pedigreed. When buying a puppy, however, purebreds offer the advantage to predict fairly accurately the basic physical and mental characteristics of the adult dog, which in turn can be passed on to the offspring.

GERMAN SHEPHERD DOG

(Deutscher Schäferhund) (originally used for herding sheep - Max von Stephanitz, a German, is the founder of the breed) Intelligence, alertness, courage, willingness, endurance, easy trainability and devotion to his master, as well as his all-weather coat and low demands on food and housing have made the GSD the "Number One Dog" for private persons and for dog-employing agencies. It is said that the German Shepherd Dog is not best in anything, but second-best in everything.

BOXER   (the name refers to the head form)

This powerful, energetic and courageous dog has a somewhat difficult behavior pattern, and he is a slow learner. He compensates, however, with devotion and gentleness towards his master.

AIREDALE TERRIER

(the breed originated in the Aire Valley in England) This dog is easily trainable but needs much exercise and grooming. He is inquisitive and full of temperament, dependable and unafraid.

GIANT SCHNAUZER

(German: Schnauze = snout, Schnauzer = beard) He is eager to learn but needs much exercise and grooming. He is sturdy, prudent, self-conscious, full of temperament, sometimes even a daredevil.

DOBERMAN (designer Karl Doberman, a German)

Hardly any other breed is as devoted and loyal to his master as a Doberman. He is alert, smart, eager, quick to learn and willing to work, and he has fast reflexes and a lively temperament. He needs much exercise and attention and does not adapt easily to inclement weather.

ROTTWEILER (from the town of Rottweil/Germany)

He is a sound working dog, originally used for herding cattle. Power, persistence, endurance, alertness and willingness give this breed its distinction.

HOVAWART (Old-German: 'guardian of the farm')

This breed is rarely found outside of Germany. The dogs have a certain resemblance to a Golden Retriever, and they are alert, courageous, protective and easily trainable.

BOUVIER DES FLANDRES

(the breed originated in Flandres/Belgium) Bouviers were originally used to herd cattle. They are strong-willed and strong-muscled, lively, courageous and loyal working dogs.

OTHER BREEDS

Working dog training is open to dogs of all breeds, and mixed breeds if they can handle the job. This was also true for Schutzhund competitions where the dog was required to be of sufficient size to clear the 40 inch hurdle, and to have enough power to do effective protection work. These requirements excluded all small breeds from competition, yet very large breeds were discouraged also. A Great Dane, for instance, is too powerful a dog so that even the police have abandoned earlier attempts to employ very large breeds. To Schutzhund training the same reasoning applies.

Under pressure from breed clubs, some European countries now restrict participation in Schutzhund trials to dogs of 13 breeds (this changes periodically). Before, there were eight officially recognized groups of service dogs, and they are still in the majority: German Shepherd Dogs, Dobermans, Rottweilers, Boxers, Airedales, Giant Schnauzers, Hovawarts and Bouvier des Flandres. GSD's outnumber all others. Bauceron, Lakenois, Tervuren, Malinois and Groenendael have now been added. Of those, Malinois have significantly gained in popularity in the last few years.

There are many others who also participate in Schutzhund training, like: Anatolian Shepherd Dog, Australian Shepherd Dog, Briard, Bulldog(var.), Bullmastiff (var.), Collie, Dalmatian, Great Dane, Great Pyrenees, Herding Dogs(var), Hounds(var.), Husky, Komodor, Kuvasz, Malamute, Mastiff(var.), Newfoundland, Puli, Picardie, Pointer(var.), Poodle, Retriever(var.), Samoyed, Setter(var.), Terrier(var.), Viszla, Weimaraner.

These, and other breeds, may also be allowed to participate in national and international competitions, depending on the country, the host club, the registration papers, FCI Rules, etc.

4. FUNCTIONAL COMPATIBILITY

While there are notable exceptions, many of the dogs that are not officially recognized as service-dog breeds have difficulties meeting the requirements for advanced working dog training, like Schutzhund, UD and TDX. Bred to serve mankind in other capacities, their particular size, weight, agility, temperament, protective instinct, fighting drive etc. make them less successful.

However, if the handler of such a dog is more interested in training than in official recognition, if he is willing to accept the additional workload required to train his particular dog, if he wants to play by rules that were developed for other breeds, and if he also realizes that for him, outstanding trial performances are more difficult to obtain, then he should not be discouraged. He and his dog will greatly benefit from participating in this training, and with a patient, knowledgeable, versatile and understanding instructor, such a person often becomes one of the most reliable and loyal club members.

Regardless of the breed, it may also be necessary to withdraw a dog from training for temperament deficiencies, structural faults such as overangulation, illnesses such as arthritis, hereditary problems like hip dysplasia and other physical impairments. Mental illness is rare in dogs and it hardly needs to be mentioned.

5. PHYSICAL COMPATIBILITY

Since training is a team effort, the partners must be compatible.

A little girl handling a powerful male Rottweiler, for instance, might look cute. Rarely, however, will such a combination be a happy and successful one. By the same token: A husky, bold-type construction worker will probably not do too well with a sensitive Airedale bitch.

The handler's age, sex, bodily strength, health, physical and mental capabilities, etc. should all be considered when selecting a dog for the sport. This is not to say that only perfect dog/handler combinations should be allowed to participate. The handler must understand, however, that anything but the ideal not only requires additional efforts but also stacks the odds against him for doing well in competitions.

The young girl, for instance, can be taught to manipulate expressions of her mood, to employ exaggerated voice control, to skillfully use her bodily strength or to refer to tools not normally recommended for training (prong collar, double leash etc.). The roughneck, on the other hand, must learn to restrain himself, to be more responsive, more considerate and more gentle than ever before.

Situations like these usually require the involvement of an experienced instructor. Under his guidance, problems can be detected and addressed more easily. In time, the serious handler will acknowledge the shortcomings of his animal and look for a more suitable dog.

6. PSYCHOLOGICAL COMPATIBILITY

For a well functioning dog/handler team, not only the bodies, but also the minds of the two partners must be compatible. A phlegmatic person is bound to be very unhappy with a hyperactive Doberman, and so will be an agile, snappy handler with a lethargic Boxer.

Breeds of working dogs differ in their general temperamental make-up, and the breed standard is often a valuable guide when selecting a team mate. Nevertheless, even within one breed we find a wide variety of different character traits. Many handlers with preference for a particular breed can be accommodated if enough effort is spent on finding a suitable animal. Fortunately, though, people seem to instinctively select the dog that suits their personalities. The keen observer will often find a striking resemblance in appearance and behavior of a dog and his master, provided a close relationship exists between the two partners.

7. TEMPERAMENT TESTING

The Roman: " A sound mind in a sound body " and Von Stephanitz's: "Function is beauty" both emphasize the interdependence of physical structure and temperament. Temperament, defined as "the manner of thinking, behaving and reacting, characteristic of a specific individual" is a combination of inherited character traits and learned behavior.

A **HANDLER** is concerned with this combination as displayed by his dog. To him, a temperament test merely means taking inventory. Since he knows his dog intimately, formal procedures to determine temperament traits are not even needed.

A **BREEDER**, or a **BUYER** of a young puppy, however, needs to separate the learned behavior from the inherited character traits. The buyer wants to predict what the mature dog will be like, the breeder needs to know what kind of offspring a dog or a bitch can produce. This group seeks objective tests to classify their dog's inherent temperament characteristics.

Several American temperament testing organizations award passing or failing grades for dogs regardless of breed, based on **one** standardized test. This is naive since breeds differ in their temperament requirements. A better approach would be to judge each dog on its suitability to serve in certain capacities, for instance as

- good breed specimen (for temperament)
- stud dog / brood bitch (for temperament)
- companion dog
- Search & Rescue dog
- herding dog
- draft dog
- guide dog
- pet
- guard dog
- alarm dog
- Schutzhund
- police dog, etc.

Test situations should be varied or unique, and unpredictable in nature, to owner and dog. They must not cause physical or mental harm to the dog, and they should not be scheduled during transitory critical developmental phases (for instance the fourth, seventh and eighth week in a puppies life).

EVALUATION

A dog can be tested in familiar and in unfamiliar/ strange surroundings, with and without his pack members, and in the presence and in the absence of his owner. Observe his response to, and recovery from, novel and familiar stimuli, neutral, pleasant and unpleasant experiences, and subtle or gross changes in the environment.

Conducting such tests is not without risk. A thoughtless person in search of a new dog can do great harm to a dog that would be an excellent choice for certain other owners. If, for instance, a dog appears to be shy and soft, then there is no justification for conducting the "Henze Courage Test" (see below).

Some of the temperament traits that will become apparent during testing are:

energy	loyalty
initiative	affection
persistence	discrimination
intelligence	curiosity
willingness	rapport
responsiveness	alertness
attentiveness	body sensitivity
tractability	ear sensitivity
trainability	nose ability

competitiveness	shyness
wildness / tameness	fear
submissiveness/dominance	sharpness
stability	fighting drive
trust	aggressiveness
confidence	protective instinct
self-confidence	courage
self-right (sovereignty)	hardness, etc.

The relative weight of each of these factors will vary, depending on dog, people, situations, et al. The observer must make sure, though, that test results are consistent. Additional probing will be needed if, for instance, the self-opening umbrella and a flag flapping in the wind produce contradictory responses.

Past experiences or earlier training will influence the behavior of a dog. The reaction to gun shots, for instance, will be different for a (police) dog trained to bite the weapon arm, for a hunting dog, for a pet, and for a dog that has never experienced such loud noises before. Only the last dog will display his true temperament. The other three will do whatever their owners have trained them to do (otherwise they would not keep them), although the way HOW they respond provides a wealth of information.

There are two practical ways to exclude learned behavior: to test only very young or unconditioned dogs, or to devise test situations that are novel and unfamiliar to dog and handler. The first option has limited applications, the second requires an extremely large repertoire of tests. Neither one guarantees complete elimination of learned behavior, however.

Listed below is a compilation of suggestions for test conditions. The stimuli shown are representative of tests described in the literature, but there is no general agreement on classifying the results because of an inherent complexity, delicacy and dependence on variables difficult to control.

Recently published methods use a numerical approach for rating predetermined responses to specific test conditions, then they try to find prevailing grades. The assignment of numbers (1-10) is based on the movement or cooperation of the dog (forward, remaining, backward), on the way how he behaves (confident, hesitant, afraid), on body language (eyes, lips, teeth, ears, tail, head carriage, fur raised or flat, etc.) and on other incidental observations. Important is not only the first, initial response of a dog to a new stimulus, but also how, and how quickly, he recovers from any surprise effect.

A more practical variation of the above concept uses the following scale for rating each one of the test conditions listed later on:

insecure	undecided	confident
uncooperative	indifferent	cooperative
(negative resp.)	(no response)	(positive resp.)
- 2 - 1	0	+ 1 + 2

EXPLANATION:

0 The dog acknowledges the stimulus but does not act on it. He is neutral, undecided, and he reserves judgment, waiting for further developments.

-2 The dog is overwhelmed, in a negative sense. He is uneasy, insecure, suspicious, afraid, uncooperative. He may retreat, observe the challenge(r) out of the corner of his eyes, lower his head, lay the ears flat, tuck his tail between the legs, and in some situations he may raise his fur, curl his lips, show his teeth, growl, snarl and bite, as a last resort.

+2 The dog accepts the new situation as another exciting part of life. He is content, confident, sure of himself, trustful, unafraid, uninhibited, inquisitive, cooperative, he advances to check out the stimulus or to face the challenge. He looks straight ahead, carries head and ears erect (depending on the breed), and his tail is wagging or up.

The +2 classification is not always the most desirable score. In confrontations with other dogs, for instance, the +2 rating shows a potential for dog fights, a +2 rating for olfactory acuity disqualifies the dog from the Seeing Eye program, the +2 rating in the Henze Courage Test spells trouble for an insecure owner, a +2 rating for having the teeth checked by a stranger identifies low potential for Schutzhund training, etc.

We suggest to compile a list of the various temperament traits (see previous page), and to enter the rating for each as testing progresses. The completed chart will then aid in determining the suitability of a given dog for a given home or working environment (see also under "RESULTS", below).

TESTS

ACTION

The DOG INITIATES the action while the tester remains a passive observer.

Select a fair size, confined area, and spread around a few novel objects, like

> rubber and wooden toys
> a wet sponge
> paper bag, cardboard box
> a bucket
> a small ball, a large ball
> a large, flat box
> a balloon
> a piece of cloth, plastic, aluminum foil
> a broom
> a knuckle bone (reserve this one for inactive dogs)
> a mechanical toy (activated)
> a few empty tin cans stacked on end, with a piece of meat hidden under the bottom can,
> a chime (hanging low),   etc.

Then the dog is, or several dogs are, admitted to the test area and given ample time to adjust and to investigate. The tester remains passive and takes notes.

The test should be repeated at some other time, with other objects.

Questions that arise, and character traits to which they relate, are:

Does the dog do something right away? (initiative)

What does he do ? (discrimination, shyness, fear)

How does he do it ? (intelligence)

How involved does he get ? (intensity)

How much effort does he spend in pursuing this activity ? (vigor, persistence)

Does he pursue in spite of obstacles ? (determination, stamina)

Does he pursue in spite of competitors ? (self-confident, competitive, shy, aggressive)

Is he startled easily ? (fear),

Does he recover quickly ? (self-confidence)

REACTION

In this group of tests the DOG IS CHALLENGED, either by the tester, or through his efforts, and he has to respond. Reactions are responses to novel or familiar stimuli that have been perceived by an organism via its five senses:

smell, taste, hearing, sight, touch.

Some conclusions on the intelligence of an animal, how discriminate, how confident, and how content it is, can be drawn from its reactions to taste and smell stimuli. A much heavier emphasis, however, must be placed on responses to stimuli that relate to hearing, sight and touch. They show best how much the individual dog has adjusted to domestication, how well he is suited to live in a human pack under often quite unnatural conditions, and how well he can serve mankind in the many different fields of engagement.

Smell: Small, secure containers with vent holes or wire cages can be used to test the reaction to the odor of: ammonia

> meat
>
> vinegar
>
> a small live animal (mouse, rabbit, gerbil)
>
> laundry bleach
>
> a piece of clothing worn (and thereby scented) by his owner
>
> freshly cut garlic or onions
>
> a piece of clothing worn (and thereby scented) by a stranger
>
> fresh or decaying fish   etc.

Taste: Small samples can be placed within reach of the dog or offered to him, like

> a raw piece of meat
>
> a small piece of a plastic meat wrapper
>
> a rubber tire with cooking grease
> > splashed on it
>
> a vegetable / fruit
>
> a block of salt
>
> a small sample of a straight alcoholic drink
>
> carbonated (bubbling) water   etc.

Hearing:

> a) familiar sounds
> > handler's voice
> >
> > food bowl handling
> >
> > barking of another dog
> >
> > car / bus / train / airplane
>
> b) unfamiliar sounds
> > tape recorder with prerecorded noises, large metal sheet to imitate thunder, tin can clatter, gun shots, fire crackers, siren, bells, whistle, exotic car horns, music box, musical instruments (drums).

Sight:

a) familiar things

> his master, food bowl, leash, toy, cat

b) unfamiliar things

> mechanical toys
>
> remote-controlled toy animals
>
> self-opening umbrella / life vest
>
> water sprinkler (erratically operated), camp fire
>
> strange dog / strange person
>
> person grotesquely dressed, or acting like a drunk

during a night excursion, the surprise by:

> - a scare crow
> - a bright light (flashlight, car headlights)

- a bed sheet, lowered from above into the path of the dog

Touch:

a) familiar (done by, or with, the owner):

> stroking, praise, correction, heeling, lifting / carrying the dog, checking teeth, clipping toe nails, administering medicine (small food pellets as a pill, water as liquid medicine)

b) unfamiliar (done by a stranger):

> same as "familiar" above

Combinations

a) Obstacles (this addresses temperament traits related to hearing, sight and touch)

- steep incline or decline in terrain
- walking on various surfaces: gravel, wood, metal, plastic, water (very large, shallow puddle), sand, mud, ice (if available),
- various jumps (easy, low heights or widths),
- stairs, ladder, seesaw,
- log walking, plank walking (flat or inclined, 1 and 5 ft. above ground),
- small room (enter a tiny closet with the dog),
- elevator, escalator, revolving door,
- wheelbarrow ride, bus / streetcar ride,
- recall through a group of 10 - 20 people,
- stepping or jumping over another dog, or over a person lying flat on the ground.

b) Friendly Challenges (this addresses temperament traits related to hearing, sight and touch)

- one passive stranger, motionless, or moving around but not paying attention to the dog
- several passive strangers, motionless, or moving around and engaged
- a friendly stranger, playing with, praising, handling the dog (tug-of-war, ball, stick)

c) Hostile Challenges (relate to hearing, sight, touch, protective instinct - tests for mature dogs):

- Guarding: The dog is placed in a down position, next to an article belonging to his handler.

  An assistant in unobtrusive protective clothing approaches in a suspicious but frightened manner, with the obvious intention to steal the article. There is no threat to the dog, nor will the article actually be taken if the dog guards well.

- Attack on the Handler: The handler with his dog on leash is harassed and then attacked by a stranger in protective clothing. The attack is directed toward the handler, not the dog.

- Double Attack: After an attack like above, a second decoy assaults the handler. He wears concealed protective gear, or he is unprotected and the dog wears a muzzle.
- Courage Test: The handler is harassed by a decoy who then runs away. After 50 feet he turns, charges and threatens the dog that was sent after him. This attack is directed toward the dog.

CLASSIC TESTS

The following classic temperament tests have been developed almost exclusively for working dogs:

Newborn Puppies

This is an old and forgotten German method, used by breeders of herding dogs: The newborn puppies, having been licked dry by the bitch, are removed and kept in a dry, warm place for about 12 hours. Then the bitch is held and comforted in one corner of the whelping box, and all the puppies are placed in the opposite corner.

The puppies that struggle, wiggle, roll and make it back to the mother are the best working dog prospects. They have demonstrated intelligence (they can not see yet), physical fitness (they can not walk or crawl yet), stamina (it is a long way for a newborn), and above all a sound survival instinct (they need warmth and food). The puppies that give up after a while and just cry will have to be nursed through life.

Dominance

Observe the interaction of very young dogs with each other, and with people. The busy, bossy, inquisitive, bold puppy will almost always be the best prospect for Schutzhund training.

Puppy's Choice

From 4 days to 3½ weeks after birth, watch for the puppy that shows the most interest in you, always pays attention to you, follows you with his eyes. This pup will - as an adult - always be interested in you.

Olfactory Acuity

A scent trail is laid, for instance with meat on a drag line. The dog must follow it to get to the food.

Manipulation Tests

- A piece of choice meat is hidden in a closed cardboard box. The dog must "unpack".
- A piece of meat is tied to a string. Only the string is within reach of the dog. The dog must scratch and claw the string in order to retrieve the meat.
- A piece of meat is suspended on a string. The

dog must push / pull a box under it to reach the meat.
- A filled food bowl is slid into a shallow, low clearance compartment with open front (a chest of drawers, perhaps). The dog must scratch or claw the bowl to get it out of the box, before he can eat.

Detour Tests

- Dog and owner are fairly close to each other but separated by a 10ft. long barrier (wall, fence). The dog has to move AWAY from the handler in order to get around the barrier, to his handler. The same arrangement is used as before but meat serves to attract the dog.

Maze Tests

The dog must find his way through a T-Maze or regular Maze labyrinth to get to the reward.

Test for Gun Shyness

Unannounced, an assistant fires a pistol about 15 paces away. There are four possibilities:

a) The dog pays no attention at all to the shots. This is not the most desirable behavior, but no points will be deducted if the test was part of a Schutzhund examination.

b) The dog acknowledges the shots, maybe even turns the head, but he remains in position. This is the behavior the Schutzhund trainer would like to see.

c) The dog leaves his position and runs toward the shooter. This reaction is the result of training. In a Schutzhund trial, point deductions will occur yet this is NOT gun shyness.

d) The dog leaves his position, shows signs of fear and runs toward his handler, another familiar person or place (e.g. the car). This is gun shyness and the dog will be excused in a Schutzhund trial.

Courage Test

The handler holds, encourages and then sends his dog while a decoy in the (not so far) distance advances with threatening gestures and sounds. The dog is expected to charge and to bite the decoy.

Hence Courage Test

Like the Courage Test above, but here the dog must charge and bite the decoy in spite of a hit with the stick which occurs just BEFORE the dog gets a hold on the sleeve.

This is a controversial test in our times. One must admit, though, that only courageous dogs will have the fighting drive to bite the bad guy AFTER having received a whack.

Civil Agitation

A decoy in civilian clothes threatens and assaults the handler. The dog should prevent the attack by biting (the decoy wears hidden protective gear) or by attempting to bite (when muzzled).

Re-directed Agitation

The dog should prevent a sudden attack on his handler by seizing the decoy's sleeve and biting hard. The decoy surrenders the sleeve. Then another decoy in civilian clothes and with hidden protective gear attacks the handler. The dog must forget about the just captured sleeve and defend his handler again.

RESULTS

The evaluator should describe tests and responses in a factual manner, and give an opinion on how pronounced various temperament traits are. Such a report will provide current and future owners of the dog with the information needed to utilize his capabilities to the fullest extend.

For example, Humphrey and Warner working with guide dogs at FORTUNATE FIELDS found that a dog can serve man best in a particular capacity if certain temperament requirements are met.

- ◆ For a police dog, they wanted a high degree of self-right, sharpness, fighting drive and protective drive, and a low degree of ear sensitivity, intelligence and willingness.
- ◆ The trailing dog was required to have a high degree of olfactory acuity, intelligence and willingness, and a low degree of body sensitivity, confidence and fighting drive.
- ◆ The seeing eye dog needed a high degree of confidence, medium ear sensitivity and low olfactory acuity.

8. SCHUTZHUND TEMPERAMENT

Based on Humphrey's studies, the temperament requirements for a Schutzhund might look like this:

high degree (+2) of: energy,
                      alertness,
                      courage,

medium d. (+1) of: willingness
                  fighting drive
                  body sensitivity
                  trainability
                  prey (play) drive
                  ear sensitivity
                  protective instinct /defense drive
                  sharpness
                  olfactory acuity.

The tester must be able to distinguish between the natural potential of an untrained dog and the image he presents as a result of training. Learned behavior is a facade which will crumble if enough pressure is applied.

COURAGE is probably the single most important characteristic of a Schutzhund dog. Finding his strength in the pack instinct, the courageous dog will challenge an aggressor not only when his own life is in danger but also when his team mate, the handler, is threatened. Instead of running away or staying at a safe distance, he will attempt to stop the aggressor by biting, without hesitation and without a command. Facing possible injury or even death, he will intercept regardless of the severity of the threat or of the chance of victory.

To evaluate a puppy for his courage is somewhat difficult. The most promising Schutzhund candidate is probably the one who vigorously plays with his litter mates, maybe even bosses them around - or the one who leads his siblings to the fence and barks at an approaching stranger.

PROTECTIVE INSTINCT is closely related to courage.

A pronounced desire to protect his master in critical situations is expected from a Schutzhund dog. How effective this protection is depends to a great deal on the courage the dog possesses. A dog biting only softly and reluctantly in an attack on the handler shows little courage. On the other hand, there are quite a few hard biting dogs around that have little courage. Their strong protective instinct has its foundation in fear, the survival instinct, or a well developed pack instinct.

In a puppy, the protective instinct is rather difficult to assess. Some information may be gained, though, from watching him guard a prized possession, a bone, for instance.

FIGHTING DRIVE is of lesser importance when compared to the protective instinct. Nevertheless, a certain level is expected from a Schutzhund candidate. Dogs with a well developed fighting drive always show a great amount of self-confidence, and they are always courageous. They enjoy the fight, they look forward to it - although not to the extent of initiating trouble themselves. Puppies clue us in on their potential fighting drive while playing with their litter mates, or when mouthing our hands.

SHARPNESS is the ability to react instantaneously to subtle artificial changes in the environment. The responses may be passive, semi-active, or active, like recognizing the change, alerting his master, or biting the intruder. Suspicion, mistrust and sensibility (bordering sometimes on nervousness) are typical for a sharp dog. The Schutzhund trainer, therefore, wants a dog with average sharpness. The characteristics of a sharp dog can be recognized fairly easily in a puppy.

A Schutzhund must show acceptable levels of courage, protective instinct, fighting drive and sharpness. In a trial, the judge is actually required to conduct an informal temperament test before the official proceedings begin. Here is a description of how one judge (the author) handles the situation:

> "I make it a point to observe from a distance dog and handler while they are getting ready for tracking. Since people, and often other dogs, are close by, I can learn quite a bit from it.
>
> I continue the observation when walking toward the tracking contestant. By doing so, we meet away from the starting flag and I have a chance to involve the handler in a casual conversation while we three - handler, dog and judge - advance to the start. During this walk the dog responds in some way to me being next to his handler, which I again record in memory. Then follows the handler's report. I try to put him at ease by chatting some more or answering any of his questions. This occupies the handler's mind enough so that he does not consciously or subconsciously influence his dog. If there was no problem so far, I will at that time quite naturally lower my right hand, and I will happen to come maybe within an inch of the dog's head. I also might decide to step to the side and make gentle body contact with the dog - as if by accident. While continuing the conversation with the handler I might pat him on the shoulder or touch his arm. I will take note of the dog's reaction, out of the corner of my eye. All these movements are quite natural on my part, neither too slow (afraid), nor too fast (threatening). An observer, and even the handler, will probably not connect them in any way with the temperament test I am conducting. All pieces and bits of information collected this way, and in the following trial, will then enable me to come up with a fairly accurate assessment of the dog's temperament."

9. WERTMESSZIFFER (see next page)

In the former Communist countries in Eastern Europe, Schutzhund and working dogs were rated by the "Wertmessziffer" (German: "measured value number"). This system was established by totalitarian regimes to secure easy access to suitable canines for military and police work, like crowd control (Border Guards, Berlin Wall, StaSi, Police, Military). It provided a uniform and fairly accurate description of an adult working dog's physical and mental constitution, benefitting not only the armed forces, but also breeders (and the breed) and buyers of working dogs. The Wertmessziffer was entered in a dog's registration papers. It has six digits, each digit describing a particular feature.

A Doberman with a Wertmessziffer 8643/33, for instance, would be a

heavy, large dog (8xxx/xx),
showing good endurance (x6xx/xx) and
good angulation (xx4x/xx),
being suspicious and aggressive (xxx3/xx) and
displaying sufficient sharpness (xxxx/3x),
courage and hardness (xxxx/x3).

These characteristics suggest that he is a good watch (alert) dog. The ideal Schutzhund/working dog, on the other hand, would have a Wertmessziffer of 5555/55. Dogs rated between xxx3/33 and xxx7/33, however, are still useful for the demanding police and military duties. Unfortunately this rating system has been abandoned by now.

10. WHICH AGE ?

Puppies are such a tremendous source of joy, and their personality is so easily influenced in a positive, or in a negative, way that the dedicated working dog owner will almost always acquire his dog at a very young age. Seven to ten week old puppies are the best prospects.

If the bloodlines have been researched sufficiently, if the parents have been evaluated personally, if earlier litters of the same pairing have been checked, if the puppy itself is healthy, active, vigorous, inquisitive and otherwise of sound temperament, and if the new owner is willing and able to provide the right environment for the physical and mental development of the puppy, then few things can go wrong.

People with more money, less patience and less tolerance prefer to buy a grown dog. This is a choice of the lower risk since structure, temperament, inherited and acquired traits of the dog are readily apparent.

These people, however, must share any sense of accomplishment with the previous owner.

WERTMESSZIFFER SYSTEM

value	first digit	second digit	third digit	fourth digit	fifth digit	sixth digit
	body type with respect to breed standard	constitution	build (structure)	temperament	sharpness	courage and hardness
0	little resemblance	delicate, weak, sensible	cryptorchid	nervous, afraid, very shy		
1	poor representative	deficient (weak) sexual characteristics	poor angulation or poor chest	spooky, timid, noise-sensitive	none	none
2	too light	teeth or pigment faulty	faulty leg proportions	insecure, fearful at times, possibly sharp	some	some
3	too high	coat faulty, weak foundation	average angulation	reserved, suspicious, or aggressive	sufficient	sufficient
4	sufficient	maturing problems	good angulation	aggressive, sharp, hard, dangerous	good	good
5	average	ideal	excellent	relaxed, friendly, very hard when provoked	very good	very good
6	powerful	coarse, resilient	good build, good chest	relaxed, friendly, hard when provoked		
7	too low	weak muscles, incl. ears	long body	relaxed, friendly, sensitive		
8	heavy	spongy	overangulation	relaxed, friendly, indifferent, little sharpness		
9	coarse	crippled	excess in all of the points 6-8 (above)	soft, indifferent, depressed, no sharpness		

SCHELLENBERG :   "TOP WORKING DOGS"

11. WHICH SEX ?

Time and experience have shown that both male and female dogs are capable of outstanding performance in the working dog world. While the choice between a male and a female becomes mostly a matter of personal preference, there are some factors which should not be ignored.

FEMALE dogs (bitches) are often more tractable, they are less likely to roam, and their performance does not suffer as much in the presence of members of the opposite sex. They require, however, time off from work: when they are in heat, or because of a pregnancy. Max von Stephanitz preferred to work with females.

MALE dogs ("son of a bitch" ??) are often bolder, tougher and more independent than bitches. Protection work, therefore, comes natural. A more pronounced sex drive, a greater tendency to roam, and a somewhat greater chance to get involved in dog fights make control over them somewhat more difficult for the handler.

12. WHICH BLOODLINE ?

All purebred dogs have "papers", but procedures regarding these registration documents differ significantly between various countries, various kennel clubs, and various breed organizations.

The Shepherd Club in Germany (SV) issues them with very detailed information, including titles earned, a description of structure, physique, temperament and breed worthiness for parents and grandparents. This information is collected and published annually for all dogs registered with the club. The same club supports and enforces its system with breed surveys, with limits for the number of litters and stud services per animal per year, with limits for the number of puppies left with the mother, with an elaborate network of breed wardens who will tattoo every puppy, with licensing of veterinarians (HD), and with a large clerical staff.

In the US, the American Kennel Club (AKC) provides the owner with just a single registration card. It is an honor system, and it has been criticized heavily since it can be, and is being, abused.

Information from the registration papers is needed to compile a pedigree which shows in an easily understood schematic all the names of a dog's ancestors, for several generations. This serves to study the genetic background, and to be alerted to certain strengths and weaknesses in a particular bloodline, provided sufficient effort is spent to secure such data. First hand information on both parents,

hopefully on the grandparents, and especially on the offspring from an earlier litter of the same pairing, is invaluable (unfortunately, it is often unavailable).

Proper upbringing is necessary to develop a dog's potential, but even the best environment can not fully compensate for hereditary deficiencies.

13. HARD or SOFT DOG ?

For Schutzhund competition, and especially for a novice trainer, we recommend to get a hard dog.

Hard dogs are strong-willed, bold types with an extrovert personality. They respond best to a firm handler and a strong correction, combined of course with love, praise and rewards. They are more resilient to rough handling, they forgive more easily and retain their happy working spirit.

Soft dogs are the very sensitive, easily impressed, sometimes even timid animals. Gentleness, carefully proportioned amounts of force and empathy, patience, as well as skill supplied by the trainer can improve the situation. A backlash, however, occurs as soon as the dog is confronted with too much pressure.

For example: On the retrieve over the hurdle a dog comes in too low, hits the barrier and knocks it over. The hard dog soon forgets the mishap and further training poses no problem. The soft dog remembers the pain and the noise of the tumbling boards for a long time. He will avoid the hurdle in the future, walk around it or remain on the other side. It requires a patient, understanding and skillful trainer to repair the damage.

14. WHICH ONE ?

Comparative shopping is very important for the prospective buyer of a working dog. The last one in a litter, the mail-order puppy, the phone order dog, or the impulsive buy have rarely met the long-range expectations of the owner. Narrow down the choices systematically, and spend enough time and effort on research at each individual step: breed of dog, bloodline, kennel/breeder, age, sex, individual dog (physical and mental health, and suitability for the need he fills).

Looking for proven track records (like SchH-titles of the parents/ancestors) and observing work and play of the prospect (and the parents, grandparents, litter mates, offspring from an earlier breeding with the same parents) can reveal strengths and weaknesses that the dog you selected might exhibit later on.

15. CARING for YOUR SCHUTZHUND

Let your dog become a member of the family. Treat him humanely, take care of his health, nutrition, exercise, training and housing, and adjust the care according to his age. You will have a friend for life.

Prime years for an active Schutzhund are age three to eight, approximately. Physical limitations will influence performance and training by the end of that time span. Even a dog in his best years may not always be in top condition because of health problems and/or premature aging. Be considerate when trial performance or training do not measure up to expectations. And be a good Samaritan when inconsiderate individuals (club trainers, decoys, etc.) mistreat your disadvantaged buddy.

Some dog owners use their Schutzhund like an expensive racing car: stored in the garage, taken out for maintenance, shown-off to friends, driven to the max at the races. They deprive the dog of companionship by housing him in isolation, because it might get them a few extra points at the trial. They push him beyond the limit to bolster their own ego, to score high in a trial. They electro-shock (electronic collar) him for punishment, because they are too lazy to get off their butt. They beat him for disobeying a command (page 98). They (ab)use the stick to test how much pain he can take, to assess his worthiness, etc.

Don't be a part of that group.

C. SELECTING AN INSTRUCTOR

Finding the right training group and the right instructor often determines if the owner enjoys the companionship of his dog over the years, or if he constantly worries about him. Dog obedience trainers do not have to be licensed, so almost anyone can (and seems to) get into the business.

Search for the best teacher available. Recommendations are often biased and not sound. Trophies and training titles do not necessarily make the owner an expert instructor. Diplomas and certificates issued by the various kennels and institutions merely attest that the owner has paid a fee and met certain minimum, often unrelated, requirements. Clever advertisements or gimmicky names like "Cat Whisperer" do not guarantee the qualification of a trainer either - as various series on national and international television, and a slew of websites have amply demonstrated. The best approach is to ask for permission to observe two or three lessons of a current class. If this is not possible, then enroll and make a decision after two sessions. Are you comfortable with that person? Do you trust him? Use common sense, ask yourself: (For simplicity we will refer to "him" as the instructor, although "she" might do just as well or better.)

DOES YOUR DOG APPROVE OF HIM ?

If the instructor can gain the confidence and the respect of all the dogs in the class (maybe with one exception), and without faking friendliness, you can trust him too.

WHAT KIND OF RAPPORT EXISTS BETWEEN THE INSTRUCTOR AND HIS OWN (DEMONSTRATION) DOG ?

If there is mutual respect and admiration between the two members of this team, if the dog works happily, if the instructor is kind but firm, if his dog trusts him, you can trust him too.

DOES THE INSTRUCTOR TEACH THE DOGS OR THE OWNERS ?

Even a mediocre instructor can make a dog perform for him, but he must tell and show the OWNER how to handle his dog.
Beware of instructors who show off with client dogs.

CAN THE INSTRUCTOR INSTRUCT ?

Can he motivate the class, make his point, do the handlers understand? Can he get people to do what he wants them to do? Does he accomplish something, do all the handlers progress satisfactorily?
Beware of the instructor who just socializes.

DOES THE INSTRUCTOR EXPLAIN ?

Does he explain why certain things should be done and others should not?
You need to know the reasons since in your particular situation and with your particular dog the approach may have to be modified. Beware of the instructor who demands: My way - or the highway.

IS THE INSTRUCTOR RESPONSIVE, FLEXIBLE ?

Each dog, and each handler, is different. Each needs a somewhat different approach.
Beware of the instructor who says: Do it my way, and only my way.

IS THE INSTRUCTOR TOLERANT ?

Watch how he handles the situation when someone gets him into a tight spot. Or test him yourself. You could, for instance, refuse to follow an explicit direction of the instructor, especially if your common sense tells you that he might be wrong. Be prepared to intelligently argue your case. See how he responds.
Beware of the instructor who blows his stack.

IS THE INSTRUCTOR KNOWLEDGEABLE ?

Ask relevant questions, get his advise on pertinent problems you have, or those you can imagine. Be prepared to enter into an intelligent discussion, read up on the subject.

Beware of the instructor who is uncooperative or who can not give - or not get - you an answer.

CAN THE INSTRUCTOR HANDLE A CRITICAL SITUATION ?

Tell him your dog bit the mailman, twice, and ask for his suggestions.

If he throws you out of class (quite a few will), or if he suggests the dog pound, leave. He just admitted to practicing a profession without the proper qualifications.

There is no such thing as a perfect instructor. Some are good, some are not so good. Get the good ones.

D. SELECTING A TRAINER

Finding a trainer or a decoy is much more difficult than to find a dog obedience instructor.

The US are the land of the "Instant Expert", at least as far as the Schutzhund sport is concerned. The novice having participated in a couple of training sessions is one, the Police Dog Handler after the introductory course is one, the fellow making a few videos on the training field (and then selling them to the public for oodles of money) is one, and on and on. Be critical of such self-proclaimed experts, learn to recognize the ignorant, inexperienced, misinformed, mud-slinging characters. They disgrace the sport, they can even do serious damage to unsuspecting newcomers and to helpless dogs ("lead pipe", see page 98).

Our recommendation is to contact the various national organizations and to locate their clubs in your area. Visit as many as you can. They all practice Schutzhund training, and their affiliation with a particular parent organization is of minor importance, at least initially. Observe before you participate. Use some of the criteria from the instructor selection above. I, for instance, have for many years driven 4 ½ hours each way every weekend, to train with a club that met my expectations.

Read the chapter about "The Decoy" (page 95). And always use common sense. If you have concerns about the performance of the trainer or the decoy, ask questions, then act, and act in the best interest of your dog.

"You play chess with your dog?
He must be very smart!"
"Oh no, he isn't. I beat him most of the time. "

III. THE STRATEGIES

A. TRAINING THEORY

Canis Familiaris, the common dog, is considered to be the oldest domesticated animal. He has been a loyal companion, guardian and servant to his master and to his master's family, generation after generation, over thousands of years. Four factors have helped the dog to become man's best friend:

1. Dogs are natural guardians and protectors.
2. Dogs are pack animals. Their livelihood depends on interacting with each other in a meaningful way, to respect a certain social protocol, and to take orders from their leader.
3. Next to primates, dogs are the most common trainable animals, considering versatility and usefulness.
4. Dogs have a pronounced play drive which we can utilize in training as a powerful motivator.

1. PACK LEADERS / PACK MEMBERS

Like their wild ancestors, dogs are social creatures. They live in groups, and a pecking order grants privileges and assigns duties to every member in the chain of command.

The playful fight for dominance with litter mates begins already during puppyhood, it leads to serious rivalry during adolescence and results in the establishment of a pecking order which the pack members will acknowledge and honor. Challenges and modifications, however, take place when the performance of any one pack member changes significantly. Especially the pack leader, the alpha animal, is in a vulnerable position. When he loses his strength or his superior instincts, he also loses respect, credibility and his dominance. For us, it is essential that the trainer assumes the role of the pack leader. You must earn and keep (!) your dog's acceptance, respect, trust and loyalty in order to be recognized as the leader. Although most dogs will strive for dominance at one time or another, they are as happy to be a follower as they are to be a leader. If challenged, you must show them their place by responding intelligently and understandably (to the dog) with a firm, yet loving hand.

> The domestication process has strengthened in dogs an innate desire to please their masters. This is a very precious asset available to a dog trainer and he should not jeopardize it. He must realize that a subordinate has rights too. Violating them will result in mutiny, and rightfully so. There is no justification for abusing a dog.
> Likewise, punishment out of sequence with the undesirable deed will ruin the best dog/handler relationship.

Unreasonable, inconsiderate, impatient or ill-tempered persons should not train a dog. Yet anthropomorphism (treating a dog like a human being) may cause just as much harm. The dog's brain operates at a different level, and the trainer must adjust his way of thinking - if he wants to communicate with his dog. There are limits to this suggestion, however. Barking back at a dog instead of giving a command, or exchanging saliva with him (as suggested by some "experts") is reserved for brain-dead characters.

Properly treated and guided, a dog will go out of his way to perform all sorts of difficult tasks within the limits of his capabilities, even though they might appear to him superfluous or ridiculous. Problems usually lie not with the dog, but with his human partner. Everyone can be a follower, but it takes a leader to lead.

2. SOCIALIZATION

Between about four days and four months of age, a dog finds his place in the world by establishing relationships with other individuals. During this imprinting period the puppy needs much attention and proper guidance which the dedicated breeder/owner, but not a commercial pet shop or a puppy mill, can give. Especially during the latter part of this period you must provide
- opportunities for him to meet a large variety of people, dogs and other pets (individuals and groups),
- contacts with different and varied environments in city, urban and rural areas,

- exposure to various ground covers, floor surfaces, buildings, machinery etc.

Whenever possible, take him along with you wherever you go. All this will guarantee that your dogs matures into a well-adjusted, well-liked pet whose company you can enjoy for life.

3. VERBAL COMMUNICATIONS

We know that dogs have no comprehension of the human language. The inflections in a trainer's voice, the loudness, soothing or harsh tones, they all signal his mood, his commitment, his determination, his approval or disapproval. A dog can NOT understand words or sentences as we understand them. He does respond to certain sounds (words) in a specific way, but this is the result of conditioning, not understanding.

It does not matter which word you choose for a command, as long as it is short (to be practical) and unique (to avoid confusion with similar commands). Say "sit" or "knit", "mitt", "fit" etc., and he will most likely do the same thing, he will sit. If, however, you change the emphasis or the manner in which you pronounce "sit", if for instance in the excitement of a trial you shout "sit" in a very stern, commanding manner, your dog will get confused, and he will probably lay down. You have "pushed the wrong button", and the dog will try to read your mind and to come up with a response that he thinks is right.

While the commands can be given in any native tongue, it is believed that the more guttural languages (like Russian) have a slight advantage over the more melodic ones (like French).

Of greater importance, though, is consistency. Once a particular word has been selected for a command, it should be used for this exercise, exclusively and religiously.

Initially, during the conditioning stage, command and physical guidance go together. The dog, for instance, is smartly manipulated ("handled") into a sitting position while the word "sit" is spoken. Once the association has been formed in the dog's mind, the guidance is eliminated, and the dog will sit with a command only. The word "sit" has become a substitute for the physical manipulation into a sitting position, the primary cue (guidance/force) has been replaced with a secondary cue (command).

4. SIGNAL COMMUNICATIONS

Dogs are keen observers. They are more likely to respond to a gesture rather than to a spoken word.

The serious trainer will avoid unnecessary body movements which he might subconsciously make while giving a verbal command (moving a hand or his feet, bending forward, bending the knees in a recall, etc.).

Intentional signal communications ("hand signals") have very limited practical use. It impresses amateurs tremendously when a dog lies down on signal, without a spoken command. But what do you do when the dog does not look in your direction? Do you call for his attention first? And what do you do when it is dark, shine a flashlight on your arm? A barely audible command beats a signal every time.

5. BEHAVIOR COMPONENTS

Canine behavior is shaped and determined by two factors: heredity and environment. The hereditary influence on working performance is often ignored. Even the best environment can not compensate for a lack of natural qualities, and it always pays to select the top contender. However, a good trainer can cultivate dormant characteristics and achieve remarkable success even with less than ideal candidates.

Most pet owners have a dog when they get seriously interested in training. They can not change their pupil's hereditary background, so they must operate the second criterion, the environment. Canines, though, belong to the group of high-ranking, intelligent mammals. This makes training, the response (R) to external stimuli (S), possible. A stimulus might be a tug on the leash, teaching the dog to move with his handler.

This S-R pattern is the basis for an adaptive system: the animal adjusts to changes in its environment. The changes must stand out, however, so that the student can notice and recognize them. It requires two things:

a) *constancy*: the environment must be constant (e.g. one trainer), so that changes can stand out, and
b) *consistency*: the changes (cues) must be distinct and consistent. If the cues vary, or if they are erratic, training results will be erratic too. For instance: say "off" and not "down" to discourage jumping up, because "down" is an already established, specific command which is given to anchor a dog to the ground in the prone position.

CONSTANT ENVIRONMENT means, for instance, one trainer instead of several family members; a relaxed, well coordinated handler who avoids body language; familiar, secluded training grounds; a regular daily schedule for feeding, exercise etc; no interferences like nasty kids from the neighborhood teasing the dog; and the like. The cues will then be easily recognizable by the student. A leash correction, for instance, interrupts the dog in whatever he was doing before. To restore the former state of no-conflict, the dog has two options:

1) *assimilation*, e.g. trying to change the environment (trying to get the handler to quit the leash corrections by playing, growling, snapping, biting)
2) *accommodation*, e.g. trying to change himself (heel properly).

A skillful trainer will, of course, discourage option (1) by making that choice even more unpleasant, and he will encourage option (2) by immediately rewarding the dog for desirable behavior.

CONSISTENCY, the second criterion, requires that the handler responds in a predictable way.
Erratic signals from the handler confuse the dog and make learning nearly impossible.
For example: A (trained) dog breaks the "long sit". Many handlers now yell "sit ... sit ... sit" (no response), then "down ... down ... down ..." (again no response), etc. Frustrated, they fetch their dog, walk him a bit, then yell "sit" again. How can a dog remember what was wrong when so many other things are done in between? It is much better to watch your dog closely. At the first indication of moving a muscle to get up, grab your dog by the fur on the top, front and rear, and slam him into the sit. Let go of the grip instantaneously, end the exercise after a few seconds, then praise. Next time, just a warning ("hey..") will be needed at the very moment the dog INTENDS to get up.
This example describes operant conditioning, e.g. learning processes which motivate individuals to do something, or to refrain from doing something, by properly linking an act and its consequences.

6. MOTIVATION

Dr. Spock of fame admitted shortly before his death that his theory is faulty and that he never applied it to members of his own family. His teachings ruined at least two generations of children. His "LOVE ONLY" doctrine was the major cause for today's world-wide drug and crime epidemic. Look around, every successful person uses von Bismarck's principle of "Ruling With Sugar Bread And Horse Whip". And yet, fashionable dog trainers still peddle Spock's follies to a trusting audience.

Obedience commands are in conflict with a dog's natural behavior patterns, and motivation is the single most important factor to get the dog to do what we want him to do. If the handler can motivate his dog, then training will be easy (see also the table on page 31). Motivation comes about for two reasons:

  a) the desire to get something pleasant (reward), and
  b) the desire to avoid something unpleasant (compulsion / correction).

Reward (maybe 80%) and correction (maybe 20%) are both needed to teach children or pets. Ignoring that fact, or drastically changing the above ratio will spell disaster, excepting some isolated instances.

REWARD

For motivation, rewards must be highly desirable. The stronger the desire, the more effective the reward.

There are basically three ways to increase the desire, and they can be used in combination:

a) select the reward that is most attractive
  - use broiled liver instead of regular dog food
  - play ball with him if that is what he likes best.

b) temporarily deprive the dog of the basic need to which the reward applies
  - food: do not feed for 10, max. 24, hours
  - play / socialization: confine the dog to a crate with little or no human interaction for 2, maximal 8 hrs.

c) do not reward unwanted, improper responses, and reserve the reward for those times when the dog has earned it. If the dog gets treats all the time, why should he "work" for it ?

When, what, and how much depends on the situation. Too much of a reward can be as harmful as too little. Ignoring your dog for two weeks, playing ball with him for an hour right before a trial, feeding him a pound of goodies at the completion of the tracking test, they all guarantee failure in a subsequent, imminent activity.

The most common forms of reward are

  a) **Praise**: a kind word, scratch on the head/chest, belly rub, pat on the shoulder, hug, dance of joy.

  b) **Play** (with the master): ball / stick / frisbee, tug-of-war, running, romping, swimming, chasing. Pick one toy, his favorite. Do a brief obedience routine and play with him vigorously afterwards for 10-60 seconds, using this toy. He must play **with you** - if

not, ignore him (see also page 38 cont.).

  c) **Food**
    highly effective: broiled liver, smoked sausage, bacon, misc. meat, fish, canned fish
    somewhat effective: cheese, flavored dog treats, dog biscuits
    less suitable: commercial dog food, cookies, sweets.

The two phases in dog training where rewards play an important role are:

  1) establishing or "**shaping**" a desirable behavior (teaching the dog what to do)
  2) "**maintaining**" a desirable behavior (refreshing the dog's memory on what he has learned).

◆ In Phase 1, we take many small, progressively more difficult steps and reward them instantaneously ("constant reinforcement", 1:1 ratio). A dog being taught to climb a ladder will at first be rewarded for the slightest attempt he makes. Then he will have to respond more distinctly to earn his reward. Make the individual steps not too small to mislead or to bore the dog (wasting time) nor too big to lose him in the process (extinguishing the desirable response). Use attractive rewards, include a "jackpot" occasionally.

◆ Once the dog understands and reliably produces the desired response, we progress to Phase 2. Here we reward only every second correct response (1:2 ratio) until reliable performance is established. Then we change to 1:4, 1:6 etc., the "fixed ratios of intermittent reinforcement".

◆ Still better results can be obtained by going to "variable ratio schedules of intermittent reinforcement". This is a completely irregular, haphazard pattern in which the dog might get rewarded two times in a row, then not at all for 5 times, then after 4, 1, 2 attempts, and so on. The student has no way of figuring out which one of his next responses will be rewarded.

     If you gamble and every bet would predictably earn you 10 cents, you would get bored quickly. If, however, the return varies, and if there is a real chance for a very large, attractive pay-out, you would continue and double your efforts. Your dog shares this kind of reasoning.

Reinforcement schedules can be adjusted for individual dog/handler teams and exercises, but the dog needs some kind of feedback from his master about EVERY performance.

CORRECTION - PUNISHMENT

"Punishing" a dog for having been bad is applying human standards to the training of animals. It is counter- productive since the dog can not understand moralistic values. We should employ a "correction" instead, an unpleasant experience/ guidance triggered by an undesirable deed. However, **we will not use "punishment" during the initial learning phase, because at that time the dog does not quite understand what we consider to be "right" or "wrong"**.

Adjustments borrowed from the behavior repertoire of animals are very effective, like the "nape grab": Take a hold of the loose fold of skin around the puppy's neck, lift him up by it and shake him, simulating a procedure that the mother dog would use to teach her offspring.   Some "authorities" recommend this for rebellious dogs of all ages; it does not work. Furthermore, they tell you to literally sit on the dog in the "alpha posture" as they call it. Don't do it, it will worsen the situation - and you probably get bitten as well.

The scale of (unpleasant) corrections is far reaching:

compulsion:
> threatening motions
> startling, loud noises
> restraining the dog's movement
> reprimanding, harsh scolding
> choking (quick choke collar correction)
> shaking (nape grab)
> pinching (quick pinch collar correction)
> slapping, hitting
> shocking (electro shock)

negative reinforcement:
> withholding the reward
> ignoring, confining or isolating the dog

The "penalty" must be tailored to the occasion and to the temperament of the dog. A soft dog is easily impressed by a harsh word from his trainer, while the hard dog may need physical adjustment. Timing is extremely important, and "punishment" is most effective when the dog can not determine who administered it.

A correction is a sequence of events, and it consists of four parts, one following the other rather rapidly:

1) your verbal command
  This, like a "warning", is very important from a learning standpoint. It allows the dog to avoid the correction in the following step by reacting quickly in the desired and previously learned manner.

2) assessment:
  Watch and see. If the dog performs as desired, skip step (3) and continue with step (4).

3) unpleasant stimulus (correction) and physical manipulation into the desired position (guidance).
  The stimulus must be forceful enough to make a lasting impression on the dog, but not cause psychological or physical harm. The stimulus must also be related to the objective of the exercise (don't pinch his EAR if you want him to open the MOUTH   for the dumbbell - as many "experts" wrongly recommend); it should manipulate the dog into the proper position.

4) reward for compliance
  The HANDLER does all the work, but the DOG gets the reward/praise as counterbalance for the preceding unpleasant experience in step (3). This helps the dog to remember where his advantage lies.

To find the right level of force required in step (3), you will want to start out gently and then, in increments, get tougher. The dog will not bother to respond to the correction until a certain level of force is reached. This level should be maintained during the initial training stage. Later on it can be lowered.

  Here is an example:

OBJECTIVE: "Sit" quickly and squarely (the dog already knows what "sit" means).

SEQUENCE: Heel your dog, in the proper position, at a brisk pace. Hold the leash very short. Then stop.

> 1) Give a short, factual instruction: "sit".
> 2) Look and see. If the dog sits nicely go to (4), else proceed with (3).
> 3) About 1/4 of a second later [this time span was used up in step (2)] , simultaneously
>   - tug the leash with your right hand, 45 degrees up/forward (lagging) or backward (forging)
>   - swiftly slap the dog on the croup, with the FINGERS of the left hand. Guide him now (not after the dog sits already) into a straight, square sit. Do not PRESS or PUSH the dog into a sit.
> 4) Praise your dog.

The reward-correction concept is very important in dog training. Remember:

- Rewards must be attractive, and they must be earned, not given out of affection.
- Corrections must be proceeded by a "warning" and followed by praise.
- Corrections must be forceful enough to get the

dog's attention and compliance.
- Timing for both, reward and correction, must be accurate (see "memory", below).

7. MONITORS

An objective assessment of progress in training is important. You can get it from friends or the training director. The best method is to have your performance video-taped from time to time. Keep a notebook, list progress, problems, ideas, actions. Discuss it with others, make changes as needed, then follow up on it.

B. LEARNING THEORY

1. MEMORY

Memory is "the faculty of retaining and recalling past experience, the ability to remember".

MEMORY PROCESSES

Compared to other animals, dogs have a relatively large brain; they can readily adapt to new and unusual situations. A highly sophisticated memory system enables them to relate new information to past experiences. There are three stages:

(1) encoding information, (2) storing information, (3) retrieving information.

1) During encoding, new information is analyzed, processed, prepared for storage in the brain (VSTM).
2) Storing involves chemical changes in the brain cells. Important information causes major changes and is stored in long-term memory (LTM), less important information (small changes) goes into the short-term memory (STM, ITM).
3) New events cause the brain to search for relevant stored information. Whatever is found is compared to the new situation and heavily influences the response of the student.

For example: A young dog is taken to the clinic for his first vaccinations. He happily greets the veterinarian, wagging his tail. Then comes the painful shot. The puppy appraises the situation: veterinary clinic, the office and the equipment, strange sounds and smells, the other animal patients, the doctor's coat, the pain. All this is "processed" and stored in the long-term memory. The dog is bewildered now and will readily retrieve that information later on. Just pay another visit to a vet, any vet!

MEMORY LEVELS

The length of time during which information is stored depends on how much the dog is impressed by the stimulating experience. Psychologists have defined four such levels on which memory processes operate:

a) Very Short Term (or Ionic) Memory, VSTM

The VSTM is the "receptionist" for the brain, accepting or ignoring "visitors" (stimuli).
A gentle tug on the leash, for instance, is ignored, while a sharp leash correction is remembered.

b) Short Term (or Working) Memory, STM

The STM is the "filing clerk" who picks up the information from the VSTM, then sorts and files it. While a normal leash correction (VSTM) captures the dog's attention for a moment, a few stern ones address the STM and convince the dog to behave properly for the rest of the lesson.

c) Intermediate Term Memory, ITM

The ITM, the "case-worker", stores information temporarily, maybe for about a week, assuming that it is of value only for a limited time: A dog introduced to tracking by the food method will remember for a few days that he found his reward at the end of the trail. However, if the next tracking lesson is given after a few weeks, and if the dog was regularly fed in the meantime, evidence of prior learning will usually be missing.

d) Long Term Memory, LTM

The LTM, the "vault manager", is the place of definitive changes in memory. After elaborate screening at lower levels, essential information finds its way into the LTM. Behavior or personality shaping, attitudes, general approaches etc. are established here, and fundamental decisions are based on information retained in LTM: If a dog has found through numerous experiences that he can please his master only by performing certain tasks - herding sheep for instance, then this knowledge becomes important to him, and he will acknowledge these tasks in his LTM as essential for his survival. He will become a herding dog, a working dog.

CONSOLIDATION

Transferring information from STM or ITM into LTM is called consolidation (or learning). The process takes time and the student should not be distracted, overly excited or otherwise disrupted.

Mice receiving an electro shock right after learning a task did forget what they had learned. However, if the shock treatment was given some hours later, then it had no effect and the animals would remember well (see Fig. 3).

Rewards, on the other hand, supported learned behavior (Fig. 4). If praise, food, play, even certain pleasant chemical or electrical stimuli were given right after a learning trial, then the student could see a connection between his action and the reward and would learn well.

Example: In the presence of other dogs and people, a trainer forces his dog to go over, and over, and over the hurdle, one time right after the other. The student is disturbed and distracted, and he gets to hate jumping because of all the repetitions.

Another trainer selects an area relatively free of distractions for the first few training sessions, rewards his dog immediately after the jump and then quits for the day. This second dog has a much better chance to learn, since pleasant and unpleasant stimuli were used effectively.

ASSOCIATIVE MEMORY

To stack the LTM with useful information, the dog must be able to connect specific commands with specific (desired) responses. Frequency, recency and arousal are important to make this association:

FREQUENCY means that the more often we practice a particular exercise, within a reasonable framework, the more reliable the dog's performance will become. One of the authorities was asked how long it takes to teach a dog to consistently track well. "2000 tracks, at least" was his answer. Of course, do not do all 2000 tracks in one week !

Constant repetitions, timed well, eventually cause the responses to become automatic, e.g. regulated by subconscious, rather than by conscious, efforts.

RECENCY is another important factor. We humans too forget things when they are not fresh in our mind. Forgetting becomes gradually worse as time goes by (physiological decay process). Practicing heeling just before entering competition helps the dog to remember what he is supposed to do a few minutes later.

AROUSAL finally refers to various, not directly related stimuli present at the time of training or immediately thereafter. For example:
- An anxious dog anticipates the reward (play, praise, food). He is a better learner than his dull counterpart.
- Emotionally toned commands (happy/stern, friendly/demanding) are more effective than monotone, neutral ones: *"Your voice is the most elegant, the most effective, and the always present training tool !" (D.Sch.)*

Different levels of excitement must be chosen for different tasks. Complex jobs like tracking require a lower level of arousal (don't use protection work as reward!) than simple jobs like heeling. This becomes obvious when we consider that - at a low level of arousal, unimportant as well as important cues are processed
- at an optimal level of arousal, only relevant (important) cues are processed
- at a high level of excitement, not all relevant cues are processed.

We must find the proper level of stimulation (arousal), refresh the dog's memory as needed (recency), and make sure that the dog has performed the exercise often enough (frequency) so that he can do it well.

LATENT LEARNING

"Latent learning" (latent = hidden) means that animals can accumulate and store knowledge for later use, without giving any indication of the learning process. Upon proper stimulation/ motivation the latent information is retrieved, and this usually results in superior performances. In the "send-out", for example, the handler might have run with the dog on leash many times to the spot to which he wants his dog to advance. Off lead, and without the handler running along, the dog acts as if he did not get the message. Now we add motivation (encouragement, praise, a toy, food) and - everything else being right - the dog will perform the first time and thereafter like an expert.

CONTINGENCIES OF REINFORCEMENT

Training principles that were discussed so far have not given much credit to the dog's initiative.

We know that success in teaching children, or in

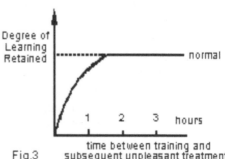

Fig.3   time between training and subsequent unpleasant treatment

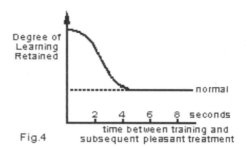

Fig.4   time between training and subsequent pleasant treatment

training dogs, is based on the student's curiosity, his personal experiences, and on opportunities to learn and to make mistakes.

CURIOSITY (learning by doing)
A curious dog (a puppy we might call mischievous) is more likely to accidentally discover the desired response than a dullhead. Accidental discovery is known to considerably enhance the learning process over manipulating (forcing) the dog through the exercise the first time. On the obstacle course, for instance, the curious dog will learn to go through the tunnel without problems. A dog that has to be *pulled* through will resent it, fight it, and learn much slower.

PERSONAL EXPERIENCE (learning by experience)
To reliably respond to the command "crawl through the tunnel" the dog must be able to relate to earlier experiences. It helps when the dog can remember situations or environments (the large conduit, for instance), where he had done something similar and got satisfaction in doing it.

OPPORTUNITIES (learning by trial and error)
Performances will remain unpredictable if the dog was never given the chance to find out what the desirable AND (!) the undesirable responses are for a given situation. For instance: going halfway into the tunnel and then coming back would be undesirable, and the dog will probably do just that at the least opportune time. Let your dog make a mistake, then show him the right way. This very basic fact of instructing is ignored by many trainers!

2. LEARNING THEORIES
Modern canine psychology refers to three general approaches for the theoretical understanding of behavior control, or learning and training. They are
 a) Obedience Theory (compulsive or force training)
 b) Reinforcement Theory (inductive or reward training)
 c) Cognitive Theory (knowledge-based training).
The cognitive theory, which includes elements of the other two, is the most effective approach.

OBEDIENCE THEORY
This theory involves moral judgements, the dog is either good or bad, cooperative or uncooperative. It uses increasing levels of force / punishment if the preceding step fails. This leads to an escalation of conflict and occasionally even to cruelty. Obedience theory has definite limitations and is generally considered to be ineffective. Look at a dog-fight situation (Fig.5): The handler who believes in obedience theory beats his dog, hoping that the dog will release the grip as a result of the punishment (it rarely works). The "forced retrieve" is another example.

REINFORCEMENT THEORY
This theory (a la Dr. Spock) can be called a "spectators approach". It does not seriously consider

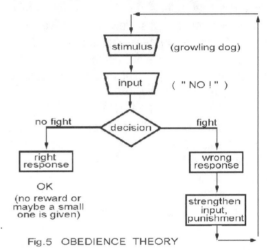

Fig.5 OBEDIENCE THEORY

the student's goals, aims or even motivations. It assumes that a certain response (R) to a given stimulus (S) will prevail when it always had been rewarded or reinforced (F) in the past (S-R-F). The "just love, no corrections" theory does not work. Dr.Spock finally admitted that, but only after his followers had incited the biggest world-wide drug and crime epidemic of all times. Even today, the majority of dog trainers happily perpetuates his follies, unable to explain why many dogs continue to choose the undesired responses, even when plenty of reinforcement for the alternative is being offered. There are no provisions made for natural ("innate") responses which are strongly engraved in the dog's mind, and which can not be substituted by unnatural alternatives. The "clicker", a clicking sound followed by an actual reward, is an example of using the reinforcement theory (it has limited applications since it works in selected training situations only).Referring to the dog fight situation, the dog's dignity, or his survival, depends on warding off the threatening attack. In the dog's view there is no alternative, reward or not, he has to take up the fight.
The reinforcement theory's "S-R-F" sequence (see above) relies on reinforcers ("F"). Dog trainers talk about:

POSITIVE REINFORCEMENT	affirmative active reinforcers:	treat given (make him a "treat addict")	"I want more of this"
NEGATIVE PUNISHMENT	negative neutral reinforcers:	treat withheld ------>	"I must do better next time"
POSITIVE PUNISHMENT	negative active reinforcers:	leash correction ---------->	"I must not do that next time"
NEGATIVE REINFORCEMENT	affirmative passive reinforcers:	nothing happens ------------>	"I must have done OK"

COGNITIVE THEORY

This theory is similar to the reinforcement theory, but it acknowledges a more complex chain of events.

Instead of working with isolated S - R pairs, it assumes the "intellectual" involvement of the animal as well as that of the trainer. Individual capacity, behavior, and reason are weighed. The trainer utilizes the proper cues and motivational forces and devises modified behavior flow systems.

Figure 7 refers to the following theoretical situation: A trainer wants his dog to sit. He gives the command. Four competing stimuli force the dog to make a decision. In all probability the dog will not sit. The trainer will eliminate the competing incidental stimuli, one at a time (cognitive theory also recognizes that not all stimuli or responses can be eliminated, as it is the case with the innate responses), by

a) satisfying the dog's needs (let him chase, eat, mate first)

b) removing the incidental stimulus (confine cat, remove food and bitch)

c) making the undesired response unpleasant (e.g. connecting the food to an electric fence charger).

With all distractions removed, chances are about 50/50 that the dog will perform as desired. To favor the outcome, a reward is incorporated, just like in the reinforcement theory. Here, however, the reward is also used as bait. Cognitive theory aims to create in the animal an anticipation, an expectation of the reward. The dog will hopefully see two possibilities:

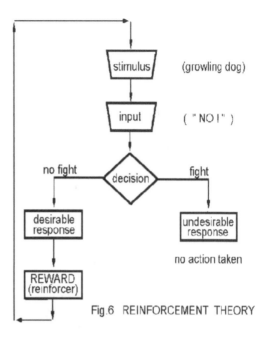

Fig.6   REINFORCEMENT THEORY

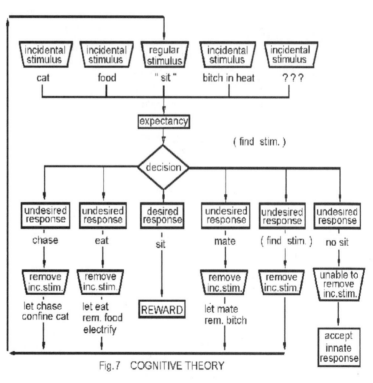

Fig.7   COGNITIVE THEORY

a) undesired reactions = ignored by his handler, no attention, no fun, maybe even unpleasantness

b) desired reaction = praise, reward, play, fun, food. The dog remembers that he always was rewarded when he sat as requested. He probably will sit now.

Having utilized the reward as a motivator, cognitive theory goes one step further: it makes the desired response a part of the behavior chain. It requests work before **AND AS A PREREQUISITE** for the permission to return to a regular activity (sleep, food, play), as shown in figure 9. Work becomes an integral part of the dog's complex behavior flow, and hopefully a pleasant one too.

C. SUMMARY

Let us try to put the theory of dog training in form of a recipe:

a) Goal: Teach a new exercise (shaping), and then practice it (maintaining).

b) Parts:
- A dog unfamiliar with the command, healthy and capable of doing the job.
- A handler capable and willing to do the job.
- Proper tools (e.g. collar, leash, reward) and proper environment (e.g. quiet training area).

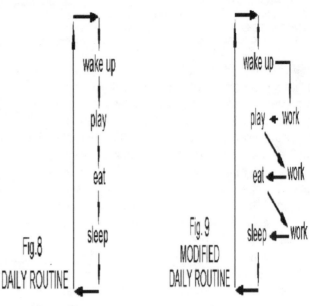

Fig.8
DAILY ROUTINE

Fig.9
MODIFIED
DAILY ROUTINE

c) Plan: Part 1: Break down into simple parts any exercise that consists of multiple tasks, e.g. in the recall teach the come, front sit and finish at random and independently of each other. Combine the three segments into a complete exercise only after the dog masters all separate parts.

Part 2: Introduce the command
- Guide your dog calmly and patiently. Motivate, manipulate, "handle" him so that he ends up where you want him to be (primary stimulus).
- Introduce the command at the same time, say it over and over again (secondary stimulus).
- Reward him once he complies, with praise, food, play (positive reinforcement).
- Repeat for days, weeks, months, until the dog understands the new command (consolidation).

Part 3: Secure reliable performance
Four rules apply to part (3):

1. DON'T GIVE A COMMAND IF YOU ARE NOT IN A POSITION TO ENFORCE IT (except for emergencies).
If your dog likes to chase cats then put him on a 30 foot leash and on a prong collar, then release the cat. If, during the training phase, you call him to you without this precaution, you only teach him disobedience (and you make a fool of yourself).

2. NEVER REPEAT A COMMAND MORE THAN ONCE (provided your dog is familiar with it).
The first time the dog has a chance to do right. The second time you make him do right, manipulate him into the desired position. Make sure that you can enforce your command, then reward.

3. AFTER EACH CORRECTION, YOU MUST PRAISE / REWARD YOUR DOG
Pick the kind of praise that works best, but there are no exceptions to this rule!

4. USE THE 1-2-3-4 RULE (see also the earlier chapter on "Correction - Punishment", p.27)
Count "one, two, three, four", to define a time frame for the following four steps:
- command: (1) During the time it would take you to say "one", give the command.
- assessment: (2) On "two", observe your dog. See if he obeys quickly, or if he does not.
- guidance: (3) Either praise him for responding well, or correct him if not, then praise.
- reward: (4) On "four", praise your dog again.

Once your dog becomes more proficient, you can count faster, thereby getting quicker responses.

IV. THE TOOLS

A. SCHUTZHUND TRAINING EQUIPMENT

Without proper tools, the craftsman as well as the dog trainer can do only a mediocre job. Furthermore, improvising, using cheap and ineffective equipment, or using no protective gear at all can cause physical harm to all involved. Here are a few suggestions for recommended equipment:

1. TRACKING

FLAGS

Aluminum poles (3/8" pipe, pointed at one end) with a small piece of white or brightly colored cloth at the top are best. Steel or aluminum ski poles (disc removed), bicycle flags (fiberglass rods) are useable too. Surveyor flags are too short, they tend to distract the dogs. Wooden poles break, regular steel pipes are too heavy.

ARTICLES

Dark gloves, cut-off fingers from gloves, pieces of an old leather shoe or belt, a leather wallet are recommended.   The beginner should use leather articles since they hold human scent the longest. Advanced dogs can be taught to find metal, plastic, glass and wood articles as well. Neutral colors discourage the dog to hunt by sight.

HARNESS

Use a light-weight, non-restrictive, adjustable leather or web material harness.

For some years now the trend in Europe has been to do tracking without a harness. Attaching the leash to the dead ring of the regular choke collar and guiding the leash under one front leg is "in". (This is actually a simplified "Boettcher harness" which cleverly guides the tracking leash along the rump, between the legs of the dog, and which forces the dog to put his head to the ground if he pulls.)

LEASH

The 30 ft. leash should be made of light-weight web or cord material. Leather tracking leashes, even the narrow-width ones, are generally too heavy. Strength characteristics are rarely important here.

MISCELLANEOUS

Clipboard, paper and pen are helpful to map out the track, to remember where it was laid, and to check on the dog's   performance. Clothes pins (spray colored) can be clipped to bushes or trees for orientation. Two-way radios (even cell phones) help the tracklayer to stay in touch with the judge or the training director. A carpenter's apron with its large pockets allows the handler to conveniently carry leash, articles, food rewards, a ball, a small water canteen and other items he might need on the track. It can also be used to store all tracking items in one place.

2. OBEDIENCE

LEASH

A six foot leather leash, ½ or ¾ inch wide, and with a medium-sized buckle, is a good choice.

The multi-adjustable leather leash (not manufactured domestically) is slightly more expensive, yet it is useful for a variety of training purposes such as exercising the dog, or in tracking (fully extended), in obedience (doubled) and in protection (partially extended and secured with the additional hooks).

A chain-link leash is tough on the hands, and its weight signals to the dog when he is on or off the hook. Nylon and cotton web leads are better than metal but they are tough on the hands of the handler as well.

LEASH / COLLAR GIMMICKS

A retractable leash or a body strap/harness is for apartment dwellers and their lap dogs only. A "Halti" and similar contraptions are useless "straight jackets". Assume that someone clips a leash to your nose and jerks you around. The moment it is taken off, you would run away from that clown as quickly and as far as you could. So will your dog.

SHORT LINE / DANGLE

A 16 inch long piece of cotton or nylon cord ("dangle"), or a nylon fishing line of the same length and with a handle on one end, is very useful during the transition from on to off lead.

LONG LINE

A 30 foot long cotton web lead, ½ inch wide, is light weight yet strong. It will not stretch, and it will not cut into your hands.   It is used for distance control.

COLLAR

Regular slip-chain collars are most effective, in some instances pinch collars might be useful.

Small-link steel collars are preferred over "fur-savers". They react more quickly and give a warning signal (click, click, click...) when activated. Nylon and leather collars (chokes) are less desirable. Spike collars (sharpened nails inside a wide leather collar) are not training tools but torture instruments. They should not be confused with the pinch collars (also called prong or German training collars).

The pinch collar consists of individual steel links with two blunt prongs each. Momentarily tightening the collar presses the prongs against the dog's neck and creates some discomfort without causing injury. If used sensibly on stubborn dogs, they can work wonders.

DUMBBELL

Get a set of 4 wooden dumbbells, standard weight (light-weight, 650 g, 1000 g, 2000 g).

Ideally, the center bar should be two inches longer than the distance between the dog's eyes.

The all-wood 2000 g and 1000 g dumbbells are impressive looking but awkward to carry around. A more compact version hides metal weights inside or on the hardwood bells. Multi-adjustable dumbbells are bothersome to use, the frequent weight changes are annoying, the tightening screws get stuck, parts get lost.

THROW CHAIN

The conventional throw chain consists of two eight inch long steel or brass link chains, joined end to end by metal rings to form a circle. A heavy-duty choke chain will be all right also. It is used to startle or to correct the dog while off lead. In most instances, a miss (on purpose) is as effective as a direct hit.

SLING SHOT

This very old training tool is used for distance control. It is a long range substitute for a leash correction, but the dog should not be able to determine who fired the shot. Dried peas or beans make suitable ammunition.

ELECTRONIC COLLAR

Radio-frequency shock treatment is used for distance control. The hand-held transmitter triggers an electric shock in the dog's specially equipped collar. Advanced models feature intensity control, and a warning sound before the electro-shock is activated so that the dog can avoid the punishment by quickly reacting in the expected fashion. Dummy collars of the same weight and size as the real thing are sometimes used during the second training phase.

Electronic collars take the fun out of dog training, any clodhopper can steer a remote-controlled toy car. Besides, they have limited applications only, they can easily be abused or misused, a mean competitor can raise havoc, and they can cause severe psychological damage. Inadvertent triggering by garage door openers or other radio-controlled equipment is a possibility. Learning to use electronic collars comes always at the expense of a few ruined dogs, and only very experienced trainers should even consider such equipment.

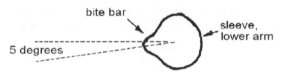

Fig.10   SIDE VIEW OF BITE-BAR SLEEVE

German Working Dog Organizations have banned shock collars. If it becomes obvious that you use one in training, you will be barred from participating in Schutzhund trials.

GUN

Blank pistols of .22 or .32 caliber should be used. Regular revolvers can be fired with blanks but they might be ruined in time. Regular pistols are not recommended since even the automatic ones have to be reloaded manually for each shot.

3. PROTECTION

SACK

Burlap or jute sacks should be washed before use. Sacks from a feed store, for instance, may contain insecticides etc. that can be harmful to dogs. In any case, the dust from an unwashed sack will annoy the animals.

BITE ROLL

A bite roll, or "sausage", is an inexpensive substitute for the puppy sleeve. It can be made from a rolled jute or burlap sack, tied together with string. Some bite rolls are also stuffed with padding.

PUPPY SLEEVE

Puppy sleeves are made from jute throughout (no leather) with some padding, for "soft" or very young dogs. They can help to make the transition from sack to hard sleeve more palatable.

SLEEVE

"Sleeves" are made from rigid leather with a flexible elbow joint, with or without bite bar. They should be strong enough so that they can not be compressed by hand, and they should be roomy enough so that the decoy can twist his arm inside without turning or rotating the sleeve (to teach a firm hold).

Sleeves with bite bar are made for either right or left arm use. Those that can be worn on either arm are a compromise, they are not recommended for work with inexperienced dogs.

For proper training of decoys and dogs use both a right and a left arm sleeve (one at a time, of course). The bite bar may run the full length of the lower arm (easier on inexperienced dogs, more realistic training situation), or it may be an indentation in the middle of the lower arm only (aim point / "target" practice, tournament style training).

Some types of sleeves weigh less (thinner materials, plastic components, modern manufacturing methods) yet have similar dimensions. They offer an additional degree of freedom for the decoy but they are not as durable as standard sleeves.

The bite bar should angle about 5 to 10 degrees downwards from the horizontal when the sleeve is worn properly and comfortably in front of the body (see Fig.10).

Sleeves made from ballistic nylon material lack the flexibility at the elbow, they are uncomfortable to wear (sweating), they are easily compressed and therefore they do not offer adequate protection for the decoy from a dog's hard bite, and some users have reported gum injuries to the dog.

Cover attachment:

To attach the sleeve covers, fasteners are provided on either the upper or the lower arm. Upper-arm attachment supposedly gives less cause to tooth injuries and offers a larger biting surface, but it limits the decoy's elbow flexibility and prohibits cover rotation (short cover life).

Lower-arm buckles are normally concealed by the upper edge of the sleeve cover. If not, cut a double-layered shield from an old tire inner tube and slip it over the metal to eliminate potential teeth or gum injuries. Lower-arm buckles give the decoy full elbow flexibility. They also allow easy rotation of the cover for a greatly extended cover life (about 4-5 times longer than a high-buckle cover).

Some manufacturers equip their sleeves with loops so that the covers can be attached with a belt (no interchange possible between buckle and belt-type sleeves/arms).

Friction-fitted sleeve covers do not need straps because of their tight fit. They are compatible with a variety of different sleeves, regardless of buckle arrangement. Friction holds these covers securely in place as long as the dog bites normally (not trying to pull the cover off at the tip). The covers can be rotated in small increments for a greatly extended useful life (5-10 times over regular covers).

SLEEVE COVERS

There are two distinctly different types of sleeves covers: standard (cuff, forearm only) and full-length (wrist to shoulder). The latter one is preferred by trainers who encourage their dogs to bite the upper arm near the shoulder, permissible even by the trial rules. In action, it looks very impressive and is useful especially in the pursuit exercises.

Proper sleeve covers are made of jute fabric or jute strands, braided covers are preferable.

For beginning dogs a burlap sack can be fastened over a used regular sleeve cover.

- Burlap covers are less durable, they are appropriate for young and beginning dogs only. Domestic burlap covers stuffed with (medical) absorbent cotton are impressive for the local police dog demonstrations but useless as training tools.

- Jute covers should be "broken-in" by experienced dogs to become readily accepted by beginners. Most clubs prefer to use a "broken-in" jute cover for the trial.

- Braided (rope) covers allow the dogs to get their teeth readily into it yet the material gives and does not cause any discomfort. Beginning and advanced dogs like the feel of it. Braided covers are the most durable ones and the best buy for the money.

- Composite covers where nylon is braided in with jute are very durable but dangerous. They have no place in training except for very hard biters, and then only when the dog owner is willing to risk gum / tooth injuries to his dog. One has to give, either the cover or the dog.

HIDDEN SLEEVE

Hidden (civilian) sleeves have a rigid, small-diameter leather forearm and a flexible leather joint / upper arm.

The sleeve should be worn under loose fitting civilian clothes, to TEST and not to train a dog.

LEATHER SUIT * OVERALL * PANTS

A leather suit offers the best protection, the overall is more flexible and comfortable to wear and provides good protection, pants with integral suspenders are risky. A decoy should never work without protective gear, there is always a bad apple in the bunch. Invest the money to buy from a reputable firm.

OVERALL

Overalls should be made of leather, double-layered and quilted. They should be flexible and have high square front and back bibs which protect vital parts of the body. Knee joints should be flexible (special sewing/quilting arrangement), zippered legs make changing easier.

Fig.12
SPRINGCHAIN

Pants without bib or those with a V-shaped bib and/or open sides should be combined with a separate jacket. Pants and jacket can be bought individually at double the expense. We find this "suit" less comfortable to wear and not necessary for all but the most demanding training situations.

Single-layer leather gear is comfortable to wear, yet it offers little protection against an "unclean" hard biter.

GLOVES

Heavy duty leather gloves (mittens are preferred over gloves) may be required for civil agitation, in the "guarding of an article" exercise, or for other special applications.

COLLAR for the decoy

A wide leather collar for the decoy is available. It offers protection for the throat / neck area.

GROIN COVER

A leather shield with preformed metal or hard plastic cup protects the genitals of male decoys. It is worn under the overall, held by leather straps and fastened around the hips or to the leather pants.

STICKS

Sticks should break before a decoy can do damage to a dog. Bamboo sticks about 3/8" in diameter and two feet long can be treated with a preservative to prevent rotting when left outside. Reed sticks can be used too.

WHIP

European companies manufacture whips for dog training. They consist of several thin reed sticks in a leather sheath. While this whip looks and sounds fearsome, it is much gentler than a bamboo stick on the dog when used properly, and with the same force. Horse whips are unsuitable, short or long, with or without streamers.

MUZZLE

Good muzzles are made from leather and have a tightly criss-crossed basket with a leather covered steel band in the frontal position (for advanced, civil agitation). Wire-cage muzzles, plastic muzzles and wide-mesh leather muzzles can not prevent an excited dog from biting. The solid, armor-style "bucket" muzzle is unsuitable as well. These imitations expose dog and decoy to injuries, and you

to lawsuits.

LONG LINE

For training purposes get a 30-feet-long, sturdy leather leash, or a nylon rope (mountaineer gear). Check it often, because just like rubber or plastic tie-outs, these materials can be chewed and break.

SPRING CHAIN

We suggest a metal chain with an integral (parallel) spring of proper tension.

This tether softens the impact on the dog's neck, and it is a safeguard against having a loose canine in case of spring failure. It is usually fastened to a stake or another secure anchor point.

A bungee cord would be a good second choice, however its full extension can not be determined exactly.

Steel cables either have no spring or an in-line coil spring which is subject to breakage under stress.

LEASH

Work with a six foot multi-adjustable leather leash, ½ or ¾ inch wide, with a medium-sized buckle.

Also useful is a very short grab leash/dangle, 18" to 24" long, leather or rope, w/o handle loop.

COLLAR / HARNESS

Chainlink, fur-saver, prong and leather collars, they all have their special uses. For passive restraint in protection work, some handlers prefer a body harness which is attached to a long line or chain.

4. SUPPLIERS

It is generally recognized that the best protective gear and training equipment comes from Germany. A few American companies have entered the market, principally trying to duplicate German models. Yet even the one American company that for many years held a monopoly on domestic protective equipment sells now mostly equipment imported from Germany.

Fig.11

B. SCHUTZHUND TRAINING MOTIVATORS

Besides material gadgets we need ideological tools, motivators that help us to get compliance.

The theoretical aspects were dealt with above (page 25 cont.), now let us consider practical applications.

1) We can not pay the dog to do a certain job, and neither can we threaten him with eviction or abandonment, but we can facilitate bonding. Caring for your dog, feeding, housing, grooming, petting, playing, treating him right, showing affection, etc. create a strong bond between dog and master. It cultivates the pack instinct which is the basis for mutual respect, adoration, cooperation. Without it, meaningful training would not be possible. Playing on a daily basis lively games that your dog enjoys just for the fun of it (ball, tug-of-war, etc.), for instance, lays the foundation for a very useful activity that can be called upon whenever a motivator in training is needed.

"**LOVE YOUR DOG, AND HE WILL LOVE YOU BACK.**" (Do the same thing for a human and you might still get a kick in the rear.)

2) We can also offer pleasant and unpleasant experiences (reward and correction), tailored to the job at hand.

Teaching a new exercise, for instance, is most effective with small rewards (little pieces of delicious food) or gentle corrections (moderate arousal), otherwise the pupil would get overly excited and forget about the task at hand.

Consolidation (practicing a learned task) benefits from a high level of arousal. Here, food rewards are often less effective than vigorous activities. Roughhousing, tug-of-war, running and ball playing, or somewhat harsher corrections, will encourage compliance without negatively affecting performance or attitude.

3) Verbal stimulation also qualifies as motivator. Loudness, tone of voice, inflection in the voice show approval, disapproval or determination/force. It will motivate all dogs, not just the sensitive ones.

I maintain:

"Your voice is the most elegant, the most effective, and the always present training tool."

4) Delayed gratification (withholding the reward until the dog performs well) is another tool at our disposal.

With an eager retriever, for instance, we demand that he flops to the ground instantaneously when given the command "down". Only then will we throw the ball for him. Here is the chain of events:

1) Command "down".   He downs slowly.
   Shove him down forcefully / Release / Relax / Repeat.
2) All as shown under 1).   Repeat.
3) This time the dog drops quickly. Throw the ball right away with much enthusiasm. Praise. Play with him.

The mailman enters this office which is totally deserted, except for a big dog emptying wastebaskets. The dog noticing his bewildered look says "Well, I can't believe it either, but this is part of my job."

"By golly, and you even can talk. I have to tell your boss what an intelligent worker he has in you!"

"Please don't.   If he finds that out, the bum will make me answer the phones too."

V. THE COMPONENTS

A. GENERAL TRAINING

Successful dog training requires a structured, systematic approach. It should, however, not be carried to the extreme where an inflexible, ritualized routine creates programmable robots. This would take away the pleasure that dog training provides for both dog and handler, and it would result in a fully trained animal which fails to react properly in non-standard situations. To avoid this, add to your training Play Time, Agility, Versatility and Variety. These are fun activities, but to avoid serious injuries (e.g. gastric torsion, "bloat") allow your dog sufficient time after meals before engaging him. Also, give special consideration to unique needs of very young, old or handicapped dogs.

1. PLAY TIME

Wolf cubs play, developing skills which prepare them for adult life. This stops as they reach maturity.

Not so with their relatives, the dogs. They enjoy playing all their lives. Are they wolves that never grew up? A dog's obsession with play is fortunate, because we can utilize it in training as a powerful motivator. There are a few things, however, we must consider:

1. All dogs play, but they have preferences, based on temperament, physical, mental and health state, age, breed, past experiences, the environment, etc. We must find out what they like best, and what they dislike.

2. We must teach the dog to play our way. We must stimulate interest, guide the activities, lay the ground rules. Only then can we use play as a training tool.

3. Play should involve the right participants (people, puppies, adult dogs), and it should be done at the proper locations (open field, busy place, dog club).

4. To be useful as a motivator, play must involve and center around the owner / trainer.

5. To be an effective motivator, play must stimulate, excite, tease, inspire, reward the dog, and play must

- be attractive: the dog must like and enjoy it, for instance play-fights, play-guarding a toy (watch puppies!), roughhousing, chase, search
- be of the right activity: tug-of-war, rabbit chase, retrieve, sniffing, running, romping, swimming
- be animated with lots of action: search, hide-and-seek, pursuit, chase a ball uphill
- use the right toys: ball, frisbee, disc, stick, kong, rope, hard-rubber toy, dumbbell, rawhide, squeaky toy, dangling toy (like a typical cat toy), etc.
- use the toy most preferred by the dog, and the trainer should always carry it with him
- be scheduled: not right after meals, but before, after and in training as an incentive and reward
- be timed: 10 second play "units" are long enough most of the time (rest ... work ... play ... rest ... work ... play... rest ... etc.)
- be rationed: too little or too much play will diminish returns. "Time-out" (confinement to a crate, or just ignoring him for a few hours) is often beneficial.

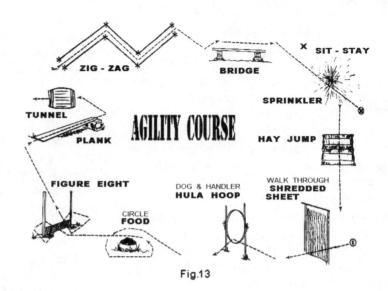

Fig.13

- be earned: If the dog gets to play all the time, why should he work for it ?
- be done regularly, preferably daily.

2. AGILITY

Agility exercises are a very enjoyable part of training, for dog and handler. Do it with a lot of enthusiasm. As a side benefit, you have a chance to show off your dog in public.

There are Clubs that offer challenging obstacle courses for training and competition. If not, you can often find the individual elements at home, in parks, at play grounds, like:

hurdles, brush hurdles, walls, fences, ramps / cat walks / slides, window jumps, hoop jumps, barrel jumps, broad jumps unusual footing, sway bridges, water ditches, sprinklers, teeter totters, weave poles, stairs, car tires, ladders, planks, logs (elevated 1 or 5 ft.), tunnels, etc.

Trick training also belongs into this category. Use treats and teach your dog to jump on a hassock and sit there ("lion tamer"), to roll over ("steam roller"), to play dead ("bang"), to find a treat hidden at random under one of three cups ("magician"), or the ball hidden in a crumbled-up large blanket ("search and rescue"), to unpack a treat from a large paper bag, to fetch the car keys from the ignition (attach a leather or cloth tab to the key ring), take a message to another family member, carry a large shovel, carry a fruit basket, open a door with European-type door handles, etc. To teach these useful tasks you need common sense, delicious treats, and lots of patience.

3. VERSATILITY

Versatility will prepare

- the service dog to pursue the fleeing criminal rather than being distracted by bystanders,
- the bomb detection dog to concentrate on finding the explosive in a confusing environment,
- the guide dog to safely steer his owner rather than fraternizing with another canine,
- the "natural protector" to defend his master rather than hiding behind him,
- the Schutzhund dog to reliably do his "stuff" in a trial.

It requires some ingenuity, and some courage too, to practice for it: The long sit in a crowded shopping mall, the courage test at a family reunion, the recall near a school yard during morning break, the retrieve near the bus station, tracking in pouring rain, doing protection work at night, sending your dog up the ladder and down the slide on a kiddie playground, enlisting the help of several cats (and their owners) for a training session, hiring a friend for a staged burglary at the dog owner's home (tell the neighbors beforehand !!), all these are things you can do to prepare your dog for the unexpected. The more distractions, the more reliable your dog will become eventually.

4. VARIETY

Confronting a dog with unusual, unexpected situations will serve to build his confidence and to stabilize his interactions with the world around him. Of course, the new situations must be tailored to the mental make-up of the canine: for a soft (nervous, shy) dog, a gradual, gentle build-up of tension is necessary, while the hard (bold, outgoing) dog does not require such a cautious approach.

The exercises and games listed below serve both the physical and the mental development of young and of mature dogs, and they provide you with a powerful, pleasant and exciting motivator your dog.

5. GAMES

A) GROUP EXERCISES   (Ideally, there are at least five handlers with their dogs, and at least ten assistants.)

a) Circle Weave

With their dogs sitting at heel, the handlers form a circle and allow about five feet spaces between teams. dog/handler team then leaves its place and weaves its way in and out of the circle, around the stationary other members of the group. Upon return to their spot, the next dog/handler team proceeds. The handler of the moving team encourages his dog to stay in a nice heel position. The stationary members of the group must keep their dogs under control. Instead of just weaving, the team can also do a "Super Figure Eight": circling the first "post" to the left, the next to the right, the next to the left, etc.

b) Reverse

All dog/handler teams form a queue, one team behind the other at a distance of about 10 ft.

The column moves out, at a normal pace. The first team at the head makes an about turn and weaves its way (right, left, right, left etc.) through the group. Having passed the last member, they turn around and join the moving formation at the end.   During all this time, the queue had continued to move straight ahead. The second team then repeats the performance of the first team and so on, until everybody had a chance.

c) Line Formation

Handlers and dogs form a line with about 5 ft. spaces between teams. The line moves forward at a steady pace. One dog/handler team at a time moves in and out of, and through, the line in an irregular pattern.

d) Super - Group

The handlers with their dogs form a line, side by side, leaving about five feet spaces between teams. Trying to maintain the line formation, they all move forward. In the meantime, the assistants have formed the 'super group', wandering aimlessly around and keeping maybe ten feet spaces between themselves.

The dog/handler formation now moves through the super group. Then they do an about turn and come back.

Next, the super group crowds a little more, getting closer together. Again, the handlers and dogs walk through the group. This is repeated a few times, until the crowd is so dense that passing is nearly impossible.

The assistants should watch out for the dogs and not bump into them. They do not have to get out of the way, but they may have to stop momentarily to make passing easier.

e) Group

At least four assistants form a group, they talk and slowly mill about. They are not supposed to get out of the way of a dog/handler team but they may have to stop momentarily to let them pass. One or two dog/handler teams work inside and around this group, taking right, left, about turns and right and left circles around a group member.

A few halts (the dog sits) should be included where a handler may want to shake hands with the assistant, pat him on the shoulder and start a brief conversation.

f) Crowd

Secure an area of maybe 40 x 40 ft with 4 stakes and a rope, for four dog/handler teams. Within its boundaries, the handlers with their dogs practice heeling, including some halts. Assistants slowly decrease the size of the ring by moving the posts closer together. Quit the exercise when the space is so crowded that dogs and handlers have a difficult time to move at all.

g) Wheel

Handlers and dogs walk counter clockwise in a large circle. On command of the instructor, they all make a left turn and move on imaginary spokes to the center of the wheel. When very close together, an "about turn" causes them to move on a radius outward again. Another "about turn" brings them back to the center, and at the very last moment a "halt" is given. The dogs must sit, and the group forms a very tight circle. Then "forward, about turn, right turn" brings all the dogs and handlers back into a circle.

h) Circle

Forming a circle, facing the center, and having the teams separated by about six feet, the handlers now command their dogs to "down". With the dogs remaining in this position, the handlers turn left and step over their own dog. Continuing to walk, they step over every dog in the round until all have returned to the starting point next to their own dog.

l) Trade

The dog/handler teams form a circle as described above.

The training director (or an assistant without dog) approaches one team, inquires about name and special habits of the dog, and takes the lead. The now dog-less handler moves to the right, inquires about name and habits of that dog and takes the lead. This exchange continues until the last handler in the circle takes his charge from the assistant. Then all handlers heel their newly acquired canines in circle formation, using lots of praise and as little correction as possible. The switching process can be repeated, or everybody can claim his own dog, on directions of the training director.

k) Channel

The assistants form two lines about eight feet apart, facing each other. Each person has another one opposite him. Dog/handler teams form a single file and walk through the channel. With the last pair having passed through, the two lines of assistants move a little closer together. This is repeated a few times until in the last pass there is barely enough room for the dog/handler team to walk through.

l) Tunnel

The helpers form a tunnel (like the channel, above): each one of two assistants grasps the hands of his opposite partner (right for left and left for right) and holds them up high. After all dogs have passed through, the assistants can lower their hands, to "lower the ceiling". Again, dogs and handlers file through.

m) Noises

Still maintaining the channel formation, all assistants clap their hands while the dogs and their handlers are moving through. This can be done loud for one pass, not so loud for another pass. As a modification, the assistants can say "booo" instead of clapping hands, or they can make other sounds at their discretion.

n) Barriers

The assistants still maintain the channel formation. One of them goes flat on his tummy across the channel. The dogs and their handlers pass through, over the barrier. For the next turn, one more volunteer goes down and so on, until it becomes difficult for dogs and handlers to negotiate the course.

o) Ring

The assistants form a tight ring, leaving very little space (maybe 4 inches) between each others feet.

One dog is held by a volunteer on a slip leash, about 30 yards away. His owner, inside the circle, calls him.

The volunteer releases the dog which now wants to get to his owner. Many dogs first try to find an opening in the human wall, then they will force their way through it. The assistants should not discourage the dog from going through, but they should not voluntarily create an opening either. All the while the owner is encouraging his dog to come to him.

p) Friends

Once inside the circle, the owner praises and pets his dog and then stands upright again, not giving his dog any attention. The assistants squat and keep their shoulders together, trying to prevent the dog from leaving. The dog should now be encouraged to investigate the circle and the people forming it: each assistant has a few tidbits in his hands or pockets. Once the dog comes to him he pets him and lets him have a treat.

q) Startling

With handler and dog (loose) in the circle, all assistants will squat suddenly, on command of the leader. Then they will stand up again, just as quickly. Repeat a few times until the dog has gained confidence.

r) Cornering

In unison, all assistants move backwards, enlarging the circle. On command they close in again. This can be repeated a few times. Then the assistants clap their hands while opening and closing the circle, or they make other distracting noises. All the while, dog (loose) and handler remain in the circle.

s) Conclusion

In conclusion, the assistants form a circle again, standing upright, shoulder to shoulder. The handler leaves the circle. His dog remains behind and is prevented from following through the tight human wall the assistants are forming. From a distance of about 30 yards the handler calls his dog which is now allowed to force his way through the barrier.

B) INDIVIDUAL EXERCISES

◆Most dogs love to run after a thrown ball (or a stick, a "loaded" kong etc.), the rest should be taught to enjoy it. Play it with much enthusiasm, run with your dog after the ball, compete with him. Once he plays the game you just have to throw the ball, giving him much needed exercise without wearing you out. Use a ball launcher (commercially available, looks like a ladle with extra-long handle) to effortlessly throw much farther. Sometimes go to an area with hills. Throw the ball uphill, to increase the difficulty, and to stimulate development of your dog's front assembly.

◆Many dogs enjoy playing frisbee. Start with two people throwing the frisbee slow and low. The dog will want to participate and try to grab it. Eventually he can take the place of the second person.

◆Playing tug-of-war is another game every dog will enjoy. Get a sock, an old pair of jeans, a burlap sack, and shake it gently in front of the dog. Move or run away with it, tease the dog, let im grab it and then gently (or a little more vigorously at a later stage) pull and give - like in the real game. Avoid sudden, jerky movements, surrender the prize in the end.

◆Secure two tennis balls to a two-foot rope, one on each end (you can buy that). Hold the rope in the middle, wiggle it and tease two dogs to each grab one ball. Then let them continue in their tug-of-war.

◆Chasing a rolling object provides much fun also. Ask your dog to bring the ball back to you. Practice in unfamiliar locations if he does not come to you, and/or run away from him. You can try a long line too.

◆Drover: Get a light-weight beach ball and place a treat near the base under it. To reach the treat, he will push the ball away with his nose. At that time say: "push", to teach him to drive the ball with his nose. Guide this action into the desired direction.

◆Slalom: Get a set of plastic traffic cones and line them up, four feet apart. Teach your dog to drive the ball through the line: right, left, right, left ....

◆Use a muffin baking pan, put five or six tennis balls into the holes and hide a small treat under each ball. Lift one ball briefly, show him the treat, put the ball back quickly. Then tell him to "take the muffins out".

◆Soccer: Place two small plastic traffic cones about four feet apart (the "goal"), step between them and spread your legs, then tease your dog (with a treat) to roll the ball between your feet. If he does well, step away and coax him to score a goal. Then trade: you move the ball, he guards the goal.

◆ Volleyball: Get a light-weight beach ball and play Doggy Soccer with him. Kick it and encourage your dog to move it with his nose or feet. Then change to Volleyball: throw it just over his head. He may jump up and bounce it. Give lots of praise and encouragement.

◆Obstacles and Challenges: See Temperament Tests (page 13 cont.), Agility and Versatility (above).

◆Get out your remote-controlled toy car and introduce it to your dog (cats will play with it, dogs may or may not). Move it, let him chase it. Attach a bacon strip to the car's antenna, to increase the fun.

◆Blow soap bubbles (non-toxic stuff) with one of those toy kits. Chasing them will amuse a lot of dogs.

◆Many canines enjoy searching for thrown objects in high grass or in underbrush. Use small potatoes or wild apples - if available. They can be abandoned if the dog does not find them. Scent them by rubbing them in your hands. Throw them first small distances, farther away later on. A "loaded" Kong might stimulate interest.

◆Short fun tracks can be a game too. Hide at the end something that the dog really wants (see chapter on "Tracking"). Be enthusiastic about it, and do not turn it into a "job".

◆Pursuit: Run away with a flapping sack or a piece of cloth tied to a string or to your leash. Encourage your dog to pursue the prey and to take hold of it. End with a happy tug of war. Let a stranger drag the prey later on, move to unfamiliar locations, etc. (see also "Rabbit Chase", page 100).

◆Race track: Get one of the blinds from the protection "Quartering" routine and drive four dowels, stakes, rods or guide rollers for a garden hose around the perimeter. Tie a toy to the end of your 30 ft. long line, guide the line around the stakes, get your dog and start pulling on the free end of the rope. The dog will chase the toy just like in the professional dog races, and you have laid the foundation for the protection "quartering" routine.

◆Chase and play-fighting between canines helps to build their muscles, fighting strategies, pack instinct.

The dog learns to submit to the stronger one, and to fairly deal with the submission of a weaker partner.

◆Play-fights with humans should also be part of a dog's early training.

At first, gently grasp, and immediately release, the dog by his scruff or clamp his snout (do not intimidate him). He probably will seize your arm and hold it in his mouth in a play-like fashion. If he bites too hard, act as if you were hurt badly. Exaggerate, vent an outcry of pain. He will be gentler from then on. In time, you can play a little rougher. Others in the family, or a friend, can take your role also.

Most dogs will play this game with much enthusiasm, others have to overcome some inhibitions first. Exercise some restraint, however, if the dog develops a passion for it.

◆Guarding: Let the puppy have a nice juicy bone. Stand right next to him to give him moral support. Then get another person (but not the owner or a family member) to approach him and to act as if he wants to steal the bone. The game is over as soon as the dog starts to growl, the dog has won and receives praise.

If the dog does not react, take the bone away from him. Repeat after a couple of days or weeks. In time, even a young, shy or insecure dog will learn to defend his possessions. The objective of the game is to teach the dog that his warning (growl) will be respected. By the way, dogs like to play this game among themselves with objects that are often completely uninteresting to them. (We should mention here, that the **owner** must always be able to approach the dog during feeding time and to take the food away.)

C) TEAM EXERCISES

◆Swim Races: Dogs swim with, or without, their handlers to compete, like crossing a small body of water.

◆Sprint: For a recall, several handlers line up and sit their dogs side by side, maybe 6 feet apart. Then they walk away and face their dogs. On signal of the leader they all, at the same time, call their dog. Winner is the dog that first sits in front of his handler.

◆Relay Races: Dog/handler teams compete, on foot or bicycle. The handler goes along, but the dog must carry a tag clipped to his collar, or carry a dumbbell, a basket, a stick which is then passed on to the next team, etc.

◆Olympics: Mark start and goal of the "race track". One at a time, the handler remains at the start, throws a tennis ball past the goal, send his dog to retrieve it. Time it. Winner is the fastest dog.

◆Slalom: see "Slalom", above

◆Obstacle Course: Set up the course (page 38), let dog/handler teams compete. Time it.

◆Drill Team: Dog/handler teams perform various obedience exercises in unison, maintaining line formation. A team leader calls the shots. Use standard obedience routines, or those from "Group Exercises" (p.39).

My favorite demo: Do a long down in line, handlers opposite their dogs. One at a time, each handler calls his neighbor's dog by name (just "Fido", not "Fido come" !!). No response. In the second go-around, each handler calls his own dog by name - he comes. Claim magic. Perform at hospitals, schools, clubs, etc.

◆Rush hour: Seek out "doggie parks", training classes or clubs that can provide playful interaction for dogs. On leash, they will often be uneasy, even hostile toward each other, but not off lead:

With the group in a small fenced-in area, maybe 50 by 50 feet, we release one dog. He will say "hello" to everyone. Then we set the second dog free and let him make the rounds, then the third dog etc. We always wait to see that the newcomer has gotten along with the others. The dog's initial caution will change into curiosity and playfulness. Do not be overly protective of your dog, roughhousing is all right. However, someone must interfere quickly when a dog gets out of control (which is very rare). Read the dogs, observe, anticipate. Use your leash to give the aggressor a well-aimed whack before a bite occurs. The troublemaker is then put on leash and walked around in the group. Curb any further aggression with a quick and not-too-gentle correction. Restart the group. Release the trouble-maker and one other friendly dog in a smaller area, but be prepared to curb misbehavior. Then add one dog at a time, as before.

In my obedience classes, we had up to 97 dogs run loose before instructions started - and I do not use assistants. Quite a sight !!

6. GUN SHYNESS   (see also pages 14, 17)
Dogs have a highly developed sense of hearing and, being smarter than the people in a disco-crowd, they detest loud noises. Ignorant and lazy people wrongly label these animals "gun shy". If a dog ignores gunshots, the dog is either deaf or genetically defective - not gun-proofed.   Most gun shy dogs are man-made by

- firing a gun too often, too loud, or too close to the dog
- teasing, upsetting or even harming a dog with a fire arm
- frightening a dog with loud noises
- transmitting the fear of a pack member to other dogs
- transmitting the anxiety of a startled handler to his dog when a gun was fired unexpectedly.

They have become gun shy because they experienced something unpleasant when a gun was fired. Retraining, replacing those earlier undesirable associations with new desirable ones, requires understanding, time, patience. The process can also be used to introduce novice dogs to gun shots.

Start by playing ball with your dog, heeling, etc. Show lots of enthusiasm and praise while someone fires a few shots in the distance. Ignore the noise. Do this for a few weeks, until the dog pays no attention to it. Then add an isolated shot at closer range. Let the dog see the shooter, be calm, pet him casually. Then ask several people to discharge a firearm (blanks) at random behind their back, without any commotion.

Some handlers use CD's or cassette tapes with prerecorded noises like gun shots, fire crackers or sounds recorded in the kitchen, in a shop, in a factory, at an airport, bus station, street corner etc. Play this not too loud for 15 minutes daily, but always when the handler and/or another member of the family is present.

It is foolish to assume that gun shyness can be prevented or cured by repeatedly firing a gun close to the dog when he is fed. This is painful, and eventually the dog will have had enough and become really gun shy.

There are some dogs that are fearful by nature, and gun shyness is one way how this trait presents itself. These dogs have a temperament problem that can not be corrected through conditioning or training, they are genetically predisposed. They are unsuitable for most service work.

"Your dog does not have a nose? How does he smell?"
"Terrible!"

B. TRACKING
1. BASIC PHILOSOPHY

Humans rely on their eyes when investigating unfamiliar surroundings, dogs use their nose.
Nose work is the domain of dogs. The objective in training a dog to track is not to teach him to use his nose, but to tell him which odorous trail we want him to follow.
All dogs can track, although some do it better than others. The trainer just has to channel their talents in the right direction. An adult German Shepherd Dog has an estimated 500 million of olfactory sensory cells occupying an area of about 26 square inches, compared to about 10 million and $\frac{1}{2}$ square inch in a human. Experiments have shown that dogs can detect the presence of butyric acid (a component of sweat) diluted at a ratio of 1 gram to $4\frac{1}{2}$ million cubic feet of air, an amount too small to be registered by the most sensitive gas chromatograph, a highly sophisticated analytical instrument.

Olfactory acuity, then, is directly related to the quantity and the quality of the detection equipment.

A long-nosed dog, like a German Shepherd, generally can handle a tracking job with much less effort than, for instance, a Boxer with his short nose and fewer olfactory sensory cells. Some SchH "experts" dispute that, but go to a few trials and convince yourself: Even the Boxers that track very well have to work much harder to finish the track then the average German Shepherd.

Teaching a dog to track is rather difficult since the handler is "left in the dark". He can not see or smell where the odor is, he has to rely on indirect means to control his dog. Serious training problems will occur if the dog is working properly on the track but gets corrected by mistake, or if he gets praised at the wrong time.

Furthermore, the dog can not be forced to track. Too much pressure from the handler, or too harsh a correction have ended the tracking career of many a promising dog. Yet, there are also those dogs that lead their handlers by the nose, literally. If the dog refuses to work (excluding justifiable reasons) or if he is taking advantage of the handler, then a proper correction from an experienced trainer is quite in order.

A ten week old puppy can negotiate a mini-"Schutzhund I" track without problems if he was started and trained the right way. An older dog requires more effort, more teaching, more skill of the trainer to accomplish the same, especially if in the past he has been discouraged from sniffing the ground.

In any way, start simple and pick the best conditions you can find: flat terrain without bushes, trees or buildings, ankle-high grass, little wind, track laid into the wind, track well scented, lots of rewards and lots of praise. Proceed from here to more difficult conditions by changing one, and only one !, variable at a time. Let the dog become confident and proficient with the new variation, then move on to the next.

Motivation is the key to a good tracking performance. For best results it should be linked to one (or more) of three basic instincts: the survival instinct (food reward), the retrieve instinct (play reward) and the pack instinct (scent of handler or another dog on the track, handler at the end of track). Using the protective instinct (biting as reward) is counter-productive for nearly all dogs (see "Arousal", page 29).

2. OBJECTIVE

The dog must retrace the path of a tracklayer, involving various track ages up to three hours, various ground covers, various weather conditions, various distractions, and he must find several well-scented articles "lost" by the tracklayer.

3. SUGGESTED COMMAND: "Find it"
SUGGESTED RELEASE COMMAND: "OK"

4. GENERAL
SCENT

A "track" is a semi-continuous ground disturbance, caused by animals, humans, or things (e.g. cars).

In finding the track, the dog is guided by vapors ("scent") which can originate from four different sources:

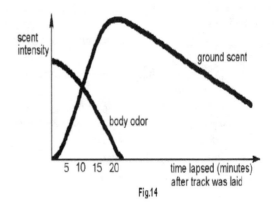

Fig.14

1. ground scent (ground disturbance, release of entrapped gases, crushed vegetation, etc.)
2. body odor (sweat, shed skin cells)
3. deposits (personal belongings, clothing)
4. contaminants (rubbed-off particles from shoes, spills of oil, blood, urine, feces etc.)

Of these, the ground scent is of the greatest importance (>95%). Body odor is highly volatile and will disappear, for all practical purposes, before the dog goes on the track. Shed skin cells are too few to be of any consequence. Air currents as well as Brown's Molecular Movement dilute and distribute the body odor and the odor from the decaying skin rafts so fast that normally all identifiable traces have disappeared after about twenty minutes. Only articles or contaminants left behind can replenish or regenerate the body odor once the track has been laid. This, however, does not hold true for the ground scent. The initial foot step of the tracklayer is only the beginning of a long series of continuing processes, generating more and more scent and reaching a maximum at about 20 minutes. Because of this "hump", a SchH I track is started at that time in a trial. There is a slow liberation of gases that were entrapped in the ground or that were generated by the crushing and the decay of vegetation, bacterial action etc. It generates little invisible "clouds" which - under equilibrium conditions - hover just above the ground. The "clouds" from several footsteps delineate a corridor (the track) which a dog is able to recognize and to follow long after any body odor has disappeared, up to maybe a couple of days under ideal conditions. European service dogs are working 48 hour old tracks for distances over 10 miles.

This theory has been proven experimentally. Dogs would, for instance, readily follow a trail made by a machine with porcelain feet (Most's wheel, weighs about 150 lbs.); dogs would quit the track at the point where the tracklayer was lifted off the ground by a cable system and hauled away without touching the ground; at intersections with a second track dogs would readily switch to the other trail laid by a second tracklayer of the same weight at the same time; and so on.

These findings indicate (and millions of dogs substantiate the fact) that a dog can be trained on his owner's track, even in advanced tracking, provided the track has aged more than twenty minutes. They also indicate that dogs do not need an article from the tracklayer to "take scent" in order to follow his trail - a widespread misconception.

TRACKER TYPES

Tracking is hard work for the dog, weight losses of several pounds have been recorded during advanced tracking tests. The demands vary, however, depending on how the dog works.

♦ The **FRINGE FOLLOWER** proceeds at the edge of the scent corridor, comparing presence and absence of tracking odors as his guide. This leads him often a considerable distance away from the track (sideways), with side wind, or with fresh tracks through lush vegetation. This is hard work and undesirable tracking behavior. It should be discouraged.

♦ The **STEP TRACKER** seeks out every individual footprint, sniffs it out, and analyses its odor. This also is hard labor and very tiring, unsuitable for long tracks. We could call this dog a perfectionist.

♦ The **LINE TRACKER** proceeds at a reasonable speed on the track, inhaling and exhaling normally. Since he advances while exhaling (when he can't sniff) he is more likely to overshoot an article or a turn, yet he is less tired, and therefore more alert than the step tracker, allowing him to quickly recognize his mistake. While his counterpart would

"die" on a long track, he saves energy and can go on to finish the job (a "green" dog?).

METEOROLOGICAL FACTORS

Canines don't mind tracking in rain, handlers usually do. The true working dog, and even a competitor in a trial, can not wait for nice weather. So one might as well get ready for the inevitable.

Atmospheric conditions (the weather) influence the scent "clouds". Their rise and fall, their lateral movement, their compression and expansion decisively influence the dog's tracking performance.

Fog

Fog provides favorable tracking conditions because of a high moisture environment. It discourages tracking by sight and limits visual distractions. Orientation is difficult for tracklayer and handler. The teaching aspect, therefore, is reduced to a minimum, the dog is more or less in control.

Dew

Dew on the ground presents a situation similar to FOG, the orientation problems, however, do not exist. This condition is advantageous for beginning dogs and handlers. Since the track is often visible, fewer chances exist to correct the dog wrongly. It also gives the handler the unique opportunity to analyze his dog's behavior when on and off the track, and it tells the handler how closely his dog is following the actual trail.

Rising sun will let the track scent rise slowly and intensify it for even more favorable tracking conditions.

Rain

There is - in general - no need to refuse going on the track while it is raining.

- *Light rain* after a dry spell will actually improve tracking conditions. Light rain onto already wet ground will do little to change the scent pattern, for the better or for the worse.
- *Medium rain* "dilutes" the odor, a heavy downpour will wash it away and make tracking difficult.

Fig.15 MOST's WHEEL

- If a *heavy rain* stops within a short time after the track was laid, tracking can proceed successfully.

If the track is laid after a heavy rain, tracking - in general - poses no serious problem (dogs can follow a track even through a shallow body of standing water).

Snow

Lingering odor in the refrigerator is a favorite subject of TV commercials. During winter, nature provides us with a giant ice box and - like in the small one at home - scents are extremely well preserved. Cold weather, some sunshine and a little snow provide ideal tracking conditions which may even spoil advanced dogs. The visible trail is only partly responsible for that fact.

Frost

Frost without snow and bare, packed ground create very difficult tracking conditions. Plowed fields or sufficient vegetation, even if dead or dormant, are needed to make tracking tolerable. While any scent is preserved rather well, biological decay processes are at a near standstill at such low temperatures.

Dryness

The olfactory process needs a solvent to function, the dog's nasal tissue must be moist. So, water your dog and wet his nose before starting on a track. For the same purpose take some water along on the trail.

Scarce or dried out vegetation can not produce a generous amount of scent, making tracking more difficult but not impossible. Dogs trained in such an area and then brought to a tracking test in colder regions usually score very high. Likewise: dogs trained in colder regions and then competing in arid climates often do poorly without extensive retraining.

Extended Sunshine / High Atmospheric Pressure

The scent-producing biological decay processes are accelerated at higher temperatures. On a sunny day more scent is generated more rapidly. The scent "reservoir", however, can deplete more rapidly.

A beginning dog will benefit from this situation. Because of the more generous supply of scent he should do well on a sunny day when allowed to work shortly after the track was laid (10 to 20 min.).

An experienced dog, on the other hand, might not perform well in the same situation. The abundance of scent will very likely cause him to track with high nose, or to follow the fringe of the scent path.

The situation changes as time passes by: An aged track under the same conditions is much more difficult to work (FH, TDX tracking tests, see "depletion" above). For training purposes, however, clever handlers use this phenomenon, to correct dogs that track with high noses. When such a dog is presented with a "sunny" track maybe 4-5 hours old, he will have to change his habit and put his nose to the ground.

Morning Hours

The earth is often much colder than the air, and moisture in the air causes dew on the ground. The tracking scent is trapped there, in a very thin layer on the bottom. This provides the dog with a constant, reliable guide to follow. The intensity of the odor and its dissipation will increase as the ground starts to warm up.

Noon Hour

At high noon, with sunshine, the ground can accumulate considerable heat. Convection currents then spread the tracking scent widely, mostly upwards if there is no wind.

Air and vegetation are often dried out, and the heat interferes with the physical activities of the dog. In the wild, the animals would normally rest under these conditions. The higher temperature does, however, accelerate the biological decay processes which produce the scent. Tracking is not made impossible at that time of the day, it is just made more difficult.

Evening Hours

The early evening hours usually show a fairly even temperature balance between the ground and the lower layers of air. This will account for rather stable tracking conditions. Everything else being the same, more scent is generated than in the morning. The scent, however, is not concentrated as much in the very low layers above the ground. This may cause the dog to track with high nose, or to air-scent.

Nighttime

Noticeable increases in tracking performance are possible during darkness. This is not surprising since the loss of one sense (sight) sharpens the others (nose ability). A problem arises, however, since the handler is very limited in guiding or assisting his dog, and he can do little to control or even monitor his dog's actions.

For service dogs, special harnesses have been designed that are fitted with a low-current light on the dog's back. This does not serve to shine on the dog's path, it just lets the handler know where his partner is.

Blindfolding the dog is a trick to create night for the dog yet leave daylight for his handler. Just like a dog can be conditioned to wear a muzzle before it is needed, he can be conditioned to wear a blindfold. Some trainers report better tracking results with this method. They also like being able to use flags alongside the track to indicate its direction.

One wonders, though, if a sportsman can really justify such a drastic measure as depriving the dog of one of his senses. If this method finds acceptance, the logical extensions would be devastating (would you surgically mutilate your dog to create a super-tracker ???).

Wind

High winds make tracking difficult, they can even make it impossible under adverse conditions, like scarce vegetation or old tracks. Moderate to light wind will shift the scent clouds and cause specific responses.

A tracking dog can encounter three conditions, basically:

a) frontal wind (Fig.16)

The wind comes from straight ahead, picking up the scent "clouds" and blowing them right into the dog's face.

Since more scent is generated all the time (see above), this odor stream is continuous. Also, the total scent carried by the wind is stronger than the scent developing at the individual footprint just in front of the dog. Therefore dogs have a tendency to lift their head while tracking into the wind (air scenting).

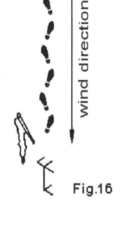

Fig.16

The first few tracks for a beginning dog should always be laid into the wind. The scent cone loaded with track odors will help to get the idea across what tracking is all about. An experienced dog, however, may be turned off by this heavy scent, or he may get into the habit of air scenting. As a corrective measure we can let the track age longer, use ground with scarce vegetation, use a light-weight tracklayer, ask the track-

Fig.17

layer to take large steps, or we can take advantage of atmospheric conditions which have been discussed above.

b) back wind (Fig.17)

The wind blows in the direction of the track and carries the scent "clouds" away from the dog. The dog must put his nose down to the footprint, to catch the freshly generated scent before it gets blown away. This condition is ideal for teaching a dog to keep the nose on the ground. The dog should, however, already be familiar with the tracking concept.

c) side wind (Fig.18)

The wind blows at an angle to the track, from the left or from the right.

The guiding scent clouds will be on the downwind side of the track and most dogs will follow the trail in this fashion. The dog's path, then, is parallel to the track, slightly to the left in the example (Fig.18). The distance between the path of the tracklayer and that of the dog will depend on wind velocity, track age, kind of vegetation,

wind direction

Fig.18

presence of windbreaks (shrubs, trees, other obstacles) etc.

During the teaching phase, the dog should be encouraged to stay on the track, to prevent him from becoming a "fringe follower". In a trial, a side shift of about two feet is usually not faulted, depending on the weather and ground conditions, and on the experience of the judge.

Since the wind direction is a factor that can be taken into account in training more easily than others we would like to re-emphasize the following points:

- Consider the wind when laying a track and go into the wind when teaching a novice dog.
- Go with the wind to force a knowledgeable dog to keep his nose on the ground.
- Use side wind to train a dog to stay on the track.
- Try to keep a distance of about 150 ft between adjoining tracks.

THE TRACKLAYER

The tracklayer and his technique have a significant effect on how well the dog performs on the track. In a trial, he can help the dog to pass a tracking test, or he can make him fail. Tracklayers should be selected carefully, and they should be trained thoroughly.

• The intensity of the "scent path" is directly related to the weight of the tracklayer who causes the ground disturbance. A heavy person will be helpful for the beginning dog, a light person will sharpen the skills of the advanced dog. In a trial, an average-weight person is called for. For a cross-track, however, a light-weight individual should be chosen, to make the difference more noticeable to the dog.

• Proper footwear, preferably water-proof boots, should be used so that the tracklayer does not have to take detours around wet or rough spots. Leather boots are often recommended, but their advantage (inherent odor) over rubber boots is either non-existent or negligible.

• Although all kinds of objects can be located by the tracking dog, leather articles of neutral color and the size of a wallet are preferable. Several hours before the tracklayer goes to work he should place them in an inner pocket of his clothing, to allow them to become scented properly. For a trial, 30 minutes is the recommended time; advanced dogs can be tested with shorter conditioning periods.

• Before going on the track, the tracklayer should be given a sketch of the proposed trail. Start, turns, article drops, cross tracks and end are indicated on it. In advanced tracking he should mark the intersections of the cross track with flags or other indicators. This will guide the second tracklayer who removes these flags in passing. Portable radios / cell phones allow the tracklayer to communicate with the instructor/judge.

• At the starting place, the tracklayer stomps down a cone-shaped area of about 1 square yard for about 30 to 60 seconds. He then remains there for another minute or so before leaving in the indicated direction.

• For the first 6-8 feet, short steps and heavy impressions, maybe even triple-laying (going forward, back on the same line, forward again) are recommended. The track should be walked at a normal pace. Large strides before, and short steps after a turn are recommended. Angles should be rounded very slightly.

• When dropping an article, the tracklayer should not just toss it to the ground but bend down in his knees and place it right behind the heel of the foot moved last, without much hesitation or breaking his stride. Some handlers prefer to drop the article in front of them and to step on it.

• Under windy conditions, a weight might have to be secured to the article, to prevent it from being blown

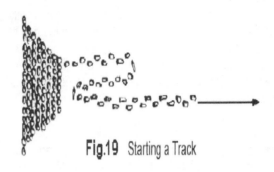

Fig.19 Starting a Track

away. There are also known instances of squirrels and birds having stolen the article.

• At trail's end, the tracklayer may want to leave the area with a few leaps, to clearly indicate its termination.

ORIENTATION IN TRACKING

When teaching a dog to track it is absolutely necessary to know EXACTLY where the track is. Artificial markers like flags, poles, discs may cause the smart dog to hunt by sight. Tracks laid alongside natural boundaries, furrows, mower lines etc. will teach the dog to use his eyes rather than his nose. A well laid track is, therefore, more difficult to trace for the tracklayer and for the handler, and both have to learn to properly orient themselves in the field. The following exercise demonstrates this point:

Novice handlers without their dogs are instructed to line up, maybe 10 ft. apart, and to mark their position. Then they are sent about 25 paces straight ahead. After a right (or left) turn and a few more paces they must place a personalized match on the ground. Then they are called back.

A little later they must retrieve the match, without the assistance of their dogs. The rate of success is usually very low, even when the exercise and its objective were explained beforehand. People count their paces, scrutinize the vegetation and try to memorize details, stomp the feet in the ground etc., without success. Maybe dropping a fifty dollar bill instead of the match would bring better results!

The only way to approach this exercise - and to lay and to find a track - is to walk a straight line toward a distinct object in the distance, one that preferably lines up with another permanent marker (don't pick a parked car !!). To walk a straight line without aiming for such a marker is impossible. An observer lined up behind the tracklayer will confirm that quickly. However, if the tracklayer keeps the first marker superimposed over the second one in the distance (just like a rifle sight), then there is only one straight line he can go.

In the sketch (Fig.20), the tracklayer would move right and left until he can find a suitable line-up, here the telephone pole and the corner of the house. This is the spot where he puts his starting

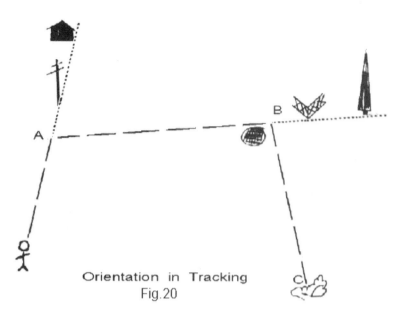

Orientation in Tracking
Fig.20

flag into the ground. When moving out, the tracklayer keeps his eye fixed on the telephone pole.

He will be all right as long as the pole and the corner of the house line up. Only once in a while, and then only very quickly, does he glance at the ground in front of him, to make sure it is safe and suitable for a track. Taking his sight off the marker for more than a very brief moment would cause a substantial deviation from the straight-line course, requiring a correction and causing a wavy track pattern.

In the vicinity of the intended turn the tracklayer will be on the lookout for two other objects that can be lined up. When he reaches point (A) where the fence corner superimposes the distant tree, he will make his turn and proceed toward point (B). There he can not find another suitable line-up. So he makes his turn at point (B) around a spot of dry grass (or another natural, untouched marker) and proceeds toward a group of bushes at (C).

Later on, when the dog works on the track, the handler knows exactly, to the inch, when the dog is on or off the track. He can influence and guide or praise his dog according to performance.

USE OF EQUIPMENT

Training problems are sometimes related to the use of unsuitable equipment, or even to the improper use of good equipment. An entangled leash, or articles blown away by the wind are examples.

Some trainers use a harness, assuming that it will allow the dog to perform better in the field. Other trainers are concerned about dependence on excessive equipment, and they maintain that tracking

with the leash attached to the dead ring on the choke collar is actually beneficial.

As long as there is no correction (jerk) given with the leash, either method is acceptable. In any event, we suggest that the dog be tracked on lead. Free tracking (off lead) forgoes a vital communication link, the leash. It is permissible, even in a trial (SchH III), but it invites problems. Without a restraint, dogs will often track too fast and superficial, overshooting turns and missing articles. In addition, control over the dog is difficult to maintain if he decides that chasing or hunting is more fun than tracking.

During practice sessions, 90% of all tracks should be done on the six foot lead. Use the 30 foot regulation leash very sparingly in training, mainly in preparation for a trial.

Working properly with the long line requires some practice. Remember:

◆The line must be of suitable, user-friendly material.

◆ The line must be free of tangles. Gather up the line in wide loops (like sailors or cowboys), or wind it on a rack (like a clothes line), or gather it in a small bucket (like a long wick in an oil lamp). Store it that way. Prior to the beginning of tracking, stretch out the line close to the starting flag,.

◆ The handler must remain at the starting place until all 30 ft. of the leash are reeled out. Most handlers are not properly prepared when the end of the line comes up. The resulting jolt (snap) is unintended, nevertheless it causes the dog to interrupt tracking and to look back. Prepare for a smooth transition from feeding the line to following the dog:

-tie a knot in the line five feet ahead of the end,

-keep hands apart and let the line run through them, straightening out tangles with the "first" hand,

-initially hold arms close to the body, then stretch them out when the knot comes up,

-have one foot in front of you and step right out when the knot comes up.

◆ Hold your end of the line high, maybe at eye level or higher.

◆ The line must be fairly taut during tracking. The tension should be such that if a handkerchief was fastened to the middle of the 30 ft. leash, it would be just short of touching the ground.

◆ Come to an immediate stop and reclaim the line hand over fist as soon as the dog backs up, circles, etc. The line naturally piles up in loops on the ground and will reel out without problems later on.

◆ Cut the corner once your dog has negotiated a turn, to maintain proper line tension.

◆ Speedily advance to any obstacle that has caught the line. While one hand holds that part of the line unobstructed that goes to the dog, the other hand tries to free the line as quickly as possible, hopefully without letting the dog feel any restrictions or jolts from the rescue operation.

◆ Let go of the leash if the dog negotiates an obstacle that is too difficult to handle for humans (hole in fence, a narrow passage way, a creek etc.). Go around the obstacle quickly and pick up the dragging leash there.

Proper line handling can be learned in practice sessions, with the trainers taking turns in playing dog or handler. Let the participants describe their sensations, actions and reactions to the person at the other end of the leash.

5. TEACHING PROCEDURE

MOTIVATION

Motivation is the key to solicit the dog's willingness to work. In obedience, the drilling and performance of artificial responses is rewarded. For tracking, we exploit and reward a canine's natural qualities and characteristics, art-specific stimuli and responses, natural instincts, innate responses, inborn motivators, native drives. The play instinct (toys), the pack instinct (handler), the hunting instinct (scents, prey), the mating instinct (scents), the survival instinct (food), to some degree even the protective instinct (bite work), they all can successfully be utilized as motivators.

We rely predominantly on praise, play and food in tracking. Each one of these motivators becomes more effective when the dog has been (partially) deprived of the basic need to which it relates. Some suggestions:

* If you use praise and play, you should give very little attention to your dog for a day or two: not playing with him, not throwing the ball or stick, not taking him for a walk, a ride or a swim. Some handlers even board their dog at a kennel for a few days before going into an important trial. After the isolation let the beginner dog watch you going out and hide a favored toy at the end of the track. Start him, encourage him, and play his favorite game at the end if he performs well. A playmate (dog) at the end of the track may work also.

* Using food as an incentive is a very effective way to teach tracking. You need a hungry dog:

Puppies should be worked just before feeding time. Feed them at the end of the track. For an older dog, cut his ration down to 50% for two days and do not to feed him at all the third day. Train with food on the forth day (you will not harm your dog, wolves and wild dogs don't live on a strict feeding schedule either).

CORRECTIONS

Strive to maintain a pleasant attitude, avoid unpleasant experiences and active punishment (no harsh scolding, physical corrections etc.). Discourage undesirable behavior (leaving the track, following the wrong scent, etc.), by saying "Hey..", or "Back", or "No....o" (easy !), or "Phooey" (from "Pfui", German). If corrections have to be given they should be of a passive nature, like restraint. For instance: Your dog may want to run after a rabbit. Instead of yanking the dog back with a "no, bad boy", quietly hold on to the leash until the dog has calmed down. Then excitedly tell him "let's track". The first approach may bring the dog back to the track, but his heart is not in it. The second approach, on the other hand, can maintain the happy tracking attitude. There are exceptions to this rule, and they apply mostly to advanced dogs who want to take advantage of their handlers. Then a proper correction from an experienced trainer is in order.

TRACK BAITING

There are two requirements that have to be met when using food as the motivator in tracking:

1. the dog must be REALLY hungry, and
2. the food must be something the dog REALLY craves.

Study your dog and find the right procedure. Determine what kind of food he likes best: raw hamburger, sausage, broiled liver, fried chicken, meat, fish, etc. Canned fish is an excellent motivator (portable, handy). Some of the commercial dog treats may work also. Regular dog food, on the other hand, would be a poor choice for baiting, although establishing the habit of feeding the dog his daily meal at the end of the track will be quite helpful, too.

- ◆ If food does not seem to work, the pupil was either not hungry enough, or the wrong bait was used.

  Experiment, try something different, try different treats (see page 26/27). Of course, there may also be other reasons why a dog does not want to track (see "Problems" page 57).

- ◆ Frequent food drops on the track (major portion of the bait at the end) will catch the dog's interest.

- ◆ You can drag the bait like fresh meat, rotten meat, rotten fish etc. on a string behind you, rub or dab it on the ground, sprinkle canned cat food or meat powder on he track, or dispense from a spray bottle broth of meat, chicken, fish, or shrimp.

Or consider alternatives:

- ◆ Some trainers drag a brick or concrete block on a string behind (to intensify the ground disturbance).

- ◆ Some trainers scent their shoes with urine from a bitch in season (very effective with male dogs).

- ◆ Some trainers fit a length of pipe with a spongy plug at the lower end and fill it with urine from a (healthy) dog. Dabbing the sponge end on the ground once in a while gets most dogs (and bitches) interested in the track. You can use a plastic fire plug on a large plate to collect the urine from your dog.

PUPPY TRAINING

The earlier a dog is introduced to scent work, the easier it is to make a good tracker out of him.

Right after birth a pup will use his nose to find his way to warmth and food (his mother) since he can neither hear nor see at that time. This skill is further developed quite naturally, and at three to five weeks the handler can already take advantage of it by letting the puppy do his first track outdoors.

We need: a) one hungry puppy
b) the puppy's mother able to nurse
c) two people familiar to the puppy
d) a grass-covered area with a sudden

slope, ditch, bushes, or other hiding place.

Someone holds the puppy about ten paces away from the selected hiding spot. The owner and the bitch (on lead) then move from there to the hiding spot, creating a scent path by taken short steps and trampling down the vegetation. Then they go into hiding.

All this time the puppy was watching. Now he is released, encouraged and praised by his prior captor, to move toward the hiding place. Upon arrival, the puppy is given a "grand reception", lots of praise from the owner, love and food from his mother. In this exercise the puppy is not doing a real tracking job. He goes more by memory and sight (he can see the trampled-down grass) than by scent. His olfactory system, however, is being conditioned. In time, the "funny smell" of the disturbed vegetation will be recognized consciously as a guide to pleasurable experiences. The exercise should not be repeated until the next day.

As a variation to this method you can

- have the bitch with her litter at the end of the track (the "tracking" pup wants to get back to his family)
- ask the puppy's most favorite person to hide (without the bitch)
- release TWO puppies at the same time (they might encourage each other, compete with each other)
- increase the distances gradually after practicing for about a week.

At 6 to 8 weeks of age, you can start with more conventional tracking conditions:

Select a grassy area, preferably cool weather and moist ground (early morning hours). Tie the puppy to a fence or tree and let him watch. Let him sniff the food reward, trample down the grass in the starting pad, drop some meat there, then lay the track into, later with, the wind. Avoid side wind, use short steps initially.

For the first few days deposit a small ball of meat or ground beef about the size of a penny behind you, directly in the footprint you just made, alternating right and left foot impressions. On later days bait every 3rd or 4th step, then still less often but totally at random. Start with a short track: After about 20 feet pick an indentation in the ground and hide his food bowl with the rest of the meat and all of his (next regular) food ration. Run back (but not on your own track !) and get your puppy, hold him on a short line (2-3 ft.), touch the starting pad with your cupped hand, move the hand on the track and then

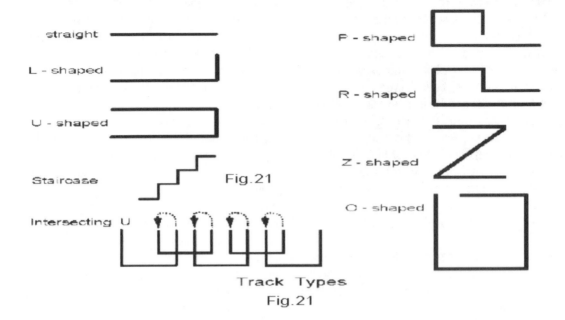

Track Types

Fig.21

encourage him to start. If needed, walk next to him bent-down. Guide him along the track with your cupped hand moving on the ground, your fingers pointing toward the dog. Offer the grand reward at the end (praise and food).

Repeat the next day, and the next day..... Then make one change at a time: use less and less food on the trail but more at the end, let the track age a little longer, increase the length, introduce a slight arc, an obtuse angle (the second leg should lead into the wind, with the final food reward 10 to 15 feet after the turn), etc.

TRAINING MATURE DOGS

To start mature dogs in tracking, modify the above procedure:

* Take the dog along while laying the first few tracks. This creates a mixed animal/human scent (in addition to the ground scent) which the dog might follow more willingly.
* At the end of the track:
  - place a FAVORED piece of food (liver, sausage etc.). This works for any hungry dog.
  - the owner hides alone (if a close relationship exists between dog and owner).
        The one-man dog.
  - hide another family member to which the dog is attracted. The typical family dog.
  - hide another dog to which the trainee is attracted, his playmate. Dog-oriented pets.
  - hide a favored toy, a ball for instance.
        Dogs that love to retrieve and to play.

Older dogs usually take longer to adopt new principles, but then they progress at a faster rate.

BEGINNER-LEVEL TRAINING
** INTENSIVE TRAINING METHOD

The so called "Intensivmethode" is used extensively by German Service Dog agencies, lending itself nicely to the simultaneous training of several beginning dogs in tracking. It offers
- to the dog the chance to work on a variety of different scents generated by other dogs and humans
- to the dog handler the opportunity to use several tracks although he lays only one himself
- to the instructor the advantage to guide several dog/handler teams with minimal effort and time.

STEP 1: Prerequisites

The group secures a suitable tracking area. Then
- find a field large enough to space the tracks sufficiently apart (100 ft. minimum).
- select a field with well established ground cover, like lawn areas, meadows or farmers' fields
- avoid dry ground or scarce vegetation, intense heat, heavy rain or high winds
- assemble the group on the up-wind side of the field so that the tracks can be laid with the wind.

STEP 2: Securing the dog

Three to ten handlers and their hungry dogs line up, spaced about 100 ft apart.

The dogs are secured in these positions, to a fence, trees, posts or stakes.

The handlers attach a tie-out chain/cable with a quick-release snap to the dead ring on the choke collar. They also clip the regular leash to the dead ring on the collar (assuming your dog does not eat the leash).

STEP 3: Starting place

Tease your dog with the meat and give him a small piece of it. Then move forward (in line-formation with the other handlers) about 10 feet away from your dog, taking with you two flags and the meat. Push the first flag into the ground. Stomp down the grass in the area to the right of the flag, about one square yard in size and slightly cone-shaped. Deposit a few pieces of meat on this scent pad.

STEP 4: Orientation

All handlers move out at the same time in a line formation, each toward an individual aim point in the distance. If sufficient aim points are not available, an assistant can approach the finish line from the rear and place the second flag from each handler opposite the first (starting) flag, to mark the endpoint of the track.

When laying the track, keep your aim point in sight (except for very quick glances at the ground).

The tracks of the group should run parallel to each other, with about a 100 ft distance between them.

STEP 5: Track laying

The track is about 150 ft. long. Take small steps during early training stages. Drop a small piece of meat (the size of a penny) directly on the track after 5 ft, another 5 ft and then approx. after every 15 ft.

At the end point push the 2nd flag into the ground and deposit a somewhat larger amount of food.

Rush back to the dog on your own track, aim for the first flag (don't create a second scent path !).

STEP 6: Start

Prepare everything beforehand (e.g. a quick-release snap on the tie-out chain) so that the following steps can proceed rapidly: Unhook your dog from the tie-out. Slide your left hand into the dog's collar.

Hold the folded-up (regular) leash in the left hand, or (less desirable) let it drag on the ground. Excitedly move with your dog to the starting place. With the dog on your left, bend down and move your cupped right hand in front of the dog's nose (fingers pointing to the dog) to the ground and then 10-15 inches along the track away from the dog. Almost all dogs will follow the meat-scented hand to the ground and start investigating it. At this time encourage your dog and tell him to "find it", or "track".

STEP 7: Tracking

Your dog should keep his nose down while you are moving along the track at a reasonable speed right next to him. If the head comes up, stop. Do not move another inch until your dog's nose is on the ground again.

You can easily prevent running and circling since you still hold your dog by the collar.

Give frequent, but subdued, praise when the dog has his nose on the track. Do NOT use your dog's name, it usually distracts the dog and causes an interruption in tracking.

Once the dog finds a piece of meat, give him time to eat it while praising him at the same time, then continue. Although you may guide your dog to the next food drop, NO action should be taken if he misses it. Just continue tracking to the next marker. Do not scold the dog, and do not make him go back to pick up the treat.

STEP 8: End Marker

Earlier, you had deposited a somewhat larger portion of meat at the end of the track. Now give your dog time to enjoy it. Show him your satisfaction and happiness about a job well done (praise, play, petting, rough-housing, etc.), but keep him on the leash.

Only after the *very last* track in a session clip off the leash, romp around, or throw a ball or stick, or do whatever the dog enjoys most. This will make the training a memorable event for the dog.

STEP 9: Return

Casually return with your dog on a short leash on your own track, being careful not to create a new scent path. Discourage tracking on the way back, but do not use punishment. During the return, drop pieces of meat on the track as replacement for the ones your dog had found. Try not to let him become aware of this.

STEP 10: Switch

Wait with your dog at the starting flag until all teams have returned. Then everybody moves one position to the right: team 1 goes to starting flag 2, team 2 advances to 3, team 3 to the old #4 and so on. The last team goes to the beginning of the line (position # 1). Since all tracks are baited, tracking can begin right away. This switch can be repeated until all dogs had a chance to work on all tracks.

Once your dog does well on the straight tracks, you can guide him on the short (2-4 ft.) leash snapped to the dead ring on the choke collar. Introduce longer tracks, turns, articles, U-shaped tracks and intersecting U-shaped (cross) tracks. Wider spaces between adjoining tracks are needed.

- When working the U-track, for instance, let the first team start and then wait until it has reached the first turn. At that time, the second team starts on the same track, etc. Bait behind you as you go.
- The "hot" scent, curiosity, and the desire to imitate usually make for good tracking performances.
- More advanced work, however, is best done on an individual basis rather than in a group.
- If no other dogs are available to participate in the basic group training, you can adopt the principles and make them suit your own requirements.
- You can also consider circle (or box) tracks.

** CIRCLE / BOX TRACKS

Circle / Box tracks are very efficient to practice tracking. The end of the track brings you right back to the start, relieving you from having to "walk a mile" to pick up the dog or to get back to the car. It also allows you to work the dog on the track and to bait the track for the next run, at the same time. The principle is actually so simple and effective that one wonders why not everybody uses it.

Novice dogs which have successfully run a few straight line tracks can work on circle tracks:
- Secure your dog at point (A).
- Walk to point (B) and lay the track in a circle, proceeding to (C) and then to (D) and (E).
- The stretch (B)-(C) can be triple laid.
- Stretch (E)-(F) is a straight line since most dogs will speed up in anticipation of the reward.
- Food can be deposited along the track, with the biggest reward left at the end (F).
- Get your dog and start between (B) and (C).
- Coax him along the track and give him time to swallow the goodies. At the same time, replace the food, without letting your dog know about it.
- Give the big reward and lots of praise at (F).

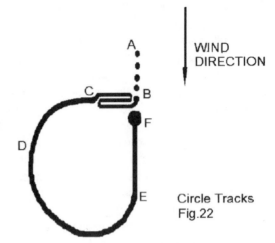

Circle Tracks
Fig.22

After a brief pause urge your dog to go on the track again. While the dog moves out, deposit another portion of food behind you at (F), and so on, to replace the food drops your dog found. It requires some skill to not let the dog become aware of this food replacement technique.

◆ Theoretically one can run the circle forever. We suggest to quit after 2 or 3 passes.

◆ Repeats on subsequent days should vary between right and left circles.

◆ Also, straight legs can be used to form a square or a rectangle (the box).

◆ The orientation of the track with regard to wind direction should be changed too.

◆ For variety:
- alternate track length between large and small circles (diameters of 60-200 ft equal 180 to 600 ft)
- extend the time between laying the first track and finding it (20 minutes)
- increase the distances between food drops from 15 to 80 ft. (see below)
- combine the rewards with the articles
- run the long tracks only once, on rare occasions maybe a second time
- switch between short/long tracks, fresh/old tracks, lush/scarce vegetation, different ground covers
- in general, the wind should not carry the scent from the last food drop to the starting place. Occasionally, however, the dog may even be shown where the reward is and then be taught that the only way to get it is to follow the track.

INTERMEDIATE-LEVEL TRAINING
Introduce one change at a time:
- Use a four foot leash on the dead choke.

- Space the food drops farther apart (double the distances once a week, advancing from 15 ft to 120 ft).
- Use each track only once, then move on to fresh ground.
- Don't return on your fresh track, take an alternate route back to your dog (single track).
- Let the track age 30 minutes.
- Lay all tracks at an angle, not parallel, to any natural boundary (fence, tree line, furrows, mower lines).
- Introduce a non-restrictive harness, if you wish.
- Switch between short/long tracks, fresh/old tracks, lush/scarce vegetation, all kinds of ground cover.
- Introduce cross tracks that were made involuntarily by people, bicycles, cars (see page 60).
- Introduce articles (glove with food in it) and unintentional "garbage" (see page 60).

ADVANCED-LEVEL TRAINING
Introduce one change at a time:
- Use a six foot leash on the dead choke or harness.
- Eliminate most intermediate food drops in favor of a larger portion at the end.
- Increase the distance gradually (add about 50% , one change per week).
- Let the track age for 40 minutes.
- Introduce an obtuse-angle turn (greater than >90 degree), with the first leg long, the second leg short, place a small food drop about 5 feet past the turn, and have the second leg lead into the wind.
- Use several articles on each leg.
- Start with larger items/articles, progress to small ones in time.
- Switch between short/long tracks, fresh/old tracks, lush/scarce vegetation, all kinds of ground cover.

All tracks in all three levels end with a large portion of food (one to two hand-fulls). Also, praise the dog lavishly at the end of the track and play with him. Throw the ball/stick, play tug-of-war, do whatever the dog likes best. He must realize that all the fun is at the end of the track, he must be able to count on that.

It can happen to the best handler, and to the best dog, that they don't find the end of the track. Be prepared for this rare occasion, have an extra article and the reward in your pocket. Inconspicuously drop the article and give the dog a chance to find it. This allows you to end the tracking session on a happy note.

The basic training is time consuming. We recommend tracking every other day, 1 to 2 tracks per day. Training more often (up to 6 days out of 7) can be advantageous during the initial phase, yet advanced dogs often show a decline in interest with such heavy involvement.

TRAINING EXPERIENCED DOGS
Train a minimum of once a week to maintain your dog's performance. Seek variety with regard to location, ground cover, track age, length, lay-out, weight of tracklayer, weather conditions, articles, distractions, cross tracks etc.   Acute angles (<90 degree), two tracklayers who separate and join again, crossing roads, or creeks, or streams, or parking lots etc., provide challenging opportunities for dog and handler.

ARTICLES
In tracking, several "lost" articles have to be found. Your dog can (a) indicate the article, (b) pick it up, or (c) retrieve it. Indicating with the dog in the down position leaves few chances for a poor performance. Indicating by standing, sitting or retrieving lends itself easily to misinterpretation and to incidental mistakes, like not remaining perfectly still.

(a) We prefer that the dog assumes a down position upon finding an article on the track, facing the article. You then drop the leash, advance to the dog, praise him briefly, and waive the article over your head (to show it to the judge). Look at your dog at this time, prevent him from getting up prematurely. You can hold up the article with one hand, and pet your dog with the other hand. Then encourage him to continue tracking in the direction indicated by the outstretched leash (remember: an article is not supposed to be dropped close to a turn).

(b) With the second option the dog would pick up the article and remain sitting or standing at the spot of the find. A nervous, excited, playful or sloppy dog might move or drop the article (which is faulty).

(c) You can also teach your dog to retrieve the article. In addition to the possibilities of a sloppy and faulty retrieve, you also lose the direction indicator (the outstretched leash), the dog has to re-do 30 feet tracked already, and he can get confused when passing the place of the find for the second time.

Teach the indication of articles independently of tracking: During obedience work, or a casual walk, drop a well-scented article without letting the dog notice it. You can also spread out several scented articles on a small field before bringing your dog onto it. When the dog approaches the article, a firm "down" command will teach him the correct response. Prevent the dog from touching or mouthing the article. Laying right on top of the article may be a problem as well. Control can best be exercised with the six foot leash: hold him back so that he stops just short of the article. Then you claim the article, waive it over your head and praise and reward the dog.

The **"Refrigerator Effect"** can be used to teach the dog to properly indicate an article. The following story describes the supposed origin of it:

> *"A dog and his master would frequently visit another family. Upon entering the house the dog would go straight to the kitchen and sit quietly in front of the refrigerator, staring at the handle. The dog would not leave his position until the home owner came and gave him **his** piece of meat."*

Applied to tracking, the "Refrigerator Effect" can be taught as follows: Obtain a glass container with a tight lid and put some meat in it. The food must be delicious, and the dog must be really hungry. Position the container on the training field or on the track, together with, or even inside of, an article. As soon as the dog has arrived at the container, teach him to go down and to wait for you to open it. After a few times, the dog will automatically assume the correct down position. Not taking an eye off the container, he will patiently wait for your arrival, and for his reward. Unpack it, be excited, excite the dog by sniffing on the reward - then give it to him.

Besides teaching a reliable indication of articles, the containers have an added bonus: other animals (wild ones or stray dogs) can not steal the food, and ants can not get at it either.

Some trainers use the baited "Kong" instead of the glass jar. This imitation of the Refrigerator Effect is ineffective: the dog does not need you to extract the reward, he will be busy for a long time working on it (and then forgets that he was working a track), and unwanted animals have access to the bait as well.

Once the dog indicates reliably, combine it with tracking: Lay a 100 ft straight track with an article (with or without glass jar) every 30 ft. Start tracking as usual. Most likely the dog will indicate the article as taught. Praise, reward. Keep him in the down position for a little while. Then restart and go on to the next article.

Unintentional "garbage" in the field may cause the dog to falsely indicate an article. Prepare for it (p. 61).

COMMUNICATION

As in all other phases of dog training, communication between dog and handler is of vital importance. Since the dog can not talk, the handler has to rely on other clues.

Learn to read your dog during practice sessions. Watch how he carries his head, his ears, his tail when on and off the track. Analyze the manner in which he moves, the steadiness, the pull in the tracking leash, the breathing rhythm and intensity, etc. Each dog is different, but there are distinct patterns each dog exhibits when on and off the scent path. Use this information in a trial with an unfamiliar track to guide your dog skillfully (see also "Loss of Track", page 58).

Encouragement ("that's a good boy, go on") is given as long as all signs indicate that the dog is on the track. Some dogs need little reassurance, others require more. When the dog signals "loss of track" yet still searches for the lost scent, encourage him again but with a different tone of voice ("find it, where is it"). If the dog is attracted by something else, stimulate him: "heeeey - look what I have found here", point to the track.

Let your dog do his job (your guess may be wrong !). Do not force him to go in a particular direction based on clues you got from the terrain layout, from visible trails in the grass, from helpful friends, etc.

COMPETITION

In tracking, the handler has little control over the performance of his dog, but he can help:
GET YOUR DOG READY.
Take your dog out of the car at least thirty minutes before he goes on the track, to switch from the fuel fumes (present in every car) to the local scent environment. Let him relax and eliminate. Prevent contacts with other dogs, especially dog fights or attraction to the opposite sex, and avoid other excitement as well. Don't let him watch protection work or do any obedience, for instance. Don't discourage him if he sniffs on the ground.
GIVE HIM SOME WATER.
Bring some water from home and encourage him to drink. Splash some on his nose just before tracking starts.
GET YOUR EQUIPMENT READY.
If you use a harness, place it close to the starting area. Unroll your leash and stretch it out on the ground, hook next to the harness. Do you wear gloves on the track? Do you have them?
Have the reward ready (ball, toy, tidbit), either at your

car or in your pocket. If you take it with you, conceal and wrap it well. If the dog smells the meat he will concentrate more on your pocket than on his track. WHERE IS YOUR NUMBERED ARM BAND / VEST?   Wear it.
REPORT TO THE JUDGE.
Get your dog, your equipment, and report to the judge how your dog will indicate an article, and that you are ready to begin tracking. Precision heeling is not required at this time, skip the "heel" command if possible.
APPROACH THE STARTING FLAG.
While approaching the starting flag, search for clues that will tell you the initial direction of the track. The experienced judge should know where it is, he will not stand on it, nor will he let anybody else get close to it, spectators or even you, while you approach the flag. (Watch out for the judges who do not know where the track is. I have seen one who let the spectators trample all over the track.)
A close-by wall, house, river, fence, road, starting pole from another track etc. will also limit the directions your track can go. Sometimes dew lines, trails in high grass or snow etc. can be seen. However, all these clues should be used to reassure the handler, not to let him take over the tracking job of his dog.
START TRACKING.
Once the dog gets close to the starting flag, encourage him to pick up the scent. A "down" there is not required. It might even switch the dog's mind from tracking to obedience. Holding him short on the leash at that time may be all he needs. Requiring a dog to stay at the start for a given number of minutes is another fallacy. Read your dog. Let him move out on the trail once you see that he has picked up the scent and is ready to go. Holding him back at this time is like telling him to forget about tracking. Feed him the lead and follow him as soon as the end of the rope comes up.

6. PROBLEMS
** LOSS OF INTEREST
At one time or another, most trained dogs go through a phase where they seem to have lost interest in tracking. They may just lay down and refuse to go on the track, they may wander around aimlessly, or they may casually walk past the article. Search for the cause.
a) **CAUSE**   Medication:
Certain medication interferes with a dog's ability to analyze scents.

SUGGESTIONS Wait until medication is no longer needed or until its effect has worn off. Consult with your veterinarian.
b) **CAUSE**   Saturation:
The dog was tracked too often, and the (small) reward was not worth the effort in the dog's mind.
SUGGESTIONS - Take a break from tracking for a couple of weeks.
- Track less often, use shorter lengths. Use difficult and simple tracks at random.
- Provide variety, motivate your dog. Try bigger, better, different rewards.
c) **CAUSE** Exhaustion: Past tracks were too difficult, the handler advanced too fast in the program.
SUGGESTIONS - Back off, work on simpler, shorter, fresher tracks.
- Use efficient track baiting.
d) **CAUSE** Boredom: The dog is not sufficiently motivated.
SUGGESTIONS - Use very short tracks, with lots of play and fun afterwards.
- Try different motivators: very special food treats, urine, play, decoy.
- Use the motivator only in connection with tracking, withhold it at all other times (use treats, or play only after the track, for a couple of weeks).
e) **CAUSE** Objectionable or scarce scent: A change in ground cover (vegetation, asphalt, water) alters or minimizes scent.
SUGGESTIONS - Practice with tracks laid over a narrow strip of the disturbance (a small foot path, a tiny creek, a narrow strip of the strange vegetation).
- Gradually increase the width of the disturbance.
- Use generous track baiting at the far side of the disturbance..
- Advance straight ahead, then cast your dog left and right so he can pick up the scent.
f) **CAUSE** Failure: In earlier training, the dog lost the track and could not earn the reward.
SUGGESTIONS - Make sure that you know where the track is. Guide your dog if necessary.
- Always carry an extra glove (and reward). Once it becomes clear that your dog can not finish the track, drop

the extra glove inconspicuously and help him to find it. Praise and reward him for completing the track successfully. Do better next time.

g) **CAUSE** Total Loss of Track, you both are totally lost.

SUGGESTIONS (see Fig.23)

- Go back to the last point where your dog lost the trail when still tracking well (Point L). Face the same direction that you were going then. Turn 90 degrees to the right, advance about 15 paces and direct your dog to go forward to the end of the leash. Then both of you turn left 90 degrees and walk on your respective radius for 180 degrees. There is a very good chance that your dog will pick up the scent. If not, see e) and f) above.

If the preceding suggestions do not help to regain interest in tracking, then re-train and apply some pressure:
Lay a straight 40 ft. track, with one article after 20 ft., and a second one at the end. Then follow this sequence:
*   Grab your dog by the collar or prong collar and tell him in a matter-of-fact way "find it". If he refuses to go, drag him forward on the track to the next article with repeated and meaningful tugs on the leash.
*   You probably taught him to indicate an article by laying down - that is what he will do now anyway when he gets to it. Praise him, then continue as described above: Grab your dog by the ....
*   At the end of the track praise him for finding the article, release him, extract the ball from your pocket and invite him to play with you. Be very excited, cheerful, make this a fun thing to do. Quit for the day.
*   Repeat this for a few days.
*   Then, in the days to follow, let him see that you deposit the ball at the end of a 40 ft. track. Lay a second trail as before, but no ball at the end. Ask him to track trail #2, after that trail #1, then play ball at the end.
*   Repeat this for 1-2 more days, then increase the length of the track gradually, introduce turns, place a regular article at the end of the track. Produce the ball and play with your dog as a reward for the successful completion of the track.

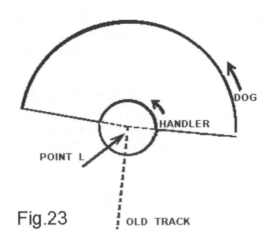

Fig.23

** LOSS OF TRACK
Your dog works steadily, yet suddenly he indicates loss of track, maybe by carrying his head high, his tail high, wagging his tail, air scenting, checking far to the left and right, circling, moving erratically, returning to you. Most likely he encountered a stretch of weaker or faded scent, unfavorable ground cover, unusual climatic conditions, a turn of the track, a freshly sprayed field, an old gasoline, oil or chemical spillage, gas leaks, other natural or artificial masking odors which might have created a "blind spot".   You should stop instantaneously, maybe even move back a little on the track, and give your dog a chance to work it out on his own.
If you are aware of such a "blind spot" when laying the track, then food-bait the trail maybe 4 paces past it. If you encounter the blind spot unprepared, then deposit the bait inconspicuously while the dog is circling.
   A clever handler will know when his dog has recovered the scent. The nose will most likely be glued to the ground again, his body, head and tail carriage indicate confidence, he moves in a straight line, and he pulls in the harness. At that time you should let him take the lead, but only then. Do not follow if he is not sure.
   On the other hand, overly long circling is pointless, and it requires that you make a decision. Rather then to give up, advance somewhat in the direction where the track is most likely to continue. In doing so cast the dog to the right and left, hoping to recover the lost track on uncontaminated, more favorable grounds (see also "Total Loss of Track", above). In a trial, you will lose points for such unscheduled assistance, however you still have a chance to find the track and to complete it,

harvesting the points assigned to that portion.

It is always a good idea to prepare your dog for the worst conditions:
Locate a large tree or a wide underpass (bridge), or stretch a sturdy cable between two elevated points (buildings, poles, trees etc.). Tie a strong rope off-center to the overhead cable and secure the lose end near the envisioned track path. Four or five days later lay your track and let the tracklayer aim for the rope. Once he reaches it, ask him to swing Tarzan-style away from the track. Upon reaching the ground again, let him continue the track, baiting it abundantly. This is the perfect "loss-of-track" situation and you can practice recovery now.

A less efficient option is to have the tracklayer make a few leaps sideways at the point of the intended loss-of-track, or to cross a road etc. (see "Dead Space" below). In any case, bait the continuation of the track well.

** HIGH SPEED PURSUIT
Too fast a pace causes missing turns and articles. Find the reason for the hurry, try one or all options below:
a) Tire him out somewhat before going on the track (running, playing).
b) Use physical restraint, hold him back with steady, constant tension on the tracking leash.
c) Guide the leash around your back and lean into it.
d) Use Boettcher's harness.
e) Use a regular choke collar on the live ring (steady pull).
f) In very severe cases consider using a prong collar for a short track, with tension on the leash.
g) Let him drag some weight. Use a good pulling harness and suitable weights like an old car tire.
h) Use more difficult conditions: older tracks, cross-tracks, hard surfaces, track down-wind.
I) Ask the tracklayer to take larger strides, or to run in leaps (diminished scent intensity).
k) Use shorter tracks.
l) Use longer tracks.
m) Track with the wind.
n) Track with a smaller (or no) food reward at the end (maybe he was anxious to get to his dinner in a hurry).
o) Bait the track with more frequent rewards of small food drops.
p) Deposit food with the articles, openly or bottled up (see "Refrigerator Effect" page 56).
q) Offer a small amount of food, or play with him a little, BEFORE going on the track.

** TURNS
Often, dogs have difficulties to negotiate a turn. As soon as he overshoots and indicates loss of track (see "Loss of Track", above) you should stop, hold on to the leash and give the dog a chance to find the continuation of the trail. Give encouragement and keep the leash reasonably taut to prevent entanglement. Follow when your dog is pulling steady in the new direction.

In training, practice for a perfect turn in the following way:
a) Know exactly where the turn is.
b) DO NOT mark the turn in any way. Chicken wire (as recommended by the "Advanced Schutzhund" experts) would teach the dog to track by sight.
c) Practice on tracks with one turn only, make the second leg very short (10ft.), have an article and the reward there at the end, quit for the day.
d) Let the new direction initially lead into the wind (change that later).
e) Place a reward just past the turn.
f) Rub meat on the ground along the first four to five paces in the new direction, e.g. *after* the turn, or use another desirable scent source (meat powder, meat broth).
g) When laying the track, take large strides just before the turn.

Triple Laying
After Turns

Fig.24

h) Triple-lay the first 4-5 paces in the new direction, using small steps.
I) Round the corner, or make an obtuse angle (>90 degrees). Then, in subsequent tracks, make the angle smaller and smaller, until it becomes an acute angle (<90 degrees; maybe even 20-25 degrees).
k) Do as many left turns as you do right turns (many handlers practice right turns only).
l) Work with a short leash (6 ft.), or shorten the leash even more just before a turn comes up.
m) Don't let the dog overshoot the turn more than a couple of feet.
n) Stop soon enough and don't end up standing on the turn that the dog is supposed to work out.
o) Avoid signaling your dog that a turn comes up, don't tighten the line. Keep a loose lead, let him work it out.

p) **Praise** your dog while on the track, **encourage** him when off or searching for it. Make the distinction.

Some trainers suggest very *short* steps (or bait) just before a turn. This is the surest way to make the dog miss it. Very big strides before the turn, and small steps after it, are called for instead. Here is the proof:

* Figuratively speaking, the tracklayer - like a scout - communicates with the dog via smoke signals: big steps = barely a scent cloud marks a footpath ("I must watch so that I do not miss anything"), small steps= "heavy smoke" (a lot of scent clouds) marks the highway ("YES !, here it is").

* Heavy scent (small steps, fresh tracks, lush vegetation) before the turn causes the dog to relax and to track casually with a high nose. He will overshoot the turn for a considerable distance and may lose the track.

* Scarce scent (large strides before the turn), an "almost" loss of track, alerts the dog and motivates him to work harder.

Each dog has a different inertia, so the scarcely scented portion just before the turn may need to be larger or smaller for different animals. Ideally the dog should be just short of the exact location of the turn the very moment he has reconfirmed that the track is still there. Considering timing elements, allowances should be made for the dog's way of thinking:

a) the alert (beginning of large strides before the turn: am I still on the track ?)

b) the verification (ending of large strides before the turn: ok, the track is still here but fading)

c) the whammy (wow !! massive scent coming from my right, or left)

Observe your dog, gauge parts a), b) and c). Then tell the tracklayer to do X big steps before the turn.

** ARTICLES

a) **PROBLEM**   Faulty indication.
   CAUSE   The dog moves before the handler shows the article to the judge.
   SUGGESTIONS - Relax and talk calmly, quietly, reassuringly to your dog (allowed even in a trial).
   - After the down, put your hand unobtrusively on your dog to hold him in position.
   - Practice the indication of articles as an obedience exercise.

b) **PROBLEM**   Article ignored.
   CAUSE   The dog did not recognize / acknowledge it.

SUGGESTIONS   - Work him slower, do not let him run on the track.
   - Use a greater variety of articles with regard to color, shape, size, material, and where you store the articles between usage.
   - Test if short or long prep times make a difference: carry the articles for 30, or 10, or 1 minutes on your body before you deposit them on the track. Then train for shorter times.
   - Cover the article with some grass or a little dirt (it happens even in a trial).
   - Place the article in a puddle of water (it could have rained).
   - Practice finding independently of tracking. Use the techniques described earlier.
   - Use a food reward for finding the article (refrigerator effect)

c) **PROBLEM**   Article missed.
   CAUSE   The article was blown away or unexpectedly covered up.

SUGGESTIONS   - Practice for it: place the article 2-3 ft. to the side of the track, or cover it with dirt.
   - Secure the article with a weight.

d) **PROBLEM**   Wrong articles indicated.
   CAUSE   The dog hunts by sight.

SUGGESTIONS - Collect small articles of glass, metal, wood, paper, leather, fabric, etc., "air them out" for 2-3 weeks - don't touch. Then use tongs and drop them into a paper bag. Lay your track with the well-scented articles as usual, but also deposit the "garbage" near it (tongs!). Discourage your dog when he gets interested in the garbage, praise and reward him when he acknowledges the real article. Clean-up afterwards (tongs), re-use the junk.
   Confirm that your dog got the message: scent a few of these items on your body - your dog should now indicate.
   - Hide the article from sight, dig a shallow hole, cover it with some grass or dirt.

** CROSS TRACKS

Very few trainers can count on an uncontaminated tracking field: people, animals, vehicles often and unintentionally generate confusing "cross tracks". This can happen in training or in a trial, and dogs familiarized with it will have an advantage over others. Prepare for it by using some of the suggestions given below. Have for instance a person on foot or on a bicycle cross the field and note the path. Then lay your track crossing the disturbance and get your dog to track and to investigate, but not to follow, the distraction.

In a trial, advanced tracking dogs must ignore intersecting trails made by another party. Investigating the cross track for a few paces is not faulty as long as the dog returns to, and pursues, the original path.

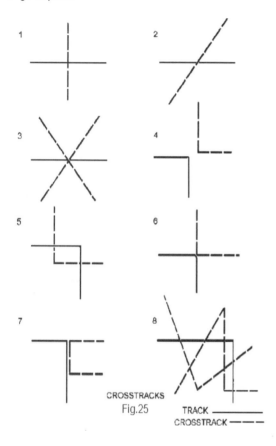

CROSSTRACKS
Fig.25

TRACK ———————
CROSSTRACK — — —

Experiments conducted by German Police Canine Units have shown that well-trained and talented dogs can differentiate between the tracks of two equal-weight tracklayers, provided there is a time lag between the two tracks of more than five minutes, at a total track age of about three hours.

Figure 25 shows cross tracks with increasing levels of difficulty. To start training, we suggest:

primary track
- 300 paces, straight, 2 hours of age
- food reward on main track 5 ft. past the cross track, and at the end
- heavy weight tracklayer (30 lbs+ heavier then the crosstracklayer)

cross track
- 5 minutes of age (e.g. laying it almost 2 hrs. later than the main track)
- intersects primary track near the end (~ 280 paces), at a 90 degree angle
- light weight tracklayer.

Hold your dog back if he wants to investigate the crosstrack for more than about three paces to the right or left. Verbally, but casually, discourage him from following the crosstrack any further. Praise and encourage him as soon as he gets back on the main track. If necessary, guide him onto the main track, and to the reward which is just 5 ft. away from the intersection. Practice similar tracks for five to ten more training sessions during the following weeks. Then introduce difficulties, one at a time, like turns and articles on the main track, other tracklayers, more crosstracks, intersections other than 90 degree etc. Increase the main track age to three hours, the crosstrack age to thirty minutes (e.g. main track 6:00 AM, cross-track 8:30 AM, tracking started 9:00 AM). Crosstracks must be sufficiently separated from articles and turns.

It is also helpful to create a super-saturated crosstrack situation: five to ten assistants, about 20 ft. apart, are asked to walk in a line formation across a U-shaped main track. The dog is worked on this track in the usual manner, with assistance from his handler, if needed (see Fig.26).

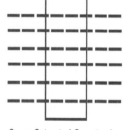

Super Saturated Crosstracks
Fig.26

** DEAD SPACES
Hard surfaces (rock, sand, concrete and asphalt) do not generate or hold sufficient ground scent since physical disturbances cause only minor changes to their inherent scent characteristics. If an experienced dog can pick up any track scent, then it is most often from material carried onto it with the footwear. Bodies of water severely complicate tracking as well.

The basic training concept for crossing a road or a body of water consists of following the track up to the edge of the dead space and then sending the dog ahead in a straight line, with an obedience command. After reaching suitable tracking ground, the dog is directed to cast to the right and left until he picks up the scent.

Start training with a small obstacle, like a narrow

road or a small creek. Make sure that you know exactly were the track continues. Use the 6-ft. Leash. Send the dog intentionally at a slightly skewed angle over the dead space, to practice casting. Give encouragement and verbal praise once the dog picks up the track.

During the teaching phase, bait the continuation of the track after one, five and ten feet.

** MAKE BELIEVE

Some dogs appear to be working, nose on the ground, pulling in the harness, yet they are definitely not on the right track.

a) **CAUSE**   The dog is following an undesirable scent. There are, for instance, cases where dogs have followed the track of the judge who instructed the tracklayer on the day before the trial.

   SUGGESTIONS - Retrain your dog (see crosstrack techniques)
- Don't show anymore under that judge, pick a better-qualified person (a good judge will stay off the field and direct from an appropriate observation point).

b) **CAUSE**   The dog has learned to please his master and avoid punishment by faking the track.

   SUGGESTIONS - Ease off on the pressure and on the corrections
- Re-start basic training, knowing EXACTLY where the track is.

** CASTING

A tracking dog ideally retraces the exact path of the track layer, as it was laid. In practical terms, however, occasional checking to the left and right is quite natural and acceptable, especially in the vicinity of turns. Yet excessive circling, excited running from the left to the right border of the scent path, and other departures from the track cause the dog to put in more work than necessary and tire him out prematurely. The problem develops most often with hyperactive, easily excitable dogs, those that are eager to work and/or anxious to please. Quite a few Dobes fit that description in their beginning stages of tracking. You need to gain better control of your dog. Use the six-foot tracking leash. Try to determine the reason for it. Common causes are:

a) **CAUSE**   The scent is too strong (offensive) - the dog needs to make wide sweeps to determine where the tracklayer has NOT been (fringe follower).

   SUGGESTIONS - change to a different ground cover. Alfalfa grass, for instance, seems to generate a scent that is offensive to some dogs.
- change to a location with scarce ground cover
- employ a light-weight track layer
- instruct the track layer to take large strides
- let the track age longer
- bait and/or scent the track.

b) **CAUSE**   The scent pattern is too weak, the dog has trouble finding it.

   SUGGESTIONS - change to a location with lusher vegetation
- employ a heavy track layer
- ask the track layer to carry extra weight (bricks, weights from the gym)
- instruct the track layer to take smaller steps and to drag his feet
- soil the track layer's boots with manure, fish etc. before he goes on the track
- don't let the track age as long as before
- bait and/or scent the track.

c) **CAUSE**   The scent path is inconsistent, irregular, confusing (the scent may be blown away in some places, trapped in others, like ditches, holes, vegetation and high ground cover).

   SUGGESTIONS - practice more often under similar, adverse conditions
- help / guide your dog over rough spots
- use more articles or bait on the confusing stretches

d) **CAUSE**   The dog shows a desire to track but he is too excited, too jumpy.

   SUGGESTIONS - use more articles
- use smaller articles
- tire him out somewhat before going on the track (running, playing)
- use physical restraint, hold him back with steady tension on the tracking leash
- if the dog is uncooperative when using the physical restraint, consider:
a) Boettcher's tracking harness
b) snap leash to live ring on choke collar and guide the leash between his front legs
c) as b) but use the prong collar
d) let him drag some weight while tracking (a good pulling harness and suitable

weights, for instance an old car tire, must be secured beforehand)

e) **CAUSE** The dog is not interested in tracking, he wants to play or to hunt.

SUGGESTIONS - if this is an isolated instance, the dog may just need a stern verbal correction
- if it happens more often, the dog needs to be retrained from the ground up. Motivate!!

There are numerous other factors that can cause a seemingly erratic tracking behavior. For instance:
- Illness.
- Conflicting tracks made by other people, animals or vehicles may confuse the dog.
- Chemicals, oil/gas spills may not be obvious to humans, but they are to dogs.
- Ground disturbances, buried chemicals, leaky pipelines, agricultural chemicals, unusual natural odors, even insect infestations (ants, wasps, spiders) can cause the dog to respond differently.
- Automobile exhaust fumes during long car rides may have temporarily impaired a dog's scenting ability.

Dogs do not always perform as expected. Find the reason, then try different and appropriate remedies until the undesirable behavior patterns are eliminated.

7. SUMMARY OF TRAINING SUGGESTIONS

- Start simple: short grass, short track, no turns, lots of rewards, then introduce difficulties gradually.
- Use positive reinforcement (encouragement, praise, reward).
- Avoid punishment, use restraint instead.
- Select the method and the motivator (reward) that is best suited for your dog.
- Don't give obedience commands before going on a track. You don't want to cripple your dog's initiative.
- Track regularly, preferably daily, but at least once a week.
- Know exactly where the track is. Monitor your dog's performance and help him when necessary.
- Restrain your dog while laying the track rather than giving the down command. You want him anxious to go out when it is his turn to track.
- Give your dog some fresh water (brought from home) just before he goes on the track.
- If you use a harness, put it on just before you go on the track. Take it off immediately afterwards.
- Read your dog at the starting place, go when he is ready. Don't remain there too long or too short.
- In practice, use a short leash and keep your dog on the track at all times.
- Always carry a spare article/reward so that you can fake the end of the track if the dog gets stuck.
- Provide variety, like longer and shorter tracks, older and fresher tracks, lay tracks with turns, without turns, track in a variety of ground covers, track during all seasons, in all weather conditions, change tracklayers, or carry some weight occasionally to alter your ground impressions, provide distractions during training like other people, dogs, cars, traffic noise, wildlife etc.

A blonde and her husband are trying to get some sleep, but the neighbor's dog in the backyard will not stop barking. The woman finally jumps out of bed and runs downstairs. After ten minutes she comes back.
Her husband is wondering:
"What have you been doing? The dog is still barking."
She says: "I put the dog in our backyard. Let's see how **THEY** *like it!"*

C. OBEDIENCE

1. BASIC PHILOSOPHY

In truth, obedience training is the drilling of artificial, sometimes even unnatural, responses. They are useful to us, however, and we consider it to be the yardstick for the talents of a dog trainer. Spirited, happy, joyful and accurate work of the dog moving in unison with his master attests to the high qualifications of the handler. Listless, dutiful, sloppy compliance, on the other hand, indicates the need for a change in training style.

This chapter aims at developing the rapport between dog and handler that makes training an enjoyable pastime for both, and it necessarily leads to superior performance. To accomplish this goal:

- start preliminary obedience training during puppyhood
- pay attention to the needs of the individual dog
- reognize every (!!) good performance instantaneously with an appropriate reward
- use compulsory guidance when needed
- have short, lively, spirited training sessions, followed by play.

2. PUPPY TRAINING

Start playful obedience training at an early age, as early as six weeks perhaps.

Play lively games with toys / balls, tug-of-war, hide-and-seek, pursuit, gentle rough-housing and other fun activities. Introduce "here" (come when called), "sit", "down", "bring" (retrieve), and collar and leash in a gentle and playful way. The puppy is very receptive at this time. He learns fast, yet his attention span is short. Do not insist on drill routines, or on perfection. For the pup, showing a desire to comply is more important than performing like a robot.

Patience, persistence, tolerance, forgiveness, gentleness are qualities that you need at this time. Other requirements are enthusiastic praise, play, tidbits as reward for good work, and very short training sessions.

* Coming when called is probably the first exercise you want to teach your puppy. Reserve the "here" (casual), later the "come" (formal) exclusively for occasions to which the puppy looks forward anyway (food, play, going for a walk etc.). Call the pup in a very pleasant, excited tone of voice, as an invitation, rather than as a command. Always reward and praise him when he comes. Never connect anything unpleasant with the recall (no scolding, punishing, confining, attaching the leash etc.). Do not practice the front sit and the finish in connection with the recall, at this stage.

* To introduce the sit, hold a tidbit above and slightly back over the dog's head. This will cause the puppy to sit naturally and voluntarily. Give the command "sit" (short, emphasis is on the "t") at the same time, and through repetition the dog will learn to follow the verbal instruction. If the dog backs up, you can try to
- move your hand with the tidbit quicker
- hold the tidbit a little lower, or a little farther back
- do the exercise in front of a wall which prevents the puppy from backing up
- hold the treat in the right hand, and use the left hand to pat the puppy's back with gentle pressure on the croup.

During early training, practice the sit-stay for very short durations only, and follow with lots of praise.

* To teach the down, move your right hand with a tidbit in front of the dog's nose toward the ground, and then a few inches away from him, forward. Most likely he will follow it and lay down. Your left hand can assist in this maneuver by physically manipulating the pup into the down position, sliding the front paws out, for instance, or applying very, very slight pressure on the shoulder or on the croup, as needed. Initially, the hand can be left on the dog for a while, to insure the down-stay. Uncooperative pups can be flipped on their sides, quickly, but still gently. As with the sit, give a verbal cue. Past the teaching phase, the appropriate "down" is truly a command, it should be given firmly. Terminate the exercise down-stay after a very short duration with a release command ("OK") and praise.

* Throwing a tennis ball, a toy or a rag and encouraging the puppy to return it for a play session introduces the retrieve at an early age. You can use a food reward to entice the puppy to bring the toy back, even to trade in the toy for the treat. Technique is unimportant, and compulsion or corrections must not be used at this stage. If you use as long line, use it with much discretion. It is all about fun and games:

Start by squatting down and rolling the ball.

Tease him, excite him, encourage him to "get it". Then invite him to approach you. A playful pup will get close enough so that you can touch him, praise, pet and hold him. Gently take the ball, then play again right away. Make this a daily routine for about two weeks. Then use a dowel instead of the ball, hold it in your hand, move it back and forth and tease the puppy to grab it. If he does, wiggle it gently while he holds it (prey drive). Hold still after a few seconds, absolutely still, make the toy life-less. This will prompt the dog to relax the grip, to release (if it does not work, use a treat for diversion). Say "out" in a matter-of-fact way, take the stick and immediately throw it a few feet. When the puppy goes for it and holds it, touch the stick a few times (without taking it !!) while moving backwards, and encourage him to follow you. You now have laid the foundation for a happy regulation retrieve, including the "out".

* Another task is to condition the puppy to collar and leash. Initially the leash is just attached to the collar and he drags it around, later you should hold on to it and encourage him to accompany you. Use a lot of verbal encouragement, and select a destination the puppy favors (the local park, for instance, and not the veterinarians office). This will help to avoid the "pulling contest" we see so often.

Start leash training away from home. Take him to an unfamiliar area and attach the leash to his collar there. The new surroundings will capture his attention, they will also increase his dependence on you, and as a result he will be more cooperative than at home. Don't tell him to heel at this point, he must just learn that you determine the direction of travel. If he disagrees, you should slowly continue in your path, cheer him on and encourage him to follow. Gentle repeated tugs on the leash can be given at the same time.

* We like to teach eye contact (command "look") as a separate exercise at a young age. When the dog looks at your eyes, he can - to some degree - read your intentions, anticipate and prepare for your next move. This increases bonding, communication, interaction, teamwork, and it is an extremely helpful tool in obedience.
a) Start by teasing the dog with a highly desirable food morsel in front of your chest, but withhold it until he looks into your eyes. Encourage him, move your hand, goad him, command "look". It is not good enough to look at the food, he must make eye contact - and it will take a while before he does. Eventually, though, he will look at you, wondering: " What's wrong ? Why don't you give it to me?" That very moment you must surrender the reward. Practice this for a few weeks.
b) Then hold the food in front of him, let him see it, move it around, tease him and command "look". Release the food only when he looks into your eyes. Be patient, this will take more than just a few minutes. Repeat this for several days until he responds reliably.
c) Go from food to toy. Throw the ball the very moment he makes eye contact - not before. Practice this.
d) At some later time use "look" while heeling. For a spirited dog, the ball will work better than food. Throw it the moment he focusses on your eyes. Only rarely will you have to remind him to "look", most of the   time he will do it on his own.
e) The reward can also be the decoy's sleeve. Tell your dog to "sit", then "look". Only after he complies and makes eye contact with you (you ! - NOT the decoy !), let him go for a brief fight with the decoy.

* A puppy must understand what "no" means. Proper timing, at the moment when he gets into mischief, a very forceful "no", an outburst of displeasure   (anger, without physical contact) convey the message best. Rarely is it necessary to physically punish the puppy, the startling and the scolding are usually sufficient. This, however, must be followed immediately by praise, provided he interrupted the mischievous behavior.

A young dog needs much attention and interaction with his caretaker. Just opening the back door and wishing him a good time in the yard will not be enough. In living with his owner, doing things together, being around, the puppy can easily be taught to behave well, and to adopt the peculiarities of the "human pack".

3. OBEDIENCE TRAINING FOR MATURE DOGS

Start serious obedience training when the dog has reached about six to eight months of age. Up to that point, training should have been conducted in a playful manner, putting more emphasis on cooperation by the dog than on precisely executing the routines. If the dog is much older than a year, more patience and skill is required of the trainer, but here too, progress can be satisfactory. You CAN teach an old dog new tricks.

** In Schutzhund Obedience, the **play** reward is the most effective motivator for the dog. A dog anxious and eager to play ball is much easier to train and will perform better than his food-oriented counterpart. You, the handler, can help to develop this play drive: pick the right

a) location: the training field is better than your back yard

b) attitude: relax, make it fun, play animated and vigorously, correct only when absolutely necessary

c) timing: short play periods are better than one long play session, like: 15 min. confinement in the crate, then 1 minute obedience training, then 2-3 min. lively play. Repeat this: 15 min. crate, 1 min. training, 2-3 min. play, repeat: 15 / 1 / 2-3 min. .... etc. (repeat a few times.)

d) linkage: only play with him before and/or after training - a very simple training routine will do.

** "Coming when called", going for a walk (not heeling!) and "down" are probably the first exercises on your list (see puppy training, above). In further training lessons provide a balance between movement (e.g. retrieve) and rest (e.g. long down), attractive (e.g. jumping) and unattractive (e.g. heeling) exercises.

** Split exercises into parts and practice them separately and randomly (sit-stay + come when called + finish = recall). Go from simple to complicated tasks (e.g. holding the dumbbell, getting it, bringing it back).

** Group training (classes) offers many benefits for beginners, it would be the preferred method of instruction.

** Some trainers will select the "down" as the first exercise with which to strive for perfection. Other handlers will pick another important and easy routine. Each dog requires a somewhat different approach, and you are encouraged to compile your own program, and to proceed at your own pace.

The routines listed below represent groups of related exercises. Their sequence of presentation does not coincide with any preferred sequence of teaching.

4. ROUTINES

** HEELING ************************
GENERAL
Heeling is the most basic and the most easily boring exercise in obedience training. Make it lively and exciting.

Many trial rules specify that the dog keeps his shoulder "in line with the left knee of the handler". This would result in a jerky, discontinuous movement. For all practical purposes "knee" is interpreted as "hip", or "shoulder".

By the way: Throughout the world, the dog is kept on the left side. Why? Service dogs were initially employed by the police, and in the old days, right-hand dexterity was uniformly enforced - which included firing a weapon with the right hand. The left hand, however, was free to control the dog.

OBJECTIVE
The dog will remain at the handler's left side, keeping his shoulder in line with the handler's left hip at all times, regardless of changes in pace or direction.

SUGGESTED COMMAND: "heel "

SUGGESTED RELEASE COMMAND: "OK "

PSYCHOLOGY
To walk at the heel position is completely unnatural to the dog, by nature he was "programmed" to scout ahead of his master. While physical restraint and punishment can force a dog to remain at his handler's left side, the sight of such a duo is always a rather pitiful one: the dog with lowered head, drooping ears and in a depressed mood, the handler tense, grim, uncoordinated. Now look at this team: the dog responds excitedly and happily to his masters every movement, glued by an invisible bond to the handler's left side, ears alert, head up, monitoring his master's facial expression so that he can anticipate the next maneuver. The handler himself is relaxed, friendly, responsive and constantly stimulating his dog's interest. They move in unison, as a true team.

The first team is a typical "drill sergeant" example:
the "soldier" has not much of a choice.

The handler in the second team, however, practices "Applied Canine Psychology". He recognizes three basic facts, and he follows three basic rules:

Three facts:
1. Roaming ranks very high on the dog's list of desirable activities.
2. Force alone may get compliance but never happy performance.
3. A motivator displayed but withheld too long will lose its effectiveness.

Three rules:
1. The handler must constantly observe his dog so that he can capture and stimulate his interest and give guidance instantaneously. This will work for relatively short periods only.

2. Correction for inattentiveness and undesirable responses must be lightening fast and pronounced.

3. Give praise immediately after each correction, and for each special effort the dog makes. The most effective level of praise and correction has to be determined for each dog / occasion.

Make training sessions short and spirited, and end with an enjoyable play period. At this time do not practice heeling and related exercises like the "down" and the "down out of motion" in the same training session. Different criteria apply to each, the dog would get confused, and both routines would suffer.

PREREQUISITES None, except a well-established dog/handler relationship.

ACCESSORIES

A) COLLAR: Push one end of the extended choke chain through its own ring and pull it through until both rings meet (Fig.27 A-D). Orient the collar so that it forms a "P" in front of you, slide it over the dog's head (Fig.27 E; point of arrow is the dog's head). The collar will free itself by gravity when the tension is released. Having the collar up high, just below the dog's ears, gives better leverage.

B) LEASH: For initial training, hold the excess length of the leash in your right hand, neatly bundled like ribbon-candy. A loop with very little slack hangs in front of you, giving the dog enough freedom to move without feeling pressure on the collar, yet allowing you to tighten the collar instantaneously.

Your left hand should be on stand-by, swinging normally (and more freely than the right hand) as you walk. If the dog leaves the heel position, then reach with your left hand for the leash and administer the correction. Immediately thereafter, the left hand releases the leash and pets the dog for now being in the correct position.

Touch/brush his nose with the tips of your fingers. Most dogs like that, they will stay close to you, and they will look up to your face then.

C) LEASH CORRECTION: Although some people consider it cruel, a forceful leash correction with the choke collar is much more humane than the slow self-strangulation of dogs who drag their owners around.

Learn to read your dog and to anticipate what the animal will be doing one second later. If trouble lies ahead which requires a correction, you should execute the following pattern in rapid succession without breaking your stride. Let us assume your dog is starting to forge ahead. Now:

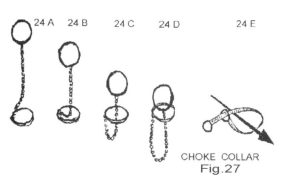

CHOKE COLLAR
Fig.27

a) Continue walking briskly. Mimic a freight train, maintain your speed, stop for nothing.

b) Feed the dog more lead. There is no tension on the line, yet.

c) Give the command "heel". If the dog responds, then omit steps d) to f).

d) Balance and brace yourself while continuing to walk. Reach for the leash with your left hand.

e) Give a forceful leash correction. It is ineffective to just gradually tighten the leash, this will accomplish nothing but a pulling contest. You must suddenly and forcefully snap (yank, jolt, jerk, slam) the leash, comparable perhaps to the sensation the dog would experience in a powerful lunge. The correction should be strong enough to physically manipulate the dog into the proper position.

f) Instantaneously release the tension and take your left hand off the leash.

g) Continue walking, speeding up a little to recover the ground lost while giving the correction.

h) Praise the dog enthusiastically for now being in the proper position and touch / pet him, with the left hand.

COMMANDS

Give the "heel" command before any correction. This "alert" offers the dog a chance to avoid the correction if he responds instantaneously. If he does, the correction is not given, of course. Sometimes it may be necessary to give a second command, but a command must never be repeated more than once (provided the dog is familiar with that exercise). The first time the dog has a chance to comply, the second time he should be made to comply. If you are unable to enforce the command, then you should not give it in the first place.

REFINING PROCEDURES

A) PRECISION HEELING

Practice precision heeling as a challenge to the dog: how well can he follow abrupt changes in pace or

a) Schedule brief but regular training sessions (two to ten minutes, 2-3 times daily). Do not bore your dog to death with endless repetitions.

b) Before a work-out, let your dog explore and sniff out the training area - on or off lead.

c) Use a light-weight leash, the dangle, and a choke collar.

d) Adjust the length of your steps to accommodate your dog: small/large dog = small/large steps. A brisk walking pace (you do not have to run) will keep the dog's attention focused on you.

e) Talk to your dog. This will make him comfortable at your side, and anxious to stay there. How, how much, how often you need to talk depends on the dog. Don't talk him to death.

f) Show enthusiasm, give lots of encouragement and much praise when he earns it.

g) Tease your dog with a favored toy, or a treat (see "look", page 66). This stimulates the dog to look at your face. Let him have the reward after a few seconds (feed the meat, throw the ball).

h) Ask the dog to make eye contact: "look" (see page 66). Reward him EVERY time he does. Encourage this by stroking with your left hand from below the dog's left ear -under the chin- up to the tip of the muzzle. Brush his nose with the fingers of your left hand, occasionally.

I) You must CONSTANTLY observe your dog, giving praise or correction the instant it is needed.

j) Make directional and pace changes in rapid succession. This keeps the dog busy. Then do a few long stretches until the dog becomes inattentive again.

k) Give timely, quick, snappy leash corrections when needed, and always follow with praise.

l) Tempt him to make a mistake whenever he is not paying attention (e.g. make an about-turn when his mind is wandering), then apply your correction. Praise him afterwards.

m) Ask for perfection. Correct even minor "violations".

n) Do not follow a set heeling pattern, improvise instead.

o) Do not adjust your pace or your position to accommodate the lazy or rambunctious dog, don't wait for him. Maintain a steady speed ("freight train"), even for corrections or praise.

p) Never let your dog lead you. When he pulls left, you go right. When he slows down, you run. When he forges, you make an about turn without hesitation.

q) Heeling alongside and close to a wall or a fence teaches the dog to stay close to you.

r) If the dog heels wide, hold the left hand "glued" to your left knee, pet the dog near the neck. Affectionate dogs will seek contact and stay close. Or quickly yank the dog toward you and praise him afterwards. Walking past a post so that the leash between you and the dog gets caught is quite educational to the dog, especially when you continue without much hesitation.

s) If the dog crowds, goose-stepping might help. Strapping spikes to your knee is a silly gimmick that does not work, it actually causes more problems.

t) Forging and lagging are discussed below under "Problems".

u) Do very brief off-lead training early-on, in a fenced-in area. Walk in a straight line for about 50 feet (no turns). Clip the lead on and off frequently and correct with the dangle, if needed.

v) During the on-lead / off-lead transition, keep a 16-inch piece of rope (a "dangle") attached to the dog's collar. After demonstratively removing the regular leash - but inconspicuously holding on to the dangle - give a harsh correction if the dog slacks off.

w) Attach a light-weight 30 ft line to the collar and let him drag it (he needs to get used to it first). You, or an assistant, can quickly grab it in case of training problems.

x) The nape-grab method is very effective for a correction during off-lead work. Quickly grab (and release) the skin fold on the dog's neck and pull, shake, and/or scold the dog.

y) During off-lead heeling you should use both hands to
   - stimulate your dog (clap, move them in front of the dog's nose, hold a toy or a tidbit)
   - reward, reassure or guide (pet, stroke, channel in turns, keep the dog close)
   - correct the dog.

z) End each training session with an exercise the dog can do well, then praise your dog and happily play with him. He will remember that and look forward to the next training session.

direction, how neatly does he sit after a halt from a run, how eager is he to stay at heel when you make a multiple right-about turn (spin twice around on the spot, or 720 degrees: the dog should almost wrap around your legs in doing that turn), etc.

You must help, of course, using verbal stimulation and encouragement, verbal correction, hand contact to guide, correct and praise your dog, as well as teasers (tidbit, ball) or a leash correction, if needed.

◆ Incorporate the sit after a halt into the heeling routines, and practice the various turns.

◆ Do most of the heeling on leash, but the lead is now generally held in the left hand, neatly folded up.

◆ In competition, the judge may require execution of the commands as he gives them. You are not expected to respond instantaneously, a little time lag is perfectly all right. Taking one or two more steps after having been ordered to stop will allow for a much smoother halt and a much more accurate position of the dog. Practice this in training and let a friend call the shots, once in a while. In a Schutzhund trial you are working on your own, of course.

Some judges insist that a particular heeling pattern be followed. While this request may or may not be justified according to the rules, we suggest not to argue with the judge on the field.

A heeling pattern does have certain advantages: you are less likely to forget any parts, and you will cover the required distances. In training, however, you should deviate from the standard often enough so that the dog can not anticipate and learn the sequence.

B) SIT

Whenever you stop during the heeling exercise, the dog is supposed to sit automatically. He has to be next to you, on your left side, sit straight and squarely, sit close and face the same direction.

To teach the sit:

- Walk forward, keep the dog on your left side.
- Continue walking and fold up the leash in your right hand, as short as comfortably possible - but not taut. For large dogs you will have your right hand near the buckle of the leash.   This gives you control over the front end of the dog.
- Come to a halt, and while doing so bend down in the knees, way down, but keep the upper part of the body straight, nearly vertical. This brings your left hand down to the level of the dog where you can guide him, without changing directions, shifting position, or leaning over him - all of

which is undesirable.

- Do not turn toward your dog, you both must face the same direction.
- Give the command SIT.
- A split second after the command, slap the dog with the fingers of your left hand on the croup. If the dog does not sit quickly, tap him harder. At the same time tug the leash, up and back (if he is forging), or up and forward (if he is lagging). Hold the leash up straight and almost taut, above the dog's head.
- Straighten up the knees and praise your dog calmly.

C) CROOKED SIT

When coming to a halt, the dog is supposed to sit next to you, straight.

- If the dog swings his rear end behind you, use the left hand to slap him on the right flank, to push him away. You can also balance yourself on your left leg (standing up straight), lift you right leg, swing it behind yourself and bump your dog's rear with the heel. This is quite effective since he can not see when and from where the correction is coming. This maneuver must be done while the dog is *in the process* of sitting down.
- If the dog swings his rear end away from you, slap him with the left hand on the left flank for guidance.

The corrections must be given while the dog is *in the process* of sitting down, NOT afterwards.

D) START UP

Some trainers suggest to move the left foot first, others prefer to move the right foot first, when starting to heel. It does not really matter since most likely the dog will lag in both instances anyway. What the dog really needs is an "early warning" system. For the start-up in heeling get the dog to sit at heel, straight. Visually check ring, ground, stewards, judges and your dog's position. Then:

Count silently 1 - 2 - 3 - 4 - 5 - 6 and do one of the following things on each count:

1. Straighten up, concentrate your thoughts.
2. Move your feet unobtrusively a little up and down a few times, as if you were walking in place. This should not be overdone. To an observer it should look like restlessness, rather than like an exercise.
3. Bend one knee slightly forward, the one you will be using in taking the first step. It does not really matter which foot starts, but the left foot (next to the dog) may offer a slight advantage.

4. Give the command "heel".

5. Maintain the posture from position 3 and fall forward, feet together, body straight. If it was not for the next step (6), you would fall flat on your face.

6. Step out.

The preceding sequence helps you to standardize one of the most tense spots in an obedience trial. The routine forces you to concentrate on a sequence of events and leaves little room for other worries. Being sure what to do here makes the rest of the trial easy.

Your restlessness causes the dog to be ready for the moment of the start. Steps 3, 4 and 5 above actually make the dog believe that you are moving already, allowing him a little head start. This way the team is perfectly lined up from the very beginning.

E) TURNS

Just before going into any turn you should slow down very slightly. This is a natural maneuver to keep your balance and it will not be faulted in a trial. Since your dog watches you closely, this alerts him to an impending change, and - reading your body posture - he will be able to negotiate the turn with you perfectly. This is a better and more natural way to communicate with your dog than to turn your head prematurely into the new direction.

Left Turn

Tighten the leash (held in the left hand) to slow down the dog while stopping on the forward movement with your extended left foot. Bring the right foot up to the left foot (both feet are side by side now) and turn the body 90 degrees to the left. Then stride out in the new direction, with the left foot first. The outstretched left leg now blocks the dog's path and guides him into the new direction. Other foot techniques are possible, but do not skip the slight hesitation and the sharp 90 degree turn. In advanced training, practice the left turn off leash. If needed, you can slide the left hand along the left side of the dog (front to back), to push his rear end around, to line it up with the new direction. Such assistance is eliminated gradually.

Some trainers favor the left hop (for the dog). They do not pay attention to their own foot work but, just like in the left-about swing (see below), they require the dog to hop up and to spin in the air backwards 90 degrees to the left. That is unnatural and it looks funny (but it gets applause).

Right turn

Stop forward movement with the right foot extended to the front. Give little tugs with the leash (held in the right hand) while at the same time petting the dog on the neck with the left hand, encouraging him to speed up and to stay with you during the turn. In the meantime, the left foot has been brought up to the right foot (both feet are side by side now). Turn right, then stride out, logically with the right foot first.

Left Turn

Fig.28

Other foot techniques are possible, but common to all of them is the minute hesitation during the turn (the dog has to walk the larger outside circle !), and the sharp, 90 degree angle the handler executes.

Done off leash, both hands should be used to pet and encourage the dog to speed up during the turn. If necessary, a tug on the collar (if you can get a hold of it quickly enough), or the nape grab can be employed to get cooperation. Follow with praise.

Right Turn

Fig.29

ABOUT TURNS

There are three ways to do an about turn: Right About Turn (AKC style), Left About Turn (Schutzhund style), Left About Swing (Circus style).

Right About Turn

This is really an extended right turn. Stop forward movement with the right foot extended to the front. Give little tugs with the leash (held in the right hand) while at the same time petting your dog on the neck with the left hand, encouraging him to speed up and to stay with you during the turn. In the meantime, the left foot has been brought up to the right foot (both feet are side by side now). Stepping in place (don't overdo it), continue to turn until you have completed a half circle (180 degrees). Then stride out in the new direction, most likely with the left foot first.

It is important that you
- hesitate a little to give the dog a chance to walk the larger outside circle
- simulate walking while turning on the spot (or your dog will stop and sit)
- keep your feet together while turning so that you do not trip the dog (trample down a

About Turn

Fig.30

1x1 ft square while you simulate walking)

- walk briskly in the opposite direction as soon as the dog has completed the turn.

Done off leash, both hands should be used to pet, stroke, and encourage the dog to speed up during the turn. If necessary, a tug on the collar (if you can get a hold of it quickly enough), or the nape grab can be employed to get cooperation. This must be followed with praise, of course.

Left About Turn

This is an extension of the "finish" from the recall exercise (page 81). Stop forward movement and turn left, facing the broadside of your dog. Hold the leash (short) in the right hand, encourage the dog to turn right, around you. Step in place to indicate motion while slowly turning to the left until you face the opposite direction, change the leash behind your back into the left hand. Encourage your dog to keep going around, resume a brisk walking pace in the opposite direction as soon as the dog has completed the turn.

During off lead training, use both hands to guide and praise the dog.

Left About Swing

This turn is seldom seen. It is best left to the owner of a small, lively, eager animal.

In training, keep the leash very short in your right hand, and use the left hand on the canines left flank, teaching him to back up and to swing backwards into the new direction while turning to the left yourself. For an eager retriever, a ball can be used to excite and manipulate the dog to hop into the proper position. During the initial training it is important to have complete physical control over the dog's front and rear end, to avoid confusion and frustration.

F) NORMAL, FAST AND SLOW PACE

"Normal Pace" is by no means a leisurely stroll. The suggested speed for most working dogs is a rather brisk 4 - 5 MPH. The length of the strides should be adjusted for harmony in movement of dog and handler (it almost always means shorter strides). Walking briskly helps to focus the dog's attention on you (and you get some exercise).

Changes to Slow or Fast Pace should not be too abrupt (ease in !), and in Schutzhund competition you are allowed a "heel" command to alert the dog.

Some dogs interpret the slow pace as a signal to come to a halt and to sit, especially when you slow the dog down with a leash correction. Avoid this confusion, eliminate the leash correction, generate

some additional body movements, for instance by swinging the front foot out with every step, like in a military parade step. If done with moderation, the technique will not be faulted even in a trial.

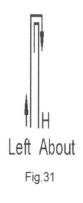

Left About

Fig.31

For the fast pace, running speed is required. Training for it, you must excite your dog sufficiently to get cooperation, with verbal encouragement, by clapping the hands, by using treats or a toy, etc.

G) THE GROUP / FIGURE EIGHT

In a Schutzhund Trial, the handler/dog team must move in and out of a group of people milling about. There is at least one halt required in this group, and the judge usually asks the handler to

ABOUT SWING

Fig.32

circle one of the people in the group to the right, and another one to the left. A sit, down, stand out of motion may also be requested. Although somewhat more difficult, this exercise is similar to the FIGURE EIGHT required in AKC obedience. The training suggestions given here apply to both forms of competition.

Place two objects (barrels, chairs, cartons etc.) eight feet apart. Begin close to the connection line and circle the object on the left first. This is the preferred choice since it gives you a chance to easily control the dog: he is between a rock (the post) and a hard spot (the handler) when YOU take the outside circle.

A good start often means a good exercise. Here are a few ideas to improve performance:

- ◆ Slow down on left circles during initial training. This forces the dog to pay attention and to adjust his pace. Use leash correction for forging dogs, and hand as well as verbal contacts for encouragement.
- ◆ In right circles speed up intentionally. Most dogs will lag here since they must negotiate the larger circle. Teaching them to accelerate whenever there is a right turn will eventually make that behavior habitual.
- ◆Use a metronome or a tape recorder with march music to maintain a steady pace in this exercise.
- ◆Circle one object twice, reverse directions, round

both objects as a unit in O-type fashion etc.

- ◆Change the objects to smaller ones and finally use just sticks, and circle them at close quarters.
- ◆Change the speed, going fast all the way at one time, and rather slowly at another time.
- ◆Place the objects farther apart, and sometimes even closer together, for variety.

Then use distractions and encourage, correct or praise as necessary:

- Stewards with and without dogs take the place of the posts suggested above.
- Add a few more people/stewards, practice in the crowd.
- Noisy spectators stand around, say "boooo", clap their hands.
- Other dogs are worked nearby: the retrieve, the send-out, or a few protection exercises are always attention getters. A caged bird, rabbit or cat are almost irresistible temptations for a dog.
- Introduce food distractions, like meat dropped on the floor or in the hands of the stewards.
- Go to public places. Shopping plazas, schools, bus/railroad stations, airport parking lots are ideal.

H) ON LEASH VS. OFF LEASH

- Even dogs in higher classes of competition should be trained on lead frequently. As soon as the dog becomes inattentive or lazy, do a few turns on lead, followed by short off-lead periods.
- A dangle works well in the transition period from on to off leash heeling. Once the regular leash is removed and thrown to the side with much fuss, you are still able to correct your dog with the dangle.
- Brush the tip of his nose with the tips of your left fingers, at random. He will look at you and pay attention.
- Employ the "look" command, use verbal encouragement, praise, food and play rewards.

PROBLEMS
A) TAKE-OFF

Some dogs say "good bye" as soon as the lead is unclipped.

- * To get him back, wait a little until the initial excitement is over - then sternly command "down" (a "come" will most likely not work). Go and pick him up, don't call him.
- * You could just sit on the ground and wait for him to return - he may or may not come back in time.
- * A less glorious way to catch your dog is to ask

everybody on the training field (that is people and dogs) to join you in walking to your car. Tell your dog you leave him there, and that you will have a marvelous time without him. You may have to start your engine, or even to drive a couple of yards. It usually works - if the dog is watching.

- * You can try to bait your buddy with food, a ball, a stick, but only a few dogs will fall for this trap.
- * Never run after your dog to catch him - he will enjoy this game, for hours on end.

The next step must be to resume leash training, for quite some time (re-read the "heeling" section). Also practice the "down" (first on, then off lead, see page 75) with any distraction you possibly can think of.

B) FORGING

Heeling correctly, a dog should always have his shoulder lined up with the left hip of the handler. When staying farther back the dog is 'lagging', when moving farther ahead the dog 'forges'. Forging clearly is a matter of the handler not having the dog's attention. He must get it, and keep it. Aside from the obvious leash correction, try

** Bribes

Use food, toys, encouragement, the "look" command. Most likely, though, you will have to use compulsion.

** Corrective Turns

For beginning dogs, or for those that forge ahead badly, do an abrupt about turn: Feed him more lead, command "heel", turn 180 degrees to the right, brace yourself and give a sudden, sharp leash correction with both hands which should propel the dog toward you. Then get going and praise him. After several tries, the command and the preparation for the correction will cause the smart dog to dash to your side.

** Bump:

For a dog with moderate forging habits wait until he is forging approximately one foot ahead. Then make a sudden **left turn** on the spot, swiveling on the ball of your left foot. While turning on the left foot, raise your right foot in the back and bend your knees at the same time, swing and bump not too gently with the extended right knee into the right shoulder of the dog. If done properly, the dog gets thrown off balance. He was forging ahead far enough so that he could not see the correction coming. After a few times the dog will try to avoid the bump and stay just a little farther back. Praise him.

Holding the dog on a short leash during this maneuver enables you to better aim for his shoulder.

However: You should abandon the collision attempt when you realize that not the dog's shoulder but instead his rump or the head will be hit. This would cause the dog to spin and to lose orientation. Try again.

** Verbal Correction

Dogs that only occasionally forge a little are usually in an advanced training stage, or they belong to the group of soft, sensitive dogs. Most likely they are momentarily distracted. Just a "hey.." might redirect the dog's attention back to you. Give praise, then do rapid changes in pace and direction.

C) LAGGING

Lagging is more difficult to cure. It can occur for several reasons: fear, shyness, habit, boredom, laziness, distractions etc. Determine the cause first, then address the problem.

Compare heeling on lead to off lead. Dogs lagging more on lead than off lead usually have had traumatic training experiences, like too much pressure or force in leash training. A better, more empathic dog/handler relationship must be developed where gentleness, encouragement, praise and reward can help the dog to overcome his shyness or fear - in time. Make training sessions short and pleasant, for instance.

If heeling on and off lead do not differ much, lagging is often the result of boredom, inattentiveness or habit. Wake them up. A moderate but snappy leash correction followed immediately by lots of praise and encouragement, a faster walking speed, sudden and rapid changes in pace and direction will usually do just that. A ball, a toy, the "look" command will often accomplish the same. It is important that you get the dog's attention and cooperation.

Consider also:

- Start happy, enthusiastic off-lead heeling early in the training program, for brief periods.
- Change often between on and off lead work, in brief training sessions.
- Encourage your dog to move up to your side (a faster pace, coaxing, baiting, teasing with ball, toy or tidbit, clapping hands, bending down, praising, the "look" command - all this while still walking). You must never slow down or wait for the dog to catch up - go steady like a freight train, no matter what.

- Make your dog comfortable while in the proper position. Reward, praise, pet him while walking.
- Use corrections as little as possible, rewards as much as needed.
- Practice in areas with lots of distractions (check local laws first), like shopping plazas, downtown areas, bus and railroad stations, airport parking lots, stores (many pet stores allow dogs inside !), school yards and factory entrances at quitting time, or in dog obedience classes.

D) INATTENTIVENESS

An inattentive dog reflects poorly on his handler, pointing to a lack of team spirit and enthusiasm. Correct the situation right away, do not let it become a habit. Change your attitude, become more excited, more spirited, more animated, more "peppy". Surprise him with short bursts of enthusiasm, walk faster, make changes in direction and speed after every 4-5 steps, do sudden halts from fast pace, do running starts from a stand still, move into the opposite direction when he is not paying attention, etc. Use meaningful leash corrections when needed - and heaps of praise afterwards.

Ask the dog to make eye contact, command "look" (see Puppy Training, page 66). Use food (reward after a short tease and when he makes eye contact), ball/toys (throw the ball after a short tease and when he makes eye contact), animation (act funny-stern, controlled-weird, quiet-loud), pet him spontaneously, slide your hand from his throat to the tip of his muzzle. Make the training sessions short and fun. Vary your training routines, concentrate on a different exercise for each separate session.

E) JUMPING UP

Dogs who jump up while heeling must NOT be punished unless you want to turn your eager, happy, spirited animal into a "drag along". Instead speed up for a few paces whenever the dog jumps. This forces him to keep all four feet on the ground in order to stay next to you.

** SIT *******************************

GENERAL

Besides being useful by itself, the sit is a part of many different exercises. Practice it early in training.

OBJECTIVE

On command, the dog will sit, instantaneously, fast, reliably, under any condition, and he will remain sitting in that spot until released by his handler.

SUGGESTED COMMAND: " Sit"

SUGGESTED RELEASE COMMAND: "OK"

(or "heel")

PSYCHOLOGY

The "sit" is a transitory state: the dog wants either to relax (lay down) or to get up (walk away). Be prepared to correct instantaneously and firmly if the need arises. The "stay" command is not needed (see there).

PREREQUISITES   None, except a well-established dog/handler relationship.

TEACHING PROCEDURE

During initial training use the leash - for control, and to prevent an escape. Later on practice off-lead.

A) INDUCTIVE METHOD   (It was described earlier under puppy training.)

B) SHOW & TELL

Start with the dog walking or standing on your left side. Hold the leash in your right hand, close to the buckle/collar, but leave a tiny bit of slack. This gives you control over the front end of the dog. Control the rear end with your left hand. Then give the command "sit". A split second after the command, tap (don't push, or he will fight you) the dog on the croup with the *fingers* of the left hand. If he does not sit, hit harder. At the same time, give a tug with the leash, up and back, or up and forward, depending on the reaction and the position of the dog. Then hold the leash up straight and with very little tension, above the dog's head.   For a lazy dog, stand up straight and balance yourself well on the left leg. Lift you right leg, swing it behind yourself, command "sit" and then bump your dog's rear from above with the top / right side of the front part of your right shoe (the toes compartment). This is quite effective, it surprises the dog since he can not see when and from where the correction is coming.

While the dog is preparing to sit, guide him into a straight position: If he swings his rear end behind you, the left hand should be ready to slap him on the right flank. You can also balance yourself on your left leg, lift you right leg, swing it behind yourself and bump your dog's rear with the heel. If he swings his rear away from you, however, slap him with the left hand on the left flank to make him slide into a straight sit. This guiding must be done while the dog is in the process of sitting down, NOT after he is sitting already.

During the sit, praise him calmly only. Offer lots of praise after the release command, however.

REFINING PROCEDURE

Practice the exercise in various locations, with various distractions, even during a casual walk. The dog may be close by when given the command, or he may be further away. Always insist on an immediate response, using correction and praise as needed.   Initially you may need to have him on a leash / long line.

A) SIT OUT OF MOTION

Practice this after the dog reliably executes the regular sit command.

In preparation for it, gather up all the lead in your right hand, while heeling. With the dog in the proper heel position, firmly command "sit", followed immediately by a light snap on the lead upward/backward and a tap (do not push) on the dog's croup with the left hand. All this is done while you continue walking in the original direction. However, in passing the dog's head you turn gradually to the left to face your dog. Come to a halt in front of him. Hold the leash (with a little bit of tension) in your outstretched hand straight up over the dog's head.   After a while return to the heel position and release your dog.

In subsequent training sessions eliminate the tap and the snap with the leash. Successively, drop the leash to the ground, move farther away, do the exercise off lead, discontinue the turn to face the dog and pretend not to watch your dog anymore once the command "sit" is given.

In training it is a good idea

- to tell the dog that he is doing fine as long as he remains sitting (calm praise)
- not to release the dog immediately after your return
- practice on various occasions, particularly at times when he is allowed to move about freely (not heeling).

If the dog does not perform well or breaks, rush back to him and position him properly, not being too gentle, too friendly or too talkative at that time.   Give him a lot of praise at the end of a successful exercise.

You can also use the long line and an observant assistant. He will quietly and unobtrusively hold the line (no tension), but he can prevent the dog from following you - if the need arises.

For reliable performances, practice the "sit out of motion" and the "stand out of motion" as the more difficult exercises more frequently, the "down out of motion" (see below) less often, but all under a variety of conditions, and always as a surprise to the dog.

B)   LONG   SIT   WITH   AND   WITHOUT DISTRACTIONS   (see "Long Down w & w/o Distractions", below).

PROBLEMS

A) NO SIT

When commanded to sit, the dog remains in place but he lays down or he stands.

Physically manipulate the dog into the sit (see above), making sure that your command "sit" is not given in a threatening manner, and that the commands "down" and "stand" sound sufficiently different.

B) SLOW SIT

Use quick corrections. The tug on the leash and the tap on the croup must come a split second after the command was given. The dog will try to avoid the correction the next time and sit faster.

When the sit is practiced in connection with heeling, you can hold a stick (maybe 2 ft. long) in the right hand behind your back, and land the end of it with a flick of the wrist on the croup of the dog very shortly after the command was given. The dog can not see it coming, so he has to associate the hit with the command. Heeding this warning, he will learn to sit quickly, quickly.

C) CHANGING POSITION

After a while, the dog may decide to lay down or to get up. Watch closely to detect the dog's first muscle movement to change position, then quickly shout a warning ("hey.." or "no"). If he still wants to move, rush to him and physically put him back into place. Do this firmly and silently (except for an angry "sit"). If the dog has a tendency to run off, attach a leash or a long line to the collar (see also DOWN, below)

** DOWN **************** **********

GENERAL

The down, when taught properly, is a life saver in more than one way. It can be used to control the hyperactive, the obnoxious, the evasive, or the aggressive dog, and it can be used to keep the dog out of the way - your way, or that of an automobile. If a dog is set on pursuing a cat, no "heel", "here" or "come" will get him back. Only the "down" - if it was practiced properly - will prevent him from going onto the road and getting hit by the car.

OBJECTIVE

On a single command, the dog will drop to the ground, instantaneously, fast, reliably, under any condition, at any time, in any location, and he will remain at that spot laying down until released by his handler.

SUGGESTED COMMAND:	"down"
SUGGESTED RELEASE COMMAND:	"OK"

PSYCHOLOGY

If you perpetuate Dr.Spock's follies, if you *invite* your dog to go "down", if you give a "sit" command as lead-in for the "down", if you use your dog's name to get his attention, if you wait until he has reached a comfortable spot to relax, you will be heading for the taxidermist soon. The "down" is one of the two commands that the dog has to obey out of fear ("out" is the other one). We utilize his natural response to a threat where he seeks cover laying down to evade a dangerous situation. A dog understanding the meaning of the command yet not complying with it must receive instantaneous and forceful correction, given in a threatening, but not cruel, manner. This approach does not allow for more than very low-key praise during the down. Afterwards, however, heap praise on him, to ease the pressure to which he was subjected .

PREREQUISITES None, except a well-established dog/handler relationship.

TEACHING PROCEDURE

Do initial training on leash - mainly to prevent an escape. Later on, off-lead training is necessary.

A) INDUCTIVE METHOD

It was described earlier under puppy training.

B) SHOW & TELL

Kneel, with the dog sitting on your left side. Reaching over the dog's shoulder, grasp the left front paw with your left hand, and the right front paw with your right hand. Then slide the feet out to the front, giving the "down" command at the same time. Place the left hand on the dog's shoulder for a short time, to prevent any attempt of getting up. Don't give any praise at this time, the dog would get excited and take it as a sign that the exercise is over. A little reassurance is all right, however.

There are a few other, more pushy, methods that can be used if needed:

C) FLIP #1

With the dog standing on soft ground, broadside, kneel next to him and inconspicuously prepare to reach for his feet on the opposite side. Swiftly pull the feet out from under him and command "down" at the same time. He will land on his side. A surprise maneuver.

D) FLIP #2

Stand broadside, relaxed, next to your relaxed dog, leaving about 2 ft. space between the two of you. Then, with lightening speed, bend down, grab the loose skin near your dog's shoulder with your L (R) hand, and the loose skin near the croup with your

R (L) hand. Command "down" and swiftly pull towards you, flip him to the ground, and immediately release the grip. If all of this takes longer than ½ sec., then the dog will prepare himself and fight (you can't win).

E) TUG #1
Reach for the live ring on the choke collar, give a tug downwards and tell the dog to go "down".

F) TUG #2
Stand next to your dog. Hold the leash, attached to the active ring on the choke collar, in a short loop. Place one foot in the loop near the buckle and step on it, giving the "down" command. Watch your balance.

REFINING PROCEDURE
Once the dog understands the command "down", you can work on perfecting the exercise.

A) RELIABILITY
Practice everywhere (quiet and busy places), anytime (day or night, rain or shine), at home, on the street, in a mud puddle, during casual walks etc. Give the down command as soon as the thought occurs to you. This prevents the dog from preparing for the down by reading your mind, gestures, facial expression.

B) SPEED
You want a very fast response. This can be accomplished by giving an angry, sharp, short, stern command. Give the command, wait no longer than ½ seconds, then quickly bend over the dog with both arms outstretched - a very dominating posture - and flip him with both hands to the ground ("Flip #2", above), provided he did not comply already. Be quick with your action, prepare yourself for it, avoid the wrestling contest. You may have to push him sideways (quickly !) if he has planted his feet to the ground. After a couple of times the dog will want to avoid the push, and he will go down quickly by himself.

C) DISTANCE
Teach the "down" at first with the dog on your side, then a few feet away, then a few yards away etc. Give the dog a chance to roam and wait until he is far enough away. Then all of the sudden command "down". If needed, enforce the command (long line, assistant, throw chain, sling shot). Be aware that the dog will run away if he sees the projectile coming his way. In any case, go back to practicing at closer range.

D) SIT
After the "down", and before releasing him, you can ask your dog to "sit". This does not only look professional, it is also a requirement according to some trial rules. Return to your dog's right side (the proper heel position, dog still down), give the command "sit" and then, after a short moment, praise him.

E) DOWN OUT OF MOTION
The down command is given during slow, normal and fast pace heeling, first on lead (the lead is just dropped), then off lead. You continue walking while the dog lays down and remains behind.

Initially, stay fairly close to your dog and observe his response to the command. A quick, well-timed correction (if needed) is essential. In a trial, however, you may not turn your head to check on the dog, and you must continue walking without hesitation for a specified number of paces.

F) LONG DOWN with & without DISTRACTIONS
Gradually increase the time during which you ask the dog to remain in the down position, maybe up to 20 minutes. Stay close by, move farther away, or even hide in the vicinity. Disappearing at one end of a building and sneaking back behind it to the other side will allow you to watch the dog without being noticed yourself. A large mirror in an elevated position, or a reflecting store window may accomplish the same trick.

Distractions during the long down, like people, dogs, cats, vehicles, noises (incl. gun shots) should be introduced sensibly and gradually. A stranger calling the dog or offering some food, and protection work by another team done during the long down are quite a temptation for any dog. In all these instances, you should be prepared to correct (or sometimes to reassure) the dog as soon as he indicates that he wants to move. Ideally, you or an assistant should correct the dog the very moment he moves the first muscle to get up. A long check cord may serve this purpose. If the dog has already gotten up, then you must rush back. Bring him firmly and quickly (but silently) back to the original spot and yank him down not too gently. Don't give any praise until sufficient time has elapsed to conclude the exercise.

Some handlers believe that screaming the "stay" command will prevent the dog from leaving his position. This is not only offending a dog's intelligence, and his delicate sense of hearing, it is also a public announcement of a handler's incompetence. Besides, it does not work. Not the loudness, but the determination in a handler's command impresses a dog. And determination can be whispered!

PROBLEMS

A) NO DOWN

When commanded to go down, the dog remains in place but he sits or stands.

Physically manipulate the dog into the down position (see above "FLIP #2", "Speed"), be firm and swift. Make sure that your commands for "down", "sit" and "stand" sound sufficiently different.

B) CREEPING

The dog inches toward you, or toward another point of interest.

Close supervision is needed to detect the dog's first muscle movement in preparation for creeping. Give a firm verbal correction at this time ("Hey.. !!"). You can also attach a long line to the collar and have an assistant operate it, or land pebbles or a throw chain about two feet ahead of the dog's nose, or set up a real barrier (a board from the broad jump on edge) or a psychological barrier (scratch line on the ground just in front of the dog's nose). Practicing just short of a drop in terrain (embankment, small cliff) or close to the edge on a raised platform (a heavy 4x8 sheet of plywood, or a table top elevated a couple of inches) may help also. It requires quite a few practice sessions, however, to eliminate creeping.

C) GETTING UP

The dog gets up and leaves his position.

Practice the down with you (later on an assistant) nearby, give reassurance, a forceful correction, a firm verbal correction (timing is very important !), or use the long check cord. During early training stages, you can guide the leash under the heel of your foot, pick up any slack, and step on it forcefully as soon as the dog wants to get up (see above, "Tug #2").

Some dogs will break as soon as the handler returns, anticipating the release or a correction. Re-program: return to your dog and circle him several times; or return/depart several times before you release the dog.

Some dogs will leave the down position in anticipation of a recall. While this is one of the exercises in a Schutzhund trial, in practice you should return to your dog most of the time, rather than calling him.

Some dogs will get up when the gun is fired. You could stand close by and reassure him. If this does not help, the problem of gun-shyness must be addressed individually (see TEMPERAMENT TESTING). Methods that should NOT be used with gun-shy dogs (they will aggravate the problem) are: electronic collars, throw chains, sling shots.

** STAY ****************************

GENERAL: You can not explain "STAY" to a dog. Every command solicits some action from the dog. What do you want him to do when you say "stay" ? Nothing. So, why say something?

OBJECTIVE: Obey the **previously** given command

SUGGESTED COMMAND: none

SUGGESTED RELEASE COMMAND: none

PSYCHOLOGY

The purpose of a command is to get the dog to do something. The "stay" command defeats this purpose: *NO action is wanted, the dog is **not** supposed to do anything.*

Don't confuse your dog. Insist that he continues to obey the previously given instruction until you end it.

** STAND ****************************

GENERAL

The "stand" has practical applications for grooming, examining, carting, backpacking, preventing the dog from sitting in the dirt etc. It is also an excellent control exercise.

OBJECTIVE

On command, the dog will cease to move (his feet, that is) and remain in a standing position until released by his handler.

SUGGESTED COMMAND: "stand"

SUGGESTED RELEASE COMMAND: "OK"

PSYCHOLOGY

Standing motionless for more than a very short moment is quite unnatural. The dog wants either to move on, or to get more comfortable (lay down, sit). "Stand" is one of the more difficult exercises to teach. It requires to mildly shock the dog with the way how the command is given, therefore do not practice it in conjunction with precision heeling. To avoid undesirable associations (like anticipating a recall), return to your dog almost all of the time.

PREREQUISITES Long sit and long down

TEACHING PROCEDURE

The most natural approach to teaching the "stand" is to prevent the walking dog from sitting, rather than telling him to get up into a standing position (from a sit, for instance).

With the dog on lead, take a few steps forward and then give the command "stand".

Draw out the word: "sta-------nd", raising the voice just a little at the end of it, to become authoritative. Practice the (AKC) "stand for examination" first.

STAND FOR EXAMINATION

To teach this exercise, walk your dog into position. Then bend over your dog, having the right hand on the collar, and the left hand with gentle pressure on the left flank of the dog. Command "stand". If the dog is responsive, then the left hand barely makes contact. If the dog insists on sitting then the left hand has to hold up the rear end of the dog as much as necessary. Male dogs generally do not approve of this procedure, it should, therefore, be used by the owner only, and with much discretion.

When you give the command "stand" be sure that the dog is standing comfortably. There is usually no problem if the dog was allowed to walk into the stand. Sometimes the front feet are not side by side. Lift up the front end of the dog a little (right forearm supporting the chest, just in front of the front legs) and set him down again.

Initially, the command "stand" can be repeated a couple of times, to accustom the dog to it.

React quickly if the dog moves. Reach for the offending foot and place it back to where it came from, saying "no, stand" at the same time. Avoid leash corrections or harsh scolding, they usually cause the dog to sit.

Once the dog understands, another person is asked to step up to him from the front, from the dog's left side, to pet him, and to slide the hand along the dog's back. The dog should be approached in a confident manner. A hesitant, fearful, bold or intimidating assistant usually means trouble.

For the first few times you will have to stay close to your dog, to correct the inevitable foot movements. Later on, you can step back further and observe the examination from a distance.

In AKC trials give the "stand" command, then walk away six feet (do not back up !) from the dog so that the judge may examine him. The situation is often tense, especially if the judge is tense himself. Prepare your dog for this in training: ask an assistant to dress strangely, walk strangely, act strangely when examining the dog.

STAND OUT OF MOTION

The dog has to come to an abrupt halt and remain standing until released by you. Give the command while heeling at normal, or at running pace, you continuing and the dog remaining behind. While you may call your dog to you, we suggest that you return to him in practice almost all of the time (90%).

Initial training is best done on leash while you walk at a slow pace. Give the command, drop the lead and place the outstretched right hand in front of the dog's face, blocking his view without touching him. If necessary, hold the left hand on the right flank of the dog. To prevent the dog from moving forward you must stay close, initially. In addition you should turn and face the dog for the first few times. Primary cues (blocking the vision, contact with the flank) and secondary cues (command "stand") are given simultaneously in the beginning, then primary right after secondary, then secondary only.

REFINING PROCEDURE

Once the dog has mastered the basic principles of the exercise, eliminate - one at a time:
the turn to face the dog, the touch on the flank, the outstretched hand in front of the dog.
Still working on leash and in close proximity to the dog, try to refine the exercise with
- a more sudden stop
- a secure and sure stand, until the release is given.

Then practice off leash, move farther away from the dog, move out of sight for a short moment, do the stand out of slow, normal and fast pace, and add distractions with other dogs, people, machinery around.

PROBLEMS

A) THE DOG IS AFRAID AND UNEASY

When introduced to the "stand", soft dogs often cringe, back arched, tail tugged between the legs.
1) Be less harsh, back off on the pressure.
2) Practice this exercise only once per session.
3) Give lots of praise, and play with the dog, afterwards.

B) THE DOG SITS WHEN COMING TO A HALT

4) Practice on leash.
5) Do not praise your dog during the stand, only after the release.
6) Stay close to your dog and repeat the stand command.
7) Together with the "stand" command gently put your left hand into the right flank of the dog.
8) Catch his rear end on the way down with your left foot under the belly, gently lift him up.
9) As 8) but use your left hand.
10) As 8) but quickly grab the loose skin on the back, near his croup, and pull him up.
11) Lay a short piece of rope loose over his back, or tie it loosely around his belly (hands off).
12) Slide the buckle of your leash through the loop handle. Put this "collar" loosely around the dog's belly / groin. Hold on to the buckle and tighten the choke if the dog wants to sit.
13) Command "stand" when your dog has just

stepped over a board from the broad jump, set on edge. The board is between front and hind legs, but closer to the rear. This discourages the sit.

C) THE DOG SITS WHEN THE HANDLER RETURNS

14) The suggestions 4-11 from above can be tried.
15) Leave your dog, return, leave, return, leave etc. for several times before you release him from the stand.
16) Before finishing the exercise with the sit command, heel your dog a few paces straight ahead.

D) THE DOG DOES NOT STAND RIGHT AWAY

He continues forward for one or more steps after the command to stand:

17) Try suggestions 4-6 from above.
18) Together with the command "stand" quickly put your cupped left hand over his snout and push it toward his chest. Release immediately.
19) Together with the command "stand" quickly grab the loose skin around his neck. Release immediately.
20) Rush back to him, put his feet back into exactly the same positions where they were supposed to stay.

E) THE DOG STANDS BUT THEN FOLLOWS THE HANDLER FOR A FEW STEPS

21) Turn to move away from him backwards, give a verbal correction (timing is important).

F) THE DOG LEAVES HIS POSITION WHEN THE HANDLER RETURNS

22) Try suggestions 4, 5, 6, 15, 16, 19 from above.

** RECALL **************************
GENERAL

The *formal* recall should be one of the last exercises taught in a basic obedience program. The *informal* recall, however, can be practiced as soon as the handler obtains his dog.

OBJECTIVE

On command, the dog will come to his handler, fast and reliably. He will stop for a sit in front of him and go to the heel position when asked to do so.

SUGGESTED COMMAND: "come" "heel"
SUGGESTED RELEASE COMMAND: "OK"

PSYCHOLOGY

Motivation is the key element in teaching the recall. The dog must WANT to come to you when called, and he must EXPECT (and get) something pleasant when he is coming in.

To avoid confusion, the command "come" should be reserved for the occasion where the dog is expected to perform competition-style. The dog must be able to count on the reward, and on the fun, in connection with this command. Use another command if you just want the dog to be closer, for instance "here".

PREREQUISITES None, except a well-established dog/handler relationship.

TEACHING PROCEDURE

Three rules apply, and they must be followed religiously:

1. The "come when called" must ALWAYS be an enjoyable experience for the dog, it should ALWAYS proceed and end on a happy note.
2. Do not use force, compulsion, correction or punishment when calling the dog.
   The Advanced Schutzhund experts recommend a leash correction - this invites disaster !
3. The dog is NEVER, never reprimanded when he comes to his handler on his own free will - regardless of what happened before.

INTRODUCTION

To follow these rules, we *invite* the dog to come in a pleasant tone of voice, we do not command him. There must be no doubt that when he dashes in he will get a reward, and that his master will be happy and pleased.

The exercise ends, and the fun begins, when the dog comes within your reach. Skip the formal front sit and the finish at this stage. Instead, reward the dog immediately: friendly words, praise, petting, playing, roughhousing, etc. Food rewards are very effective, especially when the dog is hungry, and when the treat is truly a delicacy in his eyes. Then set him free. The dog must not form the undesirable association between being called and being put on a leash. If he has to be restrained, you should call and receive him with a long, big hug, then - a few moments later - clip on the lead in an inconspicuous and casual way while still petting him. Do not give any leash corrections for a short time thereafter.

For **PROGRESSION**, call from close distances at first (tease the dog with the reward), from larger distances later on. Squatting, clapping hands, excitedly calling and backing up or running backwards, AWAY from the dog, entice a reluctant pupil to approach his master.

To **REINFORCE** the recall, take your dog to a remote field which is unfamiliar to him, far away from cars and other people. Set him free and allow, even encourage him, to roam. Hide quickly once he is not paying any attention to you. Then call him from hiding, once only. Remain silent and motionless until the dog finds you. It will take some time on the first try, it may even require a second call. You should, however, not reveal your location prematurely. The dog, having ignored your call, must experience the feeling of being left behind. This will teach him to respond quicker to the call, and to keep an eye on you while roaming. After two tries, you will probably have a tough time to ever hide again without being seen by your dog.

COMPLETION

Practice the front sit and the finish independently of the recall. They require some correction and would spoil the fun for the dog. Likewise, we teach a very young puppy the "come when called" but reserve the front sit and the finish for later on.

FRONT SIT

Use a different command, like "front". This will leave the "come" reserved for an experience of pure fun.

During a casual walk, with the dog on lead, give the command "front". At the same time quickly walk backwards, away from the dog, and encourage him to follow. Stop after a few paces and guide your dog into a sitting position in front of you, using, as needed, the leash, both hands on the sides of the dog's neck/cheeks, and maybe an outstretched foot (to prevent him from sitting sideways).

Once the dog is closer, reach with one hand for the collar, under the chin, and slightly lift the front end of the dog up and push it back a little. Stroke the back of the dog with the other hand, towards the croup, to urge him into a sitting position. This way the command "sit" can be avoided. If it were given and the dog would not comply, force would have to be used, spoiling the fun for the dog. If the dog does not sit, you must improve upon your technique for coaxing him into a sit. Try again.

Food (or a toy) can also be very effective: Skillful teasing gets the dog to come close, to sit close, to sit straight, to sit attentive. To accomplish that, call and tease him, offer the food held with the arm outstretched towards him. Once he is close, drop your hand to (his) eye level, then move your hand with the food toward your stomach, then slightly above and backwards over the dog's head. Only then, when he is manipulated into a sit in front of you (later on only when he sits correctly) is the food actually given to him.

Another method is to hold the food in your teeth and release it from there after bending slightly forward. This has several advantages:

- the dog is being taught to look up into your eyes ("look" command)
- the dog is being taught to sit close (otherwise he would miss the food when it is dropped)
- you can keep your hands in a natural position (you must, however, learn to speak with a full mouth).

You can also fasten a clothes pin to your belt which holds the meat. This leaves your hands and mouth free, but the dog must be taught to take the meat on command only.

Some trainers suggest two barriers for the straight sits, one each to the right and to the left, in front of the handler. This chute leaves the dog not much of a choice but to sit straight - as long as the barriers are in place.

The chute, the long line, or even the leash are very inefficient and unreliable training aids for the recall. While skillful use of line or leash can leave the dog in doubt if he at the moment is restrained or not, the chute is either there ("I must obey") or it is not ("catch me if you can !").

FINISH

There are at least three options to get the dog from a front sit to the heel position (see **"TURNS"**, p.71 cont.).

- One is for the dog to jump up and just land in the heel position (circus style).
- Another one requires that the dog makes a relatively large sweep to his right and then comes back to the heel position via a left circle (error-prone).
- The third approach is more practical and more reliable then the others: The dog advances forward, along the handler's right side, around and behind him in a close circle, and then shows up on the left side of the handler for a straight sit, in heel position.

In preparation for this third variation you should practice leash handling WITHOUT the dog:

a) Loop the leash into a neat, compact bundle like ribbon-candy, hold it in the right hand.
b) Go into a slight knee bend (the smaller the dog, the deeper the bend).
c) Move your right hand straight back and then to the rear.
d) Pass the leash to the left hand, behind your back but at about the height of your (bent) knees.
e) Move the left hand forward, at the same time bring the right hand quickly in front your body to the left hip.
f) Both hands meet below the left hip. The right

hand then accepts the leash and moves straight forward.

g) Use the left hand to guide your (imaginary) dog into a straight sit and to praise him.

h) Straighten up.

Now: Practice this sequence to perfection without the dog, then clip the leash to the dog's collar and

a) Give the "sit" command and step in front of your dog, so close that there is almost contact. Face your dog. Fold the leash into a bundle, as short as comfortably possible. With the larger breeds the leash is completely folded up so that your right hand (which holds the leash) touches the end of the collar.

b) Go into a slight knee bend (the smaller the dog, the deeper the bend).

c) Give the command "heel", and with the right hand (which holds the leash) snap/tug the leash forward. This motion is horizontal towards your back. It gets the dog on his feet and moving forward.

IT IS IMPORTANT NOW to keep the dog in motion up to the completion of the finish, therefore all of your subsequent actions must be performed swiftly and smoothly.

d) Guide the dog around your back in a tight circle. Keep the leash still very short, and change it from the right to the left hand behind your back, as described earlier.

e) Continue pulling with your left hand and move the right hand quickly toward your left hip.

f) Transfer the leash (still short) and continue to pull, forward at this time. The dog is on your left side now.

g) Use the left hand to guide your dog into a straight sit and to praise him. Straighten up.

The inductive method to teach the finish would require food, or a ball. It is best done off leash.

Step in front of your dog and show him the treat in the cupped right hand. Then lead him "by the nose" forward, around you, and to the heel position at your left side. Change the food quickly from one hand to the other, just as described for the leash above. Give the reward only after he sits straight at heel, not before.

With this last approach the dog has a tendency to swing around too far, almost to the front to face you. Position the reward at the end well to your left, and/or have your left hand ready to guide him into a straight sit. This correction must be fast since it is necessary to catch him in motion, not after he is sitting already.

REFINING PROCEDURE

After the initial training, the three parts of calling, front sit, and finish can be combined into the complete recall exercise. However, practice the individual parts frequently out of order, to maintain a happy recall, and to prevent anticipation.

◆ Practice the recall as the last routine in a training session, most of the time. A good trainer will play with his dog after a work-out. In anticipation of this, the dog will be anxious to come to his handler, fast. Dogs have a competitive spirit, too:

◆ The novice dog, having watched another dog do a couple of fast recalls and receive a reward, often is quite eager to come quickly when called.

◆ Two dogs, called at the same time, may also do a better recall if a small but tasty treat is offered as a reward. However, this does not work with all canines, since the desire to compete is influenced by the pecking order, by experiences from past competitions with this rival or with other dogs, and by other factors.

There is another approach to firmly establish a fast, happy recall. It utilizes an isolation effect which increases the dog's desire to be with his master as he gets farther and farther away (pack instinct).

◆ Sit (or down) your dog at one end of a field 300 to 400 feet long, free of obstructions - isolated from other people and other dogs. Then back away from him, but watch him constantly and very closely. That moment is critical where the dog moves the first muscle to get up. You must recognize it and call your dog in a friendly, inviting tone. Call him even though you may have gotten away only a few steps, and praise/reward him lavishly when he arrives. A moment later repeat it.

Quite naturally and without any additional effort, you can increase the distance between you and your dog before he breaks. Within a week or so you should be able to walk away 200, 300 or even 400 feet before the dog moves. Again, it is important to call the dog at the first sign of getting up, and to reward him for coming with praise, food, toy.

We have never found any difficulties with the long sits and downs because of this training approach.

PROBLEMS

A) THE DOG DOES NOT WANT TO LEAVE HIS POSITION

Probably the "sit" (or "down") command was too forceful, or the "come" was given too harshly.

- Give the "come" in a more pleasing tone, as an invitation.

- Run away (away from the dog).
- Have an assistant inconspicuously throw a throw chain or a tin can behind the dog. Then quickly call your startled dog.
- Build a pyramid of empty tin cans on a board and attach a long line to that. Tell your dog to sit, maybe six feet in front of it, then walk away. After a moment, call your dog excitedly, clap your hands, snap the line.
- Restart with the motivation process: food, toys, praise.

B) THE DOG COMES TOO SLOWLY

- Make him stay longer before you call.
- Call him from farther away.
- Run backwards, away from the dog.
- Kneel, and clap your hands.
- Excitedly call your dog.
- Show him the treat.
- Call from a spot that is of interest to your dog (the exit, your car, other people or other dogs).
- Restart with motivation: food, toys, praise.

C) THE DOG WANDERS OFF

All the suggestions that were given for the slow dog can be used. In addition, try the following:

- Attach a long line to the collar, to prevent him from leaving the field.
- Withhold food and/or ALL attention to the dog for 24 hours (with adult dogs only). Then tease him with the reward and call him. Give genuine praise, let him have the treats when he comes.
- Exclude distractions, initially.
- As a temporary measure, command "down" and fetch your dog (refer to the "down" section).

D) THE DOG SLOWS DOWN WHEN COMING CLOSE TO HIS HANDLER

All the suggestions that were given for the slow dog can be tried. In addition:

- Give little praise during the first part of the run, more praise and excitement as the dog gets closer.
- The "drop on recall" (AKC) may interfere here. Do the "drop" rarely, the straight recall more often.

E) THE DOG DOES NOT SIT IN FRONT, OR SITS CROOKED

- Practice the sits independently of the recall.
- Nudge the dog into the proper position, if necessary. Never give a harsh correction after, or in connection with, a successful recall.

F) THE DOG ANTICIPATES THE "HEEL" AND FINISHES ON HIS OWN

- Do most recalls without the finish, practice the finish independently.

- Let the dog wait (maybe 20 seconds, but vary the time) before you tell him to heel.
- Do the finish yourself. Keep the dog sitting and walk around him, to end up in the heel position.

** SEND AWAY *********************
GENERAL

The "send away" (or "go out") has various useful applications. The dog can be asked to scout ahead (quartering in protection work), to retrieve articles from a location known only to the handler (directed retrieve in Utility work), to deliver a message or an item to a specific person or location, to move out (conformation show ring). Herding dogs, police dogs, military dogs, customs dogs etc. must go out in the direction indicated by their handlers to accomplish certain tasks.

PREREQUISITES A reliable "down" or "sit", controlled from a distance.

OBJECTIVE

On command, the dog will leave the heel position and move away from the handler, at a fast pace and in a straight line, in the indicated direction, and until commanded to "down" or "sit".

SUGGESTED COMMAND "go" or "go out"
SUGGESTED RELEASE COMMAND: "down" or "sit"

PSYCHOLOGY

A dog wants to be with his handler, not to be sent away by him. It takes time to teach that concept, so start early (the puppy) and practice often (but not endless repetitions). There are two ways to reach the goal:

a) scouting, sending the dog *away* from you, or
b) aiming, sending the dog *toward* something.

While b) is easier to teach, a) is the intended meaning of the command, but always point your outstretched arm in the desired direction and make sure that your dog looks that way before sending him off. Use an aim point: a person, a large building, the shade of a lonely tree, an attraction which the dog knows waits at the goal (toy, ball, treat), etc. It prevents him from "running in circles". Without such a marker, people and dogs can not walk a straight line (close your eyes, walk 100 paces!). Then guarantee an instantaneous reward at the goal (run up to him and play ball right away!).

In general, dogs are more willing to go out in an open area, rather than in an enclosed field.

TEACHING PROCEDURE

You may give both a signal and a command. Raise one outstretched arm and give the command at the same time. The arm should be kept up as a signal until the dog has complied with the "down" (or "sit") command. Lowering the arm any earlier can be faulted in a trial as an additional signal/command.

It is better to use the "down" instead of the "sit" command at the end of the run. He will be more willing to do that, and a refusal to sit would complicate your job tremendously. We suggest, however, to skip the terminating "down" or "sit" command during the early training phases.

Scouting:

* Even a very young puppy can be taught to go ahead of you - on or off lead: chase, shove, push him.
* Playfully run and encourage the excited dog to move ahead, away from you.
* Teach the dog to get out of your way, moving forward.
* Get right behind the dog after commanding "go", and chase/push the dog with both hands ahead of you. A dog hates it when someone steps on his tail (even if it was docked). Be quick, do not let the dog evade to the side. Don't stop if he throws himself to the ground, just keep pushing! Chase him toward an easily identifiable orientation marker. He will eventually take note of it and move out straight. This method is startling to the dog but it is also quick and effective.

Aiming:

* Leave the dog on a long down in the same spot to which you want to send him in the go out. Then collect him, walk with him maybe 30 ft. away and send him without delay. During the following days (or weeks, or months) pick the same field, the same spot, the same routine. Eventually increase the distance.
* One dog can learn from the other. The "expert" is being sent out first and commanded to go down while the "student" is being held by the collar. When released and sent, the new dog is usually eager to join his playmate out there. If the dog does not want to leave, run with dog #2 to dog #1. Heap lots of praise and encouragement during and after the exercise on your dog, you want him to go out happily. "Down" or "sit" can be skipped during initial training. Repeat.
* Tie your dog to a post and tease him with a reward (food, toy). Walk away for a small distance. In full view, and while talking to the dog, place a marker (jacket, chair, box, plastic traffic cone) with the reward on top of it. Hurry back to your dog, excite, release and send him. Verbally praise him

for finding the reward, run to him. Let him eat, or play a lively game with him. Repeat right away, use the same drop point but start the send from farther away. Repeat 4 or 5 more times, then quit. During the next few days continue where you left off. Use the same drop point, but increase the distance gradually. Then switch to smaller and smaller markers, leaving finally just the reward, then nothing at all, in the field. At that point carry the reward in your pocket and use it as soon as the dog reaches the destination. Now practice the exercise in different locations, following the same procedure as above. Skip the down or sit during initial training.

* You can also use the "Refrigerator Effect" (see Tracking, page 56). Secure a glass jar with lid (about ¼ gallon size), or a five-gallon plastic bucket with lid, put some tasty treats into it, tease your dog with the food and give him one piece. Tie your dog to a post and walk away. Let him see the jar/bucket when you place it at the designated drop point. Then proceed as described before. Most likely the dog will lay down at the aim point automatically, since he needs your help to get the treats.
* For an eager retriever use the same procedure as in the previous exercise, except no food and no prop-up, just the ball. Let the dog bring the ball to you, then throw it for him and continue just as above.
* Here is another way for an eager retriever: Hold him by the collar. Throw an article, point and send the dog. Change to smaller and smaller articles until finally only the gesture of throwing, or pointing, remains. Some trainers throw wild apples or potatoes, they do not have to bother to collect them if missed or lost.
* Family members, or fellow club members with their dogs, might serve as attraction too. The dog is sent toward them, rather then away from them.
* Dogs that enjoy protection work can be sent toward a decoy who stands quietly in the field. The decoy moves only if the dog lacks enthusiasm. Command "down" when the dog reaches the decoy. If he obeys, reward him with a bite.

Methods we do not recommend for the "go out" because of questionable training or moralistic values are: - a "race track" with little picket fences
- the long line attached to the collar, no matter for what purpose you plan to use it
- a rope/pulley arrangement (with an assistant running the rope)

- tying the dog to the bumper of a car (which is driven away by an assistant).

After a few trial runs introduce the "down" or "sit" at the end of the send out, while the dog is still moving away from you at a reasonable speed. Do not accommodate him, don't give the down command when he slows down or hesitates to go out further. Make him go again and stop him in motion at your will.

Return to your dog at the conclusion of the exercise. While it is more convenient to call the dog back, it conditions him to anticipate the recall. Most likely he will break, and problems with the down (sit) arise.

REFINING PROCEDURE

Advanced dogs should go for greater distances, at a faster speed, and in a straight line. Practice on various fields, chose each time a different direction for the go out, incorporate distractions such as people, animals, vehicles, noises etc. Stop training for he day after a successful go-out, but follow up with enthusiastic play.

PROBLEMS

A) THE DOG DOES NOT WANT TO LEAVE THE HANDLER Refer to "Teaching procedures" above.

B) THE DOG DOES NOT GO IN THE INDICATED DIRECTION and/or he may change direction.

- Select an obvious aim point, possibly one of interest to the dog. This can be the shade of a lonely tree, the exit from the field, a familiar person, an unfamiliar person, your car, etc.
- Line up your outstretched arm with an aim point next to the dog's head. Make sure he faces and looks in this direction.
- Goal-baiting: show him that wherever you point and send him, there is a reward waiting.
  Go from 1-5:
  1. Show him the reward and where you drop it, then point toward it and send him.
  2. Show him the reward. Don't let him see where you drop it, then point toward it and send him.
  3. Don't let him see the reward or where you drop it. Just point in the right direction and send.
     Practice that sequence for several weeks. Use food initially, then switch to ball at the goal, then to ball in your pocket which you produce at the goal. Rush to the goal once your dog has arrived there, then play with him a lively game.
  4. Use several goal points spaced apart, let him see when you (supposedly) bait them but

put the reward only in one location. Point to the jack pot and send your dog. If he goes to the wrong goal, ignore him, do not reward. Repeat. Eventually he will figure out that only the indicated goal gets the reward.
  5. As before, but bait two goals. Play with him only if he goes to the indicated goal, otherwise ignore him.

C) THE DOG GOES OUT TOO SLOW
- Run after him, clap your hands, excite him.
- Follow your dog quickly, release him right after the down at the target, reward him (food, play).
- Try other rewards. A ball game might create more enthusiasm and a faster go-out than the food reward.
- At random, do the "go out" without the "down" at the end.
- Command "go out" and two seconds later "down" (he is still close to the starting point). Enforce the "down", if necessary with the long line. Then send him on. The penned-up anticipation of the ball game will make him move faster now.

D) THE DOG DOES NOT GO FAR ENOUGH
- Vary between short (maybe 20 ft.), long and overly long (maybe 200ft.) distances in the "go out" at random.
- Do re-starts: send, give the "down" when the dog has covered a short distance only, send again, give another "down", then send to the final destination. Use this procedure only during initial training.
- Run behind him, repeat the "go" command as soon as he slows down. Even though you may not be able to keep up with him, the shortened gap is to your advantage.
- Never give the "down" or "sit" command when the dog slows down or stops. Make him go out further, if necessary several times, and command "down" or "sit" while he is at full speed.

E) THE DOG IS DISTRACTED
- In training, put many distracting objects on the field. Send your dog past them.
- Ask a decoy in full protective gear to stand on the field. Send your dog past him.

F) FAULTY "DOWN" (OR "SIT")
The dog does not go down, or only part way, or too slowly, or he gets up again, creeps, wanders off.
- Practice the "down" (or "sit") independently of the "go out" (see page 75).
- Practice a few rather short "go out", control the "down" from close up.

- Return to your dog after a go out, don't call him back to you. He may otherwise come to expect the recall.

** RETRIEVE ON FLAT ************

GENERAL
The playful retrieve of ball, stick or rag during puppyhood laid the groundwork, now we want to use a small, light-weight dumbbell to make the distinction between play and work. The dog should associate the dumbbell with a routine that must be carried out in a specific manner. If you start this early in a dog's training program, then sufficient time can be devoted to each step in the exercise, without causing frustrations either in the dog or in the handler. The second lesson in the first obedience training class is about the right time.

OBJECTIVE
With the dog sitting at the heel position, the handler throws the dumbbell. On command, the dog goes out, picks up the dumbbell, and returns to the handler, all at a fast pace. The dog sits in front of the handler, releases the dumbbell on command, and does a smart finish to the heel position.

SUGGESTED COMMAND   "get it" "out" "heel"
SUGGESTED RELEASE COMMAND   "OK"

PREREQUISITES   None, except a well-established dog/handler relationship.

PSYCHOLOGY
Some dogs are happy retrievers, they can easily be trained to do the regulation retrieve. Other dogs show initially a strong disliking for this exercise. They require a little more effort on the part of the trainer. All dogs of all breeds, however, have the inborn instinct of carrying things in their mouth from one place to another. If you convey to them a feeling of ease by talking in a soft tone all the while, they will be more cooperative.

The most effective motivator here is the play instinct. Always play a lively ball game as reward. You might even want to withhold attention for some time and reserve playtime for those days on which you practice the retrieve, **ONLY** the retrieve. At the least, do the retrieve as the last exercise in a session, then play vigorously.

TEACHING PROCEDURE
The retrieve is taught in three separate parts:
1. taking the dumbbell ("take it")
2. carrying the dumbbell ("hold it")
3. releasing the dumbbell ("out").

Work on holding and carrying the dumbbell first, before steps one and three are dealt with.

A) INTRODUCING THE DUMBBELL
* Keep the dog on your left side, leash in the left hand.
* Hold the dumbbell by the bar in your right hand, between the base portion of thumb and index finger.
* Slide four fingers of the right hand into the choke collar (over the dog's head, pointing to his rear).
* Release the leash and hold the dog with the four fingers of the right hand, as described above.
* Reach with your left arm over the dog's shoulder and, from the left side of the dog, slide the left hand under his head.
* With your left thumb, push the dog's lower left lip onto the lower left teeth near the base of the mouth.
* With your left middle finger, push the dog's lower right lip onto the lower right teeth.
* A gentle squeeze from the last two steps will cause the dog to open his mouth. (This procedure avoids covering the dog's eyes which would bother the dog and generate additional resistance). At that time release the collar and quickly scoop the right hand with the dumbbell in front of the dog's mouth. The fingers of the right hand point toward the dog's throat, palm up.
* With a push of the palm roll the dumbbell into the dog's mouth, then release the two fingers which had pried the dog's mouth open. At the same time say "hold it, good boy".
* Keep the right hand scooped under the dog's head, barely maintaining contact with the dog's lower jaw.
* Talk to him reassuringly and slide the left hand into the dog's collar, fingers pointing toward the dog's nose, or just have your left hand behind the dog's head, praising and caressing him.
* Do not touch the dumbbell anymore, holding it is now the dog's responsibility.
* Make the dog hold on to the dumbbell for a few seconds initially, longer later on. Backing out of it is prevented with the left hand in the collar and/or behind the head. Spitting the dumbbell out is countered by scooping the right hand which holds the lower jaw up, and by the lower portion of the right arm which is in an upright position and squarely just in front of the dog's mouth. The dog will balk at this procedure, but don't give in.
* Insist that he holds the dumbbell for a short moment before YOU tell him to release.
* Heap love and praise on your dog for doing such a

marvelous job, give him a food reward.

Don't repeat the exercise for at least another hour, but practice this for several weeks or months, and gradually increase the time for holding the dumbbell. Then ask him to carry the dumbbell for a short distance:

Keep your left hand in the dog's collar and the right hand barely below his lower jaw, as a precaution. Urge him to move forward and advance a few steps. Quickly command "out", take the dumbbell, praise and reward him lavishly. In the following days and weeks do short heeling patterns first, more elaborate ones later on, all with the dog carrying the dumbbell, without any assistance from you.

B) TAKING THE DUMBBELL

Do early training on lead. Progressing in stages, tell him first to "take it" while you hold the dumbbell in front of his nose. Very rarely will you have to push his head toward the dumbbell, and to force his lips against it (move his head, not the dumbbell!).   In subsequent sessions bring the dumbbell closer and closer to the ground. Then rest one bell on the ground while you hold the other bell up. Then drop the dumbbell just in front of him and kick it a little away from the dog, then throw it farther, etc.

In the beginning it is helpful to get the dog going while the dumbbell is still moving, 'living' things are, by nature, of much more interest to the dog than inanimate ones. You may have to push the head of your dog toward the dumbbell a little.

Important is a certain firmness. Do not give in to an uncooperative dog when you know that he understands what is asked of him. Also, a command should only be given once. The second time you pronounce it, the dog must be made to obey (provided the dog knows what he is supposed to do).

C) RELEASING THE DUMBBELL

Reach for the dumbbell, one hand for each end, and command "out" in a pleasant but still firm tone. Don't play a game now. Unspoiled dogs will release willingly since their attention shifts from the dumbbell to the excited handler. Praise your dog. Dogs that have already developed bad habits require a more firm and determined "out", but still without yelling or being harsh. A food bribe, followed by praise, may help.

D) COMBINING THE PARTS

Work on leash at first, using a proper mixture of firmness and praise. Keep the training session interesting and short. Practice in a variety of locations and with various distractions. Avoid leash corrections while the dog is holding the dumbbell.

REFINING PROCEDURE

Training for advanced dogs should include the retrieve of leather, metal and wooden dumbbells. They should be of various sizes, shapes and weights: 2000 grams are required in the Schutzhund III retrieve.

Introduce distractions gradually, insist on exact performance. For variety and usefulness, teach your dog to bring a basket, a shovel, keys, shoes, a purse etc. He can also learn to drag a heavy object (box, tire) by a handle; this is just another variation of the retrieve. Sending him after an object thrown in the water (make sure that he can handle the current and that he can get out of the water by himself) will serve a multitude of purposes: variety, dependability, courage, physical exercise.

FORCED RETRIEVE

Some trainers maintain that the inductive method (described above) is inefficient, and that only the forced retrieve will guarantee a reliable performance. This may be so, but if I want my dog to be quiet I would not just shoot him!

There are various flavors to the forced retrieve. In the true version, two leashes (restraint and correction) and a prong collar are used. An assistant violently jerks the prong collar and stuffs the dumbbell into the dog's mouth when he cries out in pain. Just like in medieval times, the one in charge tortures the subject until he complies with whatever is asked of him.

The approach is wrong, for moralistic, and for psychological, reasons. It also manifests the dog owner's incompetence and his inability to properly train a dog.

We disapprove of the true, forced retrieve. A somewhat related approach, however, will benefit dogs who have mastered the retrieve earlier and who now have decided that they do not like it.

I want to apply psychological rather than physical force: When the (trained) dog refuses to pick up the dumbbell, then I convincingly play the role of a very angry, violent person who is just about to pick up a 2x4 to clobber him over the head. I would not do it, of course, but I want the dog to understand the seriousness of the situation. Rushing to the dog, angrily pushing his head toward the dumbbell and making him pick it up, or shoving it into his mouth if he still refuses, usually does the trick. Then comes the big praise and reward.

PROBLEMS

Use food rewards *after* a good performance. Timing and technique are important. When you hold the food *and* the dumbbell in your hand, there is no question which one he will take.

A) ANTICIPATION

Some dogs dash out to get the dumbbell before the command was given; they have learned the sequence of events. Vary the routine in training: throw the dumbbell, do another exercise, then send your dog to retrieve. Or force him to obey: leash corrections; nape grab; varying time intervals between throwing the dumbbell and sending him.

B) DISTRACTION

If the dog refuses to retrieve because of distractions, then prior training was not versatile enough.

Practice dumbbell work in busy places, under simulated trial conditions, with a decoy standing motionless next to the dumbbell, or while another dog does protection work. Keep your dog on a long leash, and demand perfection. Be firm, get the job done in a hurry, and then reward your dog lavishly.

C) NO FIND

The dog may have trouble finding the dumbbell. Paint the bells white so that it can be seen easier, and throw the dumbbell so that it lands in the desired spot. If the article was thrown too far or too much sideways, the dog may have to search for it.

Landing the dumbbell on the ground in exactly the spot where you want it is quite possible(see Fig.33/34).

* Hold the dumbbell by the edge of the bell, between thumb and the four fingers.
* Throw it and give it a twist the moment you release it, so that it spins around its center point.
* On landing, spin and inertia of the dumbbell will offset each other and the dumbbell will remain at the spot where it first touched the ground.

D) NO PICK-UP

If the instance is isolated, then a firm command, maybe a firm correction, will straighten things out.

If the dog repeatedly refuses to pick up the dumbbell, you have probably progressed too fast. Review and practice the introductory exercises again, at a slower pace.

Different methods have been used by trainers with varying degrees of success:
- rubbing meat on the center bar of the dumbbell
- rubbing your hand for a while on the center bar

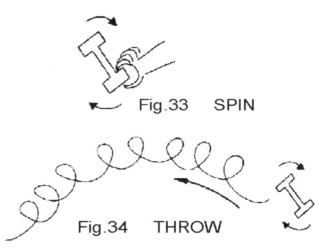

Fig.33   SPIN

Fig.34   THROW

- tying a glove or handkerchief with the handler's scent around the center bar
- gradually converting from ball to dumbbell in the following sequence: rubber ball, -> rubber ball with dowel pushed through it, -> as before, with small bells on the dowel, -> as before, with larger bells, -> as before, but with portions of the ball removed, then with just a little rubber left from the ball, -> dowel with bells alone (=dumbbell).
- pinching the ear or stepping on his toes (wrong from a psychological standpoint, useless and harmful)
- forced retrieve (unethical / cruel, only a sadist would use it).

Dogs objecting to retrieve certain objects only need re-training, a firm command, maybe some persuasion.

E) PICK-UP BY THE BELLS

There is a greater chance that the dog will drop the dumbbell, or mouth it, if he picks it up by the bells. To discourage this, nails with the heads protruding by about one inch can be driven into the bells.

F) MOUTHING THE DUMBBELL *(db)*

- Be gentle and use quick motions, but spin, wiggle, push, move the *db* when the grip is not firm.
- Make one of the bells heavier (screw a metal plate to it) - the unbalanced weight encourages a firmer grip.
- Gently kick the *db* out of his mouth, at the same time intentionally but gently slap the side of his mouth.
- Tie a short string to the *db* and wiggle it lightly when he is not holding on tight.
- Use a *db* without the bells, a stick. Tie a short string to it and quickly but gently whip it out of his mouth when he is not holding on tight.

- Wrap metal wire around the center bar - dogs don't like to bite into it.

G) DROPPING THE DUMBBELL (db)

- Practice "holding" at close range, on leash, and quickly correct the dog before he can fully eject the db.
- Walk/heel the dog while he holds the db as a separate exercise, see above: "Introducing the db".
- Try to kick the db out of his mouth just before he wants to spit it out, at the same time intentionally but gently slap the side of his mouth in the process.

H) NO RETURN

The dog may decide not to return with the dumbbell but to take off instead. He wants to play.
- Give the "down" command, then re-train.
- Use verbal correction, and practice on a long leash, or in a fully enclosed area, for a while.
- Practice with meat in a glove or in a small wooden or plastic tube, e.g. a piece of pipe with caps. The dog needs to return it to you so that you can unpack the reward and give it to him (see also page 56).
- Drill a large hole into one of the bells and close it with a plug. Let your dog watch when you hide some meat in it, throw the dumbbell. He needs your help to get the meat, so he will bring the db back to you.

I) NO OUT

Don't let the dog tease you with the db. Do not rip the db out of his mouth, he will get to hate retrieving.
- Offer a tasty morsel of food which he can only obtain after releasing the dumbbell.
- Practice on lead, press the dog's lips onto his teeth with your thumb (see "Introducing the Dumbbell", above), press your fingers against the dog's jaw to open it gently, or give a threatening "out" command.

** RETRIEVE OVER HURDLE/ JUMPING **************

GENERAL

Retrieving and jumping are activities which most healthy dogs enjoy - but don't overdo it: jumping once is fun, twice is work, three times is slave labor. Even a healthy dog will eventually get to hate, and eventually refuse, the jump for an unreasonable handler. Nevertheless, a fitness program is a good idea: swim and run with your dog, or road work him from a bicycle, to get him in shape. Include some easy jumps over natural obstacles. This can be started with a young dog already, if done within reason.

OBJECTIVE

With the dog sitting at the heel position, the handler throws the dumbbell over the hurdle. On command, the dog goes out, jumps, picks up the dumbbell, jumps back and returns to the handler, all at a fast pace. The dog sits in front of the handler, releases the dumbbell on command, and does a smart finish to the heel position.

SUGGESTED COMMAND   "get it" "jump"
                               "out" "heel"

SUGGESTED RELEASE COMMAND   "OK"

PSYCHOLOGY

With the retrieve over the hurdle we prepare our dogs for clearing obstacles and barriers of reasonable height. This, however, is not obvious to the dog at the time of training. He only sees a narrow hurdle that can easily be bypassed on the side. In his way of thinking it is ridiculous to go over it.

Since you insist on the jump, and since you (initially) go over it too, the dog will comply to please you, but his cooperation should not be abused. You must make sure that the dog can do a satisfactory performance on the second try in a row: use encouragement, guidance, or temporarily lower the height of the jump somewhat. When the dog finishes properly you should praise him lavishly, quit training for the day and play with him.

PREREQUISITES   Running (roadwork).
                           Retrieve on the flat.

TEACHING PROCEDURE

Jumping can be started very early in a dog's life. A small board placed in a doorway which the dog passes frequently is a convenient solution for you, and a reasonable way for the puppy to learn jumping.

Already at two or three months of age you can casually approach a small obstacle while playfully running with your puppy, like a board in a doorway, a tree trunk or branch, a board, a long piece of pipe, a miniature creek etc. With a friendly, inviting "jump" or "hop" (not an order) both you and your dog clear the obstacle. If the dog is playful and excited enough, if the obstacle is small enough, and if you do not make an "exercise" out of it, there will be no problems. If he wants to, let him explore and sniff out the barrier, initially. Keep the "hurdle" quite low for several months so that you and your dog can concentrate on technique.

Once the dog masters the long sit, place him in front of the hurdle. Attach a long leash to his collar,

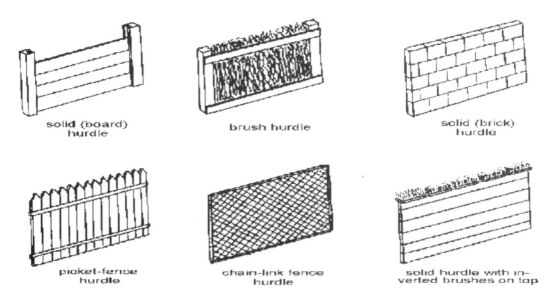

Fig.35   HURDLE TYPES

solid (board) hurdle

brush hurdle

solid (brick) hurdle

picket-fence hurdle

chain-link fence hurdle

solid hurdle with in-verted brushes on top

guide it over the barrier, and go to the other side of the jump. Call the dog and guide him over the obstacle. In the next step, throw a favored toy over the low hurdle. Jump with your dog (on leash) both ways, let him retrieve. Finally do the complete retrieve on the long leash, later on off lead, with you remaining at the start.

Use a low jump throughout this training. Continue with it for at least several more weeks, maybe even months of daily exercises. After the dog has matured (usually over one year of age), the build-up to recommended heights can be accomplished gradually and quite quickly.

REFINING PROCEDURE

Advanced dogs will retrieve leather, metal and wooden dumbbells of various sizes, shapes and weights: 650 grams are required in the Schutzhund III retrieve over the hurdle. Restrict jumping with heavy articles to a bare minimum. The forces acting on the joints of the dog upon landing can cause irreparable damage, in time.

Introduce distractions gradually, and insist on an exact performance.

Different types of hurdles have are available (see Fig. 35). The most common "jump" uses boards that slide into the grooves of two posts. This type is preferred by many for its portability and ease of height adjustment.

The brush hurdle, a framework filled with vertically oriented twigs, resembles more closely natural obstacles but its height can not be changed easily. This is the hurdle preferred in SV trials.

The board jump with bristles on top (broom) is a

viable compromise between these two common hurdle types.

The picket fence obstacle could be considered a variation of the brush hurdle, it too forces the dog to clear the barrier without stepping on it.

Chain-link fence material stretched over a tubular metal frame builds the transition to the bar jump, insofar as the dog can see through it. The bar jump itself is considered by some the ultimate obedience criterion since the dog jumps on command even though he could walk around or underneath the bar.

Many variations can be found to these four basic types of hurdles, like the solid jump made from stacked logs or from bricks, jumps fitted with a window frame or potted plants on top, oil drums, railing fence, etc.

Try to use as many of these different types of hurdles as possible, to keep your dog's interest awake.

PROBLEMS

Refer also to the problem section under "Retrieve on Flat"

A) NO JUMP

If your dog has cleared the hurdle in the past without problems, and if you are sure that there are no physical or health problems which cause the dog to refuse the jump, then you will have to return to basics:

Start by walking up to the full size hurdle, dog on leash. Tap the upper edge, climb over it and encourage your canine to follow. Most dogs will cooperate, but if he refuses and fights, you must shorten the leash and

coax / pull / drag him over the barrier. Do not give in,

do not release the leash, do not spend all day with it. He must go over the hurdle, now. Reward him royally afterwards and quit jumping for the day. Repeat the procedure once each, for the next 3 or 4 days.

Then, during the following session, run with your dog at a rather fast speed straight toward the hurdle, your dog approaching it dead center (this gets you somewhat off to the right). Just before the hurdle, maybe 4 ft. away from it, give the command "jump" and a quick snap on the leash. Run around the hurdle like in figure 34, below, encourage the dog to go over. Repeat this in subsequent training sessions, but instead of running around the hurdle stay on the departure side, feed your dog enough lead for the landing, and then call him back, aiding him with another quick snap on the leash.

It is possible that you stand too close to, or too far away from, the jump, or that the dumbbell lands too close to, or too far away from, the hurdle. Too close means that the dog has not enough room for the take-off, too far means that the dog can see an advantage in walking around the obstacle. Adjust the distances.

B) NO RETURN JUMP

The return jump is often refused when the dumbbell lands too far to the side so that the dog can then see you. The hurdle does not block the dog's direct route back to you, and smart as he is, he chooses the easy way.

You must prepare for this in practice by throwing the dumbbell purposely to the side (or by throwing the dumbbell straight and then stepping to the side), and then forcing the dog to jump both ways (long line). You should also practice throwing the dumbbell so that you can place it exactly.

C) STEPPING ON, OR TOUCHING THE HURDLE

Stepping on the hurdle, or touching it, costs points in a trial. There are several tricks available to prevent that:

- Make the hurdle slightly higher for all training jumps.
- Build the hurdle with a top panel that swings when the dog steps on it.
- Stretch a string over the top of the hurdle, maybe with small flags attached to it (to make it visible).
- Put a loose broom stick on top of the hurdle.
- Fasten brushes/brooms to the top of the hurdle, with the bristles sticking up, or use a brush hurdle.
- Remove all of the horizontal boards and stretch brown wrapping paper around the two upright posts. This looks like a solid board hurdle, but it is not (buy a big roll of brown paper!).

** RETRIEVE OVER WALL / CLIMBING *************

GENERAL

The "Guinness Book" has credited GSD "Danko" with holding the world record in scaling an upright wall: 11' 3". The six foot wall in Schutzhund competition should then pose no problem for healthy working dogs.

A few years ago the specifications for the wall were changed from an upright to an incline, because many dogs jumped from the top to the ground and got hurt in the process. They still jump down from the top of the new wall. The change was not really necessary, it just established a new, lower standard. Dogs can be taught to climb down the upright or the inclined wall so that they don't get hurt on the descent.

OBJECTIVE

With the dog sitting at the heel position, the handler throws the dumbbell over the wall. On command, the dog goes out, scales the wall, picks up the dumbbell, climbs back and returns to the handler, all at a fast pace. The dog sits in front of the handler, releases the dumbbell on command, and finishes to the heel position.

SUGGESTED COMMAND   "get it" "jump" "out"
SUGGESTED RELEASE COMMAND   "OK"

PSYCHOLOGY

With the retrieve over the wall we prepare our dogs for climbing barriers and obstacles of reasonable height. This, however, is not obvious to the dog at the time of training. He only sees a narrow obstacle that can easily be bypassed on the side. In his way of thinking it is ridiculous to go over it. Since you insist on the jump, the dog will comply to please you, but his cooperation should not be abused. You must make sure that the dog can do a satisfactory performance on the second try in a row: use more encouragement, more guidance, make the incline less steep (adjust the wall), or lower the height of the wall somewhat. When the dog finishes properly, you should praise and reward him lavishly, quit training for the day and play with him.

PREREQUISITES   Running (road work).
                         Retrieve over the hurdle.

TEACHING PROCEDURE

There are four phases to the exercise:

1. START   The dog jumps up, in a nearly vertical direction. Most dogs can do that easily and naturally. It is, therefore, wrong to position dog and handler more than maybe 6 feet away from the wall for take-off. With a longer distance the dog has a tendency to build up speed and then to crash into the wall.

2. ASCENT Reaching for the cleats with his paws, the dog pushes and pulls himself up to the top. Enthusiasm, encouragement and praise will help the dog. Early on, prevent the dog from sliding back with some gentle pushing from behind (sending), or some gentle pulling from the other side of the jump (calling), for instance by reaching into the collar.

3. CLIMAX Once the front feet have reached the top edge of the wall, the dog brings up the hind feet too and balances himself, all four feet resting on the top edge for a moment. The dog makes a quick assessment of the situation (how to get down, where to land, location of the dumbbell) while preparing for the descent. He should not be rushed at this point.

4. DESCENT Aided by the cleats, the dog climbs down the wall 2/3 or maybe 3/4 of the way. Then he pushes himself off the wall for a (nearly) horizontal landing. The dog must be taught not to jump from the top, to prevent injury. Younger or beginning dogs need all the help they can get.

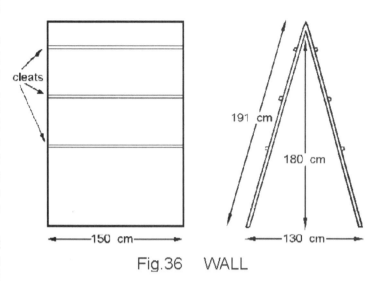

Fig.36   WALL

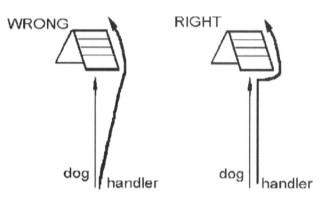

Fig.37   APPROACH to the WALL

TRAINING PROCEDURE

An inclined wall is hinged at the top and can be spread to various angles. Adjust it to a rather wide angle (secure properly!). With a lot of enthusiasm and encouragement run with your dog on a short leash towards the wall. Line the dog up dead center (this gets you somewhat off to the right). Just before the wall give the command "jump" and a quick snap on the leash. Go with your dog over the wall. (The Russian trial regulations require the handler to go with his dog over the six foot upright, vertical, scaling wall). Do this once, or maybe twice, then play with the dog and quit training for the day. After a few days of practice set the wall up at a steeper angle, use a longer leash, and run past the wall, guiding your dog over it. Make the dog believe up to the last moment that you will go with him over the wall (Fig.37). Execute the detour only after the dog has committed himself to jump. Speed, timing, your hesitation and deflection are critical. After several days of practice,

exchange the leash for the dangle (a 16 inch piece of rope), attached to the collar. Let go of it just before the dog jumps. Later you can do it off leash.

Then sit the dog at one side of the wall, walk around to the other side, climb halfway up the wall and call the dog excitedly. Tap the wall or tease your dog with a favorite toy or a tidbit, to encourage him to climb up. If the dog responds, praise him and get off the wall in a hurry to make room for him to come down. You may have to use a leash here.

Then all the parts of the exercise can be put together: First ask the dog to go over the wall both ways, without, and then with, a toy or a light-weight dumbbell. A long line can be helpful if it is handled properly: feeding enough lead for the landing, and then calling him back, aided by a quick snap on the leash.

REFINING PROCEDURE

Introduce distractions gradually, practice on a variety of training fields with walls of different built.

PROBLEMS

Problems common to the retrieve on the flat and to the retrieve over the hurdle were covered there.

A) REFUSAL TO CLIMB

- Use the dog's favorite toy, make it a fun game.
- See suggestions for "No Jump", Retrieve over Hurdle.
- Go with your dog over the wall (Russians do it).
- Offer a very small piece of meat once the dog reaches the top of the wall.
- Unpleasant experiences on the descent may have discouraged the dog. In this case, install a platform with removable hinges/brackets on the far side of the wall, about 3 ft down from the top. The dog can then get to the ground easily.

Concentrate on climbing technique, and only for about 10-20% of the exercises remove the platform to practice the regulation descent.

B) JUMP FROM THE TOP

Use the following training suggestions one-way only, to teach technique. Do not do a return jump at this time.

- Throw the dumbbell so that it lands closer to the wall.
- Temporarily install a deflecting chute (Fig.38).
- Place obstacles (flowerpots, waste baskets, cartons, lawn chairs) on the ground about 6 ft. away from the far side of the wall. The dog will not want to jump onto that.
- Position two people familiar to the dog on the far side of the jump, close to the wall, to guide him down.
- Run around the wall during the natural pause the dog makes at the top position. Stand close to the wall, right in the middle, so that you can receive and guide your dog between yourself and the wall. Reach with your outstretched hands for the dog's shoulders to keep him on the wall. This way you can prevent him from jumping off the wall, you guide him to climb down. Only at the very last moment do you step to the side quickly and allow him to jump to the ground. This is a very effective and humane method.

** SPEAK ON COMMAND **********

GENERAL

A dog that knows how to speak on command can more easily be taught to indicate a find (persons, narcotics, explosives), to announce visitors, etc. He also can more easily be taught not to bark.

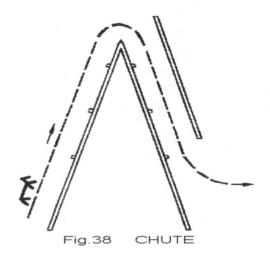

Fig.38   CHUTE

OBJECTIVE

The dog will bark authoritatively (even aggressively) and repeatedly, until told to be quiet.

SUGGESTED COMMAND   "speak" (also use a signal, the flicked, pointed index finger)

SUGGESTED RELEASE COMMAND   "quiet"

PREREQUISITES   None, except a well developed dog/handler relationship.

PSYCHOLOGY

With the exception of one breed (Basenji), or an ill animal, all dogs can bark. The problem is not to teach the dog how to bark, but when to do it. This takes time, and starting the training at an early age will eliminate many problems that normally arise because of time pressure.

The kind of barking we want to reinforce is caused by angry frustration: a forceful, demanding staccato.

TEACHING PROCEDURE

- ◆ The simplest approach, but also the most time consuming way, is to wait until the dog barks on his own and then to praise him: "good boy, speak".
- ◆ Teach your puppy, or even an older dog, to bark for his food: At feeding time, set the food bowl down, hold your dog back by the collar, tell him to "speak" (or "find it" = a sneaky way to command the dog to bark during quartering in protection work). Since your dog can not reach the food, he will eventually make some sound. Let him go this very moment. With repetition, this will lead to reliable barking on command. Transfer this to protection work, command "find it": He must bark before he gets a bite.
- ◆ Let your dog watch others on the sleeve, or let him participate in line or circle agitation. Encourage him: "speak, good boy", and reward him after a

few barks verbally ("good boy, speak") as well as with a bite.

- ◆Learning through imitation: ask a trained canine to speak, and then reward him in front of the novice.
- ◆The dog can also be stimulated to bark by teasing him with a tidbit, a favored toy, the invitation to go out etc. Holding him by the collar usually has a beneficial effect.
- ◆Restrained by a fence or a chain, many dogs will bark when teased or harassed by a stranger. Give the command "speak" repeatedly and reward your dog the moment he does.
- ◆Young dogs will often speak when you give a tug upwards on the lead, together with command and signal.
- ◆Tie the dog up in an isolated area. Walk away and call him, also give the command "speak". You may have to walk quite a distance, but eventually the dog will whine, yelp or bark. This is the moment when you joyfully run back to your dog and praise and pet him. Soon the dog will have figured out that barking prevents you from getting away too far.
- ◆There is still one other, less pleasant way to teach the "speak on command" which should be used only as a last resort: Hold the dog by the collar and use a stick to lightly hit him on the front legs. Command: "speak" and praise him when he does. The stick is gradually shortened until just the motion of an outstretched finger reminds the dog of the pain and the invitation to speak on command.

REFINING PROCEDURE

Once the dog understands what "speak" means, it is simply a matter of establishing the desired response by repetition. Ask your dog to speak before you throw the ball or the stick, before you give him his tidbit or his meal, or before you take him for a walk. Practicing with distractions is also a good idea.

PROBLEMS

A) THE DOG DOES NOT BARK, HE JUST YAPS

- There was not enough stimulation. Excite the dog more, maybe by using a different training approach.
- Try withholding the reward a little longer.

B) THE DOG DOES NOT QUIT BARKING WHEN TOLD TO DO SO

- Give the command "quiet" more firmly, or change to another activity (another exercise, play, etc.).
- Startle the dog, with exuberant praise, with noise, or with a sudden movement.

...darned cat !

Fig 39

"Say, your puppy just bit me in the ankle."
"Well, you don't expect a little dog to bite you on the neck, do you?"

D. PROTECTION WORK

1. BASIC PHILOSOPHY

Protection work is considered by many to be the ultimate accomplishment in dog training.

Some people will disagree, but the fact remains that no other phase of dog training exposes so much of the true temperament, the working spirit, the strengths and weaknesses in a dog than properly conducted man work. Obedience tells how good the handler is, protection work tells how good the dog is.

Training procedures for man work depend on the final goal the handler has in mind. A police dog, a military dog, an area protection dog, a personal protection dog, a competition dog - all require a somewhat different approach. The most universal and basic type of training is the Schutzhund sport.

Schutzhund protection training benefits practically every dog of the working breeds in a certain way, provided the attitude of the handler compliments that of the decoy / trainer. A somewhat shy dog, for instance, gains self-confidence, and an overly aggressive dog becomes more manageable. Optimum results, however, can only

be obtained when the dog, as well as the owner/handler and the decoy/trainer meet certain minimum requirements. Improperly done, man work can create tremendous stress for both dog and handler. It can also be the cause of severe injury, it may require financial restitution for damages inflicted, and it can lead to serious legal problems.

.

A WEAPON

Dog owners who get involved in Schutzhund training expect - at least subconsciously - that the dog will come to their rescue if a dangerous situation should arise. They want a bold, courageous canine. This is quite all right, even desirable, provided the dog has a nice, even tempered, good natured disposition.

Some trainers do not understand that concept. They discourage strangers from approaching their dog and swell with pride when "Killer" growls and snaps at anybody that comes within reach. They might even *teach* their dog to become suspicious of every acquaintance, to become hostile and aggressive to every stranger.

This attitude is borrowed from a trainer of attack dogs and has no place in our sport. The dog owner who can not let his friend and his dog ride in the same car, or who can not have visitors at home without first caging his dog, is not only ill advised, he is a disgrace to the Schutzhund sport. Schutzhund dogs should be alert, reserved, discriminating, but they must also be sociable. The Schutzhund dog lives with his owner, and while he will do well as a protector, he must never become an aggressor. This is even true for police dogs.

Following his natural instincts, a wild dog would rather flee than fight a giant enemy, the human. Domesticated dogs have inherited that disposition to some degree, and in general, unconditioned canines do make poor protectors of their owners in a real life-threatening situation. Dogs have to be taught to be effective in such a challenge.

It is to our advantage that canines are not bothered by personal or moralistic inhibitions like we humans are. They can instantaneously switch from a friendly, likeable pet into a convincing, effective protector as a new situation may require. They do, however,

need the proper guidance and training to master such situations. Schutzhund training is the method of choice, especially when conditions, locations, decoys, protective gear and routines (civil agitation !) are being changed frequently.

With that in mind, owner agitation (owner decoying for his own dog) is somewhat problematic. Although the dog will learn to bite the sleeve, he may not understand the reason for it, and he may fail in a critical situation.

PREY vs. PROTECTIVE INSTINCT

There are two factions in the world of Schutzhund trainers, as far as the introduction of novice dogs to bite work is concerned:

- those who utilize the prey or hunting instinct (also called prey drive), and
- those who utilize the protective/fighting instinct (also called defense/fighting drive).

The supporters of the first group maintain that Schutzhund is a sport where technique is of greater importance than motivation. They state that very few of the average dog owners could justify training and harboring a personal protection dog, and that there are few recorded instances where a Schutzhund dog has had the need, or the opportunity, to bite in defense of his master. They also state that the prey instinct is better developed in most dogs, and that man work can be taught much easier and faster on the basis of this approach. They point to the fact that prey-driven dogs generally are more dependable, more spirited, and that they usually bite with a full mouth.

Supporters of the second group maintain that man work becomes a farce if a dog just goes for the sleeve and does not care at all about the person carrying it. They claim that protection work based on the prey instinct becomes unrealistic, and that dogs trained this way will not be able to protect their masters when the need arises. They are willing to take the risks that come with a "sharp" dog which is typically more often on edge, less sure of himself, less predictable, and favors to bite with mainly its canine teeth.

There is some truth to each one of these claims. We believe that both instincts can be used as motivators with advantage, each one where it is most suitable and most beneficial. The "Search/Find/Bark" and the "Escape" would be good examples for utilizing the prey instinct. The "Attack on the Handler" should be geared to the protective instinct, on the other hand.

The most successful trainers use the prey instinct to teach fighting technique to young and novice dogs, to "sharpen their tools" so to speak. During that phase the decoy is merely carrier of the prey. He usually moves away from the dog, and during a bite he often has the dog behind him, or on his side.

At a later stage the decoy would change from carrier of the prey to an adversary, fighting with the dog for the possession of the sleeve. This is a natural and logical switch from prey to protective instinct.

As soon as the dog is ready for it, the decoy will employ still more open hostility toward handler and dog. Now the dog is usually worked in front of the decoy, and the decoy moves forward, pushing / driving the dog in a self-confident manner rather than moving backwards defensively. Yet even at that stage the agitator must solicit the prey instinct and surrender the sleeve as soon as the dog is considering to give up the fight.

Schutzhund dogs need a pronounced prey instinct (usually present) and a convincing protective drive (sometimes not well developed). The responsible trainer will give his dog every opportunity to cultivate both.

In Schutzhund training we do want our dogs to bite the padded arm, nothing else. Our dogs are not processed to be service dogs. Schutzhund is a competitive sport. Each sporting discipline has its rules and standards, to allow comparison and rating of a performance of one individual against that of another one. To this end, and also to avoid any unduly dangerous situations a decoy might not expect, the VDH Rules have selected the (padded) arm as the target (prey). In Ring Sport, the dogs go for the decoys belly and other parts of his anatomy, but then the agitator knows that and is prepared for it.

TRAINING PHILOSOPHY

Biting a human does not come natural to a dog, as we pointed out earlier. He must learn to do it.

There are a few basic guidelines that apply to this teaching process:

1) Start the novice dog in bite work using the prey drive, later switch over to the defense / fighting drive.
2) The owner of the dog must be involved to excite, encourage, support and reward his dog, particularly when introducing a new or different technique.
3) Building anticipation through frustration always leads to better performance: tease the dog, let him "almost" bite a few times before he is allowed to get to the sleeve.
4) The dog always wins: carrying the sleeve off the field, chasing the decoy away, catching the bad guy, "overpowering" the agitator, barking to get the helper to move and to re-start the fight, etc.
5) Never wear out your dog. Quit or change to a different task as needed.
6) Never work the dog when he is indisposed, ill, tired, exhausted.

THE DECOY

One of the most important keys to success in man work is the decoy, also called helper or agitator.

A good decoy can make even a poor dog look good. A mediocre decoy can easily ruin even a good dog.

The decoy should be a kind person. He must be in good physical condition, with quick reflexes and responses. Participation in a fitness program, regular exercises on the weight bench, with a chest pull, with other equipment strengthening the upper torso, practice with the "false dog" (40 lb., later 70 lb. boxing bag, strapped to the sleeve and manipulated like a real dog) etc. is highly recommended.

The decoy is expected to have a certain amount of courage. A fearful person would be unduly concerned about his own safety, and training techniques would suffer as a result. This does not mean that the decoy should play "steam roller". On the contrary, it is his primary job to instill in the canine opponent the belief that the dog can subdue any human aggressor. The secret recipe is for the decoy to switch, as needed, between aggressor and carrier of the prey, and to display at the right moment the proper mixture of threat and fear, advance and retreat, aggression, defense and defeat.

The decoy must have experience in the training of (his own) dogs, and he must be able to read and understand canines, operate on their level of thinking, so to speak. His attitude, his demeanor, his timing, his movements, his posture, his eye contact with the dog should demonstrate that he can relate to his adversary. It should be beyond any doubt that he can communicate with his adversary, and that he is able to develop the dog's potential to the fullest.

The decoy must have imagination, he must be able to improvise. Schematic, standardized routines inhibit the dog's reliability and efficiency. He must be dependable and self-confident, but he must also be willing to sacrifice his own glory for that of the dog. His calling card is the performance of the dog. The dog always wins. If a person can not lose, he should not be a decoy.

It takes a lot of experience to become a good decoy, and while learning, we all make mistakes. However, you as the handler have a moral obligation to protect your dog from an abusive decoy. A very well - known American trainer and high - ranking American Schutzhund official, for instance, teaches the "find and bark" exercise by hitting the biting dog over the snout with a lead pipe. Impressed by this man's credentials, you may hesitate to act. Don't. Take your dog and leave, don't become an accessory to the crime.

Every dog handler should once in a while get into the leather suit and "take the sleeve". For one, it gives him a better appreciation of what the decoy is doing for him all the time. It also shows him what is going on at the other end of the leash. He becomes a better and more effective handler in the process.

THE TRAINING DIRECTOR

The training director is another person essential to progress in protection work. Not being directly involved in the physical activities, he can observe and analyze the performance better, and he can offer suggestions based on his own experience and knowledge. He can also act as a negotiator between decoy and dog handler if an argument should develop. He should see to it that training is conducted in a safe manner.

PLAY IT SAFE ("CAP")

Schutzhund training involves certain risks. "CAP" is the safeguard: Consider, Anticipate, Prepare.
Consider the decoy's position:
- Is he properly protected (overall, sleeve, cover, shoes) ?
- Does he know your dog's age and experience to customize his agitation work ?
- Did you inform him of your dog's unusual biting habits (if any) ?
- Does he work the dog properly ?
  Is there a safe distance between your dog and the decoy while he works with another animal ?
Consider the position of a bystander:
- Was he directed to a safe observation spot and instructed not to move, especially when a dog is approaching him ?
Consider your own position:
- Can you control your dog, can you hold him, or should you stake him ?
- Are you far enough away from the other dogs to avoid getting bitten accidentally ?
Anticipate:
- Watch your dog closely, read him to avoid any close calls.
- Yell "loose dog" when your animal or another one gets off the hook.
- Call your dog off if the decoy should slip or fall.
- Catch and correct your dog quickly when he intends to go for the decoys leg, shoulder, face etc.
- Hold your dog securely when the decoy comes back without the sleeve for the civil agitation.
Prepare yourself:
- Read up on the subject, inform yourself. Discuss problems with the training director, the decoy, others.
- Get and use the proper equipment, check its condition before each training session, use common sense.

2. PUPPY TRAINING

Serious protection training should not be started before the dog has matured. It takes about ten months of a puppy's life to naturally develop the protective instinct. The foundation for man work, however, should be laid at a much earlier point in time, and it is here where the prey instinct can be utilized with much advantage. Develop the fighting TECHNIQUES, and at a later time, combined with the motivation to protect his master, they will give the dog a definite advantage over others who did not receive this preliminary training.

To insist that a dog be fully obedience trained before starting manwork is wrong. Both branches can very well compliment each other. The average dog needs about two years to reach a high level of proficiency in obedience. At that time he is less able to adapt to new mental and physical stimuli, he is normally too dependent on his handler, his initiative is often dwarfed and his protective instinct is nearly always suppressed. He has - for too long - been reprimanded when he barked at strangers, or when he was alert and suspicious of them. It takes special efforts and lots of patience to make a good Schutzhund out of such a dog.

STARTING THE PUPPY

Introduce your puppy to protection work at a young age. Use an old tee-shirt at first, then a piece of burlap, a soft sleeve cover later on. You, or the decoy, can drag it over the floor, wiggle it, bring it to life, release it to the dog when he grabs it, or play a gentle tug-of-war. Always surrender the prey in the end. A couple of socks left with the youngsters can provide hours of pleasure as well, for them and for the owner watching their play. However, do not engage a puppy between about 4 and 7 months of age in a power struggle that involves biting. During this time dogs lose their first teeth, and you want to avoid unpleasant experiences.

Older puppies you can take along to the training field. Tied to the fence or post (use a chain !), they can watch protection training even when you are not around. They learn by imitating the "older generation" (like people).

Proper upbringing includes early conditioning to strange people, to strange dogs, to strange places, to strange sounds, etc., playful fights with litter mates, home and not kennel raising, an understanding master, close bonds to their owner, enough attention, and feeding regularly raw meat that the dogs have to tear apart.

PROGRESS

Older puppies have much fun with the "Rabbit Chase". This is best played with three dogs held on leash by their owners. An assistant ties a burlap bag or a used sleeve cover to a rope and informs one of the dog/handler teams that they are going to be the winner. Then he teases the dogs with the prey and starts running away, dragging the "rabbit" behind. All three dogs follow close yet the handlers prevent them from actually getting a bite. Once everybody is excited, the handler of the predetermined winner goes faster and allows his dog to catch the prey. The assistant lets go of the string and releases the "rabbit" to the dog. It is very important that the dog be allowed to hold and to carry the prey, and to brag with it in front of the other two contestants. This has a tremendous psychological effect on all three dogs which becomes quite obvious when the next (and then the next) dog has a chance to get the quarry.

RAG AGITATION

The decoy wiggles a soft piece of cloth, a towel or a burlap sack close to the ground. He moves sideways and away from the dog to simulate an escaping animal. Most likely the puppy will want to follow and grab it. Tease him, pull the rag away at the last moment before he can get it, but eventually let him bite. After a moment of gentle struggling, let go of the sack - yet sneakily make (futile) attempts to grab it back. Praise the puppy and let him carry the sack off the field. Repeat. Move the sack at ground level,

but when the puppy lunges to bite, pull the rag upward about 2 to 3 feet off the ground. The dog must jump up to bite, and he will have to struggle a little more before he gets possession of it. Do this a few times.

To start sleeve work, the decoy can tie a 3ft. long rope to a used sleeve cover. He swings it in a circle, about 3ft. above ground. The handler encourages his (leashed) dog to grab and to fight.

SLEEVE AGITATION

At roughly seven months of age, more serious bite work can be started with a soft puppy sleeve. The skillful decoy will build on the prey drive used in rag agitation and develop the fighting and protective drive needed for more realistic Schutzhund work. He will challenge the puppy up to reasonable levels, he will teach him fighting skills, but he will also let the dog win in the end. The puppy will have to show more effort to get the prey, more effort to hold on to it, more effort to take it away from the decoy, more effort to guard and defend the prey - but in the end he will always be the winner. Stake agitation, line and circle agitation and other techniques described on the following pages are used with some modification to accommodate the younger (and weaker) contestants.

3. TRAINING TECHNIQUES FOR MATURE DOGS

Not every dog of the working breeds will be suitable for protection work. Some lack the physical or mental capabilities, others lack the desire to get involved. This is most often caused by poor breeding or bad upbringing. The natural talents of those dogs should be channeled into other directions. However, temporary handicaps like maturing, or minor health, skin, bone, teeth and muscle problems may justify the special efforts needed to introduce these candidates to man work.

Generally, maturing dogs are exposed to real protection work at the age of eight to ten months. Conditions must be chosen carefully. We know, for instance, that the readiness for combat (fighting drive) increases

- in an area with shrubs, trees and/or other objects, as compared to a wide open field (hunting instinct)
- in the presence of the handler (pack instinct)
- on the home grounds (territorial instinct)
- when the dog is restrained by leash or fence (defense / survival / protective instinct), etc.

BAD GUYS

While most of his contacts with mankind have been friendly so far, the dog now encounters bad guys as well. For some, that poses no problem, but others can not believe that people would threaten or harm them.

An overly friendly, soft dog does not make a good Schutzhund. Yet even most dogs with good Schutzhund potential will initially refuse to bite. Their owners had reprimanded them for any sign of hostility, usually severely, and as a result they now let their master handle all threatening or dangerous situations. The "Schutzhund Experts" then advise you to get another dog. Fortunately, that is usually not necessary. A good decoy (playing skillfully the role of an aggressor), supported by an understanding handler (playing convincingly the role of a helpless victim) can turn things around. If this does not work, then "flanking" may wake up the fledgling: The decoy sneaks up to the dog, quickly grips, pinches or pulls the loose skin on the dog's flank (the skin between hind leg and stomach) and then runs for cover. If you support your dog properly, the decoy will never get another chance to flank your dog.

Securing a good, experienced decoy for the beginning protection work is quite important since the initial confrontation may well determine success or failure in the long run. The dog must be challenged but not overpowered, he must be threatened but not defeated. "The dog always wins" is probably the most important rule a decoy has to obey.

Depending on the temperament and the courage of the dog, the decoy can be more or less aggressive. Depending on the personality of the dog, the aggression must be directed predominantly against the handler (for many German Shepherd Dogs, for instance), or against the dog (for many Dobermans). It is a very fine line the decoy has to tread, and he must back off as soon as the dog becomes insecure. The sequence of menacingly and cowardly approaching the beginning dog, and fearfully running away from him at the slightest sign of the dog defending himself or his master, is the trademark of a skillful decoy. The diagram (Fig.40) shows the response of a dog in time as an agitation exercise progresses:

- First, the decoy sets the stage, and the dog acknowledges that a hazardous situation exists (confirmation).
- Continued harassment will solicit appropriate hostile responses (conformation).

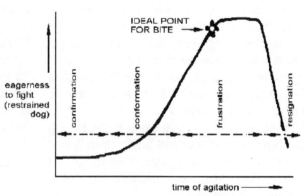

Fig.40   Agitation vs. Response

- The desire to fight the bad guy increases with each unsuccessful lunge of the restrained dog. At the same time, however, frustration builds up and reaches - eventually - a plateau.
- If on repeated tries the reward (bite) is withheld, then the dog resigns. A good decoy will sense this stage before it happens and he will give the dog a chance to bite.

THE FIRST CONFRONTATION

Both you and the decoy have to be good actors to stage a threatening situation where the dog's assistance is needed - and generously rewarded when given (with praise).

The decoy will approach you and the dog, advancing sideways. This projects to the dog a narrow profile rather than the more intimidating frontal "broad side". The decoy acts fearful, suspicious, moving slowly, crouching, growling low and lightly wiggling a burlap sack hanging from his hand. He will not shake the sack into the dog's face, nor will he vehemently move around or actually attack you or your dog.

Most dogs are still uncertain at this time and they have to find the proper reaction that also has the approval of their master. In response to the decoy's suspicious behavior the dog will normally bark and/or take a step forward, but then he will turn his head, to look up to your face to ask for approval. This is the moment where the decoy fearfully runs away, it is also the moment where you must praise your dog lavishly.

When repeating this exercise you should become aggressive yourself. Shout at the decoy, make threatening or hitting motions. The dog will most likely "assist" you, and you should praise and encourage him as soon as he does. Conclude the first training session by letting the dog chase the decoy off the field.

Dogs which do not respond should be given another chance at another location. When challenged by an intruder on their own grounds (car, or home, or kennel), the combination of the various instincts (pack, protective, territorial, survival) will often be sufficient to stimulate aggression. A fearful approach of the decoy, retreat upon the slightest response from the dog, and encouragement and support from you are important, to let the dog know what is expected of him.

Developing self-confidence:
- Kneel next to your dog, hold him by the collar. Alert him to the decoy who approaches slowly in a fearful-threatening manner. The decoy will hastily retreat as soon as your dog shows any signs of aggression. Support and encourage your dog.

If the dog does not respond, the decoy will come closer, suddenly attacking you or your dog, maybe even stinging him, or you (!), with the switch. Jump up, assist your dog in chasing the decoy off the field.

The decoy will **provoke** the dog to bite without **intimidating** him !
- Tie your dog to a post and go out of sight. The decoy, approaching as before, is careful again not to be too overpowering. He will run away as soon as the dog barks or lunges forward. At that time, rush back and praise your buddy.
- If the previous exercises went well, then the decoy walks toward the staked dog in a neutral manner (handler out of sight). Once he reaches the critical distance of about 6 ft, he will suddenly become hostile and attack, maybe even lightly sting the dog. The canine should respond in an aggressive way which will prompt the decoy to retreat hastily. Return, praise and reward your buddy.
- Dogs that stay inactive, non-committed in these exercises may, in time, come around with more support from their handler. Rush out and kick and beat the bad guy off the field. Your dog, hopefully, will help you.

TEAMWORK
The involvement of the handler is important, especially for inhibited or soft dogs.

Much too often do we see novice handlers holding their end of the leash, smiling and watching the decoy's efforts to get a bite or a growl out of their dog. These people are not really "handlers", they are spectators: interested, indifferent, amazed and finally disappointed.

Dogs are pack animals. They play, work and hunt together, under the direction of a leader. By nature, they would not volunteer to fight a giant enemy (the decoy), they would instead try to avoid him. If the pack leader, however, decides to take up the fight, they will follow suit and do the job, together. Besides the pack instinct which causes the pack members to come to the assistance of their leader, the "Risk Shift Principle", plays a role here. It states that a group as a whole is willing to take more chances than each individual by himself. On the other hand: If you as the pack leader don't commit yourself, if you just stand there and want to be entertained, your dog will do exactly the same: he will wait and watch.   Get involved. Act as if the situation were real. Don't smile, instead get angry at the "bad guy" who is harassing and threatening you. Alert the dog, shout at the decoy, hit his sleeve with your hand, push him, punch him in the shoulder.

At the slightest indication that your dog is willing to assist, give him lots of praise and encouragement. Let him know how much you appreciate that he comes to the rescue. Tell and reassure him with words and a pat on the flank that you approve of his initiative. Encourage him to help you to chase the bad guy away.   Particularly the pat on the flank is important at this point. Without it, the novice dog will take his attention off the decoy and look at you, just to make sure that you are still there to help, and that you still approve of the action.

The decoy should always give the dog a chance to win, by surrendering the sleeve, by running away, or by quitting the fight before the dog gets tired. This strengthens the dog's self-confidence. It also enables you to lavishly reward your dog with praise, laying a solid foundation for future protection work.

STAKE AGITATION
In stake agitation, the tied-up dog is on his own, handler out of sight. It should not be confused with the all-or-nothing test in which the dog is cornered and pushed to the extreme, leaving him no choice but to defend himself or to face destruction. Stake agitation is a training approach to build confidence.

Novice dogs need reassurance when introduced to this new situation, and we want to modify the exercise by having the handler present, supporting his canine.

We use a sturdy collar or harness for the dog (leather collar or choke chain on the dead ring) and a long line (30 ft.) or flexible spring chain. The spring softens the jolt on the dog's neck/body during agitation, yet there is a safety catch in case the spring should break.

Stand next to your dog and encourage him to fend off the would-be aggressor. The decoy uses sack, sleeve or stick to excite the dog until ready for a bite. While having stayed out of reach originally (Fig.41), the decoy now moves into the sphere controlled by the dog (Fig.42). He approaches at an angle (sideways) and gives the dog a chance to bite while moving AWAY from him. Sack or sleeve are held and moved ABOVE or near the waist line. This encourages the dog to reach for the prey with a firm bite. During the ensuing short fight the decoy must remain well inside this circle so that the dog, while biting, never feels any pressure on the collar/harness from a tightened chain.

The decoy then surrenders sack or sleeve and runs away, and you praise your dog without taking the sleeve away from him. As a matter of fact, you should encourage the dog to "kill" (shake) the prey, to reinforce this innate response.

This modified stake agitation is a very comfortable arrangement, well suited for novice dogs, novice or physically not so strong handlers, and novice decoys.

- The handler does not have to worry about his dog getting out of control: a secure anchor, a good spring chain, and a sturdy collar or harness take care of that. He can pay full attention to the reactions of his dog and give him encouragement, reinforcement and praise.

- The dog gets the undivided attention and the supportive involvement of his master and gains confidence.

- The decoy, lastly, is assured a safe operating arena as long as he stays outside of the circle controlled by the dog. He does not have to fear handler errors or unexpected reactions of the dog. He knows that after the fight he can just step back and be perfectly safe again.

To make things interesting, stage a little fight between yourself and the decoy, just out of reach of the dog. By "coincidence" the decoy then happens to get into the circle, allowing the dog to bite the sleeve.

To prepare for the regular stake agitation, you move farther and farther away in subsequent exercises. The decoy works the dog just like above. This might take a few days or a few weeks, depending on your dog. You might also have to go back to your dog to give him assurance when needed.

In general, we suggest the angled rather than the

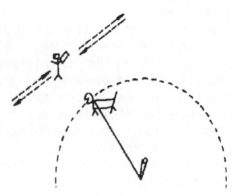

Fig.41   STAKE AGITATION

Fig.42   STAKE AGITATION and BITE

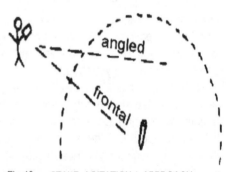

Fig.43   STAKE AGITATION / APPROACH

frontal approach (Fig.43), short fights, and to let go of the sleeve (sack) occasionally, while the dog is biting it. The decoy then runs away. Retreat and civil agitation just outside the circle conclude the exercise.

SLEEVE HAPPINESS

A "sleeve-happy" dog is more interested in the sleeve, the "prey", than in the person carrying it. For young dogs, this may be all right. Mature dogs, however, should be taught that there is more to protection work than just chasing a piece of cloth.

Sleeve-happy dogs are usually man-made, trained with the help of a stereotype. Any deviation from the

normal pattern confuses these dogs. It is, therefore, advisable
- to change decoys frequently
- to work with two decoys on the field, taking turns
- to change the protection gear frequently
- to use concealed body protection with street clothes over it
- to have the sleeve worn on the decoy's left arm, at other times on the right arm
- to work with two sleeves, one on each arm. The decoy hides one behind the back and brings it out when the dog does not want to let go of the first
- to agitate sideways, having the unprotected arm face the dog and to quickly change sides (presenting the sleeve) barely a second before the bite occurs
- to do civil agitation with the dog on leash. Here is what to do: After a regular fight the decoy surrenders the sleeve, runs away, but then comes back to re-agitate the dog. Without equipment or protective gear, he shows hostile behavior, trying to get the dog's attention. He might threaten or lightly tap the dog with a stick, especially when the dog is still busy with the sleeve and does not want to let go of it. Encourage your dog to be aggressive, but you must hold him securely since the decoy is unprotected.
- to do muzzle agitation (with advanced, hard-biting dogs only; refer to that section).

LINE AND CIRCLE AGITATION
Line and circle agitation are best suited for novice and intermediate dogs. Advanced dogs should rarely participate. In these exercises the dogs are exposed to high intensity stimuli for a rather long time before they get a chance to bite. This is desirable for beginning dogs that need the time to "warm up". Advanced dogs, on the other hand, may wear out and get bored, or they might get conditioned to an extensive amount of agitation before the actual fight takes place. Neither one is desirable.

For the decoy, group agitation saves energy and time since several dogs are watching the stimulating movements simultaneously. With more than 10 dogs, split the group and get a second decoy.

For **LINE AGITATION** the handlers line up, leaving maybe 12 to 15 feet spaces between them. They are instructed to check collars and leads and to hold their dogs securely, to prevent close contacts with neighboring handlers and dogs. If a sturdy fence or a row of trees is available, the handlers can grab it with one hand and hold the leash in the other hand, to prevent being dragged forward. You could also draw a line on the ground and tell the handlers not to let their dog go beyond it. It is also desirable to alternate dogs and bitches in the line, and to have a novice (or weak) dog between two more experienced/sure dogs.

Then the action begins: The decoy arouses the first dog in line, waving his sack, the sleeve, the stick, hitting the ground, hissing, retreating, advancing etc. At the same time, the handler encourages his dog to fight off the bad guy. The decoy stays out of reach of the dog, however, and advances to the next dog after a short while. He now agitates dog #2, then dog #3, and so on. The last dog in line gets a little more attention and then he is finally allowed to follow the escaping decoy and to bite the sleeve or the sack. Note that while the whole line is in uproar, only the last dog gets the opportunity to bite.

At the completion of the fight the handler tells the decoy to "get lost" and moves with his dog to the start of the line. Then the game begins anew until all the dogs had a chance to take the sack or the sleeve.

CIRCLE AGITATION requires that the dog/handlers teams form a ring, leaving enough working space between themselves. The decoy operates in the hub of the wheel and for his safety, all handlers must maintain their position. No-one is allowed to close in to the center. Instead, the decoy approaches the dog that he has selected to be worked.

Circle agitation allows for a little more flexibility. The decoy can see all the dogs all the time, and he can more easily spot and relate to problems that individual dogs and handlers have. He can change equipment (sack, sleeve, stick) and methods (fearful or forceful approach) more readily, he can devote more time to problem dogs and handlers, he can agitate dogs out of sequence as needed etc.

During circle agitation the decoy must be on his toes constantly. He is the absolute center of attraction, for all the dogs and all the handlers. In circle agitation, the dogs are more involved and more intense than in line agitation, and usually more things can be accomplished more quickly.

FROM SACK TO SLEEVE
The use of sack and sleeve was mentioned in the preceding exercises without further qualifications.

While the choice is left pretty much to the discretion of decoy, training director and handler, there are certain guidelines which should be observed (refer also to the equipment section):

- During initial training, a soft burlap or jute sack is used until the dog eagerly tries to get and bite it.
- The bite roll (sausage) or the soft sleeve cover (by itself, not on the arm) are used next, both are operated just like the sack. A puppy sleeve is not necessary, but if available, it would be used in this phase.
- Transition to the (hard) sleeve with (soft) sleeve cover is often aided by draping the sack over the cover and pulling it away with the free hand at the very last moment, when the dog is already committed to the bite. A soft, broken-in sleeve cover rather than a hard, new cuff should be used here, of course.
- For this transition it is especially important to get the dog angry and really excited before giving him the opportunity to bite. Once the dog has gotten a hold of the sleeve, after a very short fight, the decoy should release it and run away without it, in obvious terror.

DEVELOPING THE BITE

Dogs that perform well in stake, circle and line agitation can be worked individually. The following is a list of points to consider which, by the way, also apply to the earlier described routines.

Preparation:

- Agitate the dog sufficiently. He must be angry and almost frustrated before he gets a chance to bite.
- Do not work your dog to exhaustion. Stop the training session even before he is ready to quit.
- The decoy should play his part realistically and skillfully (hostile-afraid, but not overpowering).
- The decoy should act as an adversary as long as the dog shows confidence and willingness to fight, however he should immediately and quickly retreat (like prey) when the dog becomes uneasy or fearful.
- The decoy should present his side view, not his frontal view to the dog (smaller, less intimidating profile).
- You, the handler, should support and encourage your dog, verbally and physically.

Initiating the bite:

- Play the "Rabbit Chase" (see page 100).
- The decoy should run past the dog at an angle (not a frontal collision), to allow the bite in passing.
- The decoy should move back a little, not push his sleeve or the sack into the dog's face to initiate a bite.
- The decoy should offer the sack or the sleeve midriff or chest-high, to encourage a firm bite.
- After the initial contact (bite), the decoy should continue to move away from the dog for a step or two, before coming to a halt and fighting with the dog.

Maintaining the bite:

- The decoy should carry the sleeve about waist- to chest-high and hold it horizontally to get the dog's front feet off the ground. This discourages re-bites or grip changes. It will also aid in the development of a firm, full bite. The decoy can lift up the far end of sleeve or sack with his free hand (watch out for the teeth!).
- A slow, gradual pull on sleeve or sack encourages the dog to maintain the bite. Hasty, sudden or ripping motions are painful and cause the dog to release the bite.
- While the dog is on the sleeve, there is a constant, gradual pull (slightly upwards and away from the dog). The decoy moves his whole body (not just the arm) back a little, the action comes from the decoy's torso. The force of the withdrawal should vary, like in a tug of war: sometimes the decoy claims the prey by an inch, sometimes the dog does. As long as the fight goes on, the decoy must not let his arm go limp.
- The decoy should move his sleeve arm slightly, maybe an inch, back and forth in any direction, or he can twist his arm inside the sleeve. Moderate body movements accompany this.
- The decoy should use his free hand to gently touch the dog's head or shoulders during the fight (be careful!). This is done in preparation for the later introduction of the stick.
- The decoy should continue to display a hostile-fearful attitude. **NO** friendly or casual talk with the handler!
- Avoid long or overly vigorous fights, they often cause weakening of the grip. Use your judgement.
- If the dog releases the sleeve prematurely, the decoy can
  a) use the prey/pursuit instinct (run away, encourage the dog to pursue and to bite again: "Escape")
  b) stimulate the competitive spirit, build up the frustration (work with another dog first)
  c) make the fight shorter (the dog may have gotten tired).
- After a firm bite, some (insecure) dogs "spin" the

decoy to avoid frontal contact, to hide behind him. As the decoy, you could quickly rotate for a face-to-face position. If you work "double", e.g. with sack AND sleeve, you could also swing the sack or the stick behind your back with your free hand (try for a hit). It should bring the dog forward. Keep him in front by bending your knees, pulling the sleeve closer to your chest, and working the dog between your legs. The pointed knees will prevent the dog from escaping sideways. I would wear leather pants and a groin protector here.

- During the fight, some dogs "claw" the decoy's body with their front feet. The decoy could move the sleeve down and up, right and left, or hold the sleeve pressed against his chest and twist his body fairly rapidly to the right, left, up, down. If nothing helps, he should make it unpleasant for the dog to claw. Attach a 2-ft. section of tin roofing to the front of the suit (fold over the sharp edges!), agitate after climbing into a top-less oil barrel (steel or plastic), or just work the sleeve closer to the ground.

Finish:

"The dog always wins." He wins by:

   a) carrying the sleeve off the field (prey instinct),
   b) chasing the bad guy off the field (territorial instinct), or
   c) having overpowered the bad guy and caused him to cease struggling (fighting drive).

Novice dogs benefit the most from the first two approaches.

The decoy should stimulate the dog to vigorously shake or yank the sleeve and reward him with the release of the "prey" (see "Delayed Victory", below). Initially the dog gets the sleeve as soon as he shakes or yanks it. Later on he has to fight a little longer, to shake it a little harder.

Only mature dogs with refined fighting techniques should be commanded to release the bite after a fight (approach "c" above). In that instance, the following suggestions apply:

 - The decoy must come to an abrupt stop, standing motionless like a post. Proper protective gear, like suitable pants, as well as the handler's cooperation, will give the decoy the necessary confidence.

 - In the initial stages of training count to ten, then get casually a hold of the dog's collar and praise and pet your pal. Often this will cause the dog to release the bite.

 - Tough dogs may require a correction, followed by praise, of course (see "Release", page 106).

THE CLEAN BITE

Schutzhund is a sport, requiring the contestants to obey certain rules. The dog should, for instance, bite the sleeve and not the throat, just like the boxer can not hit his opponent below the waist line.

In a confrontation with a real criminal anything goes, but a dog shown in Schutzhund competition must not endanger the well-being of the decoy. If this happens, the dog has to be removed from the field at once, and on leash. The owner will most likely disagree, he might even think of himself as a hero. The fact is, though, that the dog has publicly demonstrated very serious shortcomings of his handler, trainer, and club decoy.

Since the dog should not be punished when he mixes up the anatomy, you must make sure that he just has no chance to bite anything but the sleeve. It is a matter of conditioning, and the process is best started with the novice dog: Initially, most exercises are done with the dog tied to a stake. This way, you do not have to concern yourself with restraining the dog, the decoy knows exactly how far the dog can advance, and the dog has no choice but to bite what he gets. He gets either the sack or the sleeve. Agitation for a sufficient length of time builds frustration, and as soon as the dog is really angry he is allowed to bite the sleeve, but only the sleeve. Repeat this for several weeks, and the dog will not even look for another place to bite. At that point switch to the six foot leash, with you controlling, and if necessary correcting, the dog's actions.

Once the dog performs reliably on a *loose* leash in the course of several (maybe 10) training sessions, he can be allowed to work off lead. Watch him closely, though, and stand nearby to fetch him in case of problems. If the dog aims for anything else but the sleeve, he was pushed too fast. Stake and leash agitation must be resumed. Minor violations, however, can often be corrected with a timely command, or with a karate chop: slice your hand between the decoy and your dog's mouth just before the bite occurs. Two other effective means are the skillfully used throw chain, or a snappy rap with the stick across the snout just before the dog actually bites (done by decoy or handler), both followed immediately with re-agitation by the decoy and a bite.

Rehabilitating those dogs that have specialized in biting particular parts of the body (leg, buttocks, unprotected arm etc.) is a little more difficult. They too must be retrained on the stake just like above, however a very slow advance to the next stage - from stake to leash to off-lead - is even more important. It is much more difficult to change a habit than to establish a new one.

IMPROVING THE BITE

Advanced, healthy dogs should show a firm bite, defined as the forceful seizure of the sleeve with the full length of the jaws (in contrast to nibbling with just the canine teeth). To reach this goal, most of the training exercises are done with the dog on leash or restrained by a 10 ft. long line attached to an anchor (tree, post). The restraint is fastened to the leather collar or a body harness on the dog. Then consider the following points:

a) Equipment
SLEEVES:
Our preference is a sleeve without a bite bar. To hold on to such a sleeve, the dog must take a full bite with full jaw pressure. The habit learned here will carry over into the trial where usually a bite bar sleeve is used, and it will result in improved performances. Sleeves with a very thin bite bar and a guard rail (to prevent slip-off) can be used to help weak dogs, but they will spoil the tough ones in time.
SLEEVE COVERS:
Sleeve covers should be sturdy yet giving, and they should provide some texture. The braided jute cover meets these requirements and helps beginning and advanced dogs in developing a firm bite.

New, plain jute covers are hard, they tend to discourage novice dogs. Advanced or tough dogs, though, learn to bite harder in order not to slip off.

Burlap is a weak, fragile material. It has very limited applications for the conditioning of young dogs only.

Nylon or nylon-jute covers should not be used since they can easily injure a dog's gums and teeth.
RESTRAINTS:
Standard restraints are a sturdy leather or fabric leash, or a spring-chain, all of them ten to thirty feet long. Their reach can be determined to the inch (in contrast to the bungee cord).

A heavy-duty bungee cord can also be used for strongly motivated dogs. The more the cord stretches, the more it pulls back. While this feature encourages a strong bite, the dog's temperament and strength must be considered, and risks must be minimized through careful planning, testing, measuring the reach of the cord.

b) Presentation
For a bite, the sleeve is normally carried horizontally, at or above the waist line of the decoy. Agitate a little longer than usual, then vary that position: high, low, vertical, angled, right arm, left arm, right side, left side, front, rear, etc. The dog must work harder to get a good grip, frustration and determination increase, and as a result the bite will improve and the dog will be better prepared for unusual circumstances that might happen in a trial. The handler encourages and praises his dog, the decoy surrenders the sleeve after a short fight.

c) Two sleeves
The decoy wears a protective sleeve on each arm, one of them hidden behind his back. The dog is sent in for a bite and the decoy switches arms at the last moment, just before contact. He can also let both arms hang down naturally and present one of them at random, at the very last moment before contact.

d) Stick
To further frustration and determination, the decoy can use the stick
- as a (horizontal) moving barrier to keep the dog away from the arm before letting him finally bite, or
- as a (horizontal) barrier, held steady. The dog must force his way through the barrier to get a bite, or
- plant its point at the dog's chest bone to push him back from the sleeve for a while, or
- rapidly move it over the sleeve right to left, to make the bite more difficult - temporarily.

e) Encouragement
While the dog is biting the sleeve, your verbal encouragement and a pat on the rump will increase his holding power. The dosage is important: the right amount reassures the dog without causing him to take his attention off the decoy, too much of it, however, will focus the dog's attention on you rather than on the decoy.

f) Counter-Balance 1
With the leash on the dead ring of the choke collar (no other restraint), the handler allows his dog to bite the sleeve. Steady tension/pull on the leash will usually toughen the bite since the dog interprets this as a signal to quit the fight - which he is not yet ready to do. He will instead bite harder and hang on with a tighter grip. Don't yank the leash, though, the dog might quit to obey your (unintentional) command.

g) Counter-Balance 2
Throughout the fight, the handler maintains steady tension on the leash, as in f) above. The decoy must avoid jerky movements with the sleeve arm to guarantee a constant pull on the leash.

h) Counter-Balance 3: Bungee Cord

The handler secures the bungee cord to the dog's body harness. The other end of the bungee cord is anchored at a secure post. Use care to determine where to place the decoy, then allow the dog to go for the sleeve. During the fight there should be just enough tension to pull the dog back somewhat, but not enough to make it unpleasant to hang on to the sleeve. Both handler and decoy can pay full attention to the dog here.

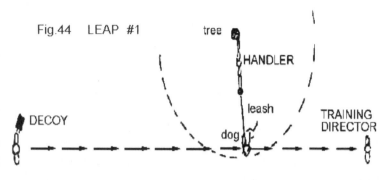

Fig.44   LEAP #1

DECOY

tree

HANDLER

leash

dog

TRAINING DIRECTOR

i) Pride

Circle and line agitation (see page 101) can help to toughen a dog's bite. Agitate long enough, then give your dog a chance to bite the sleeve - while all the others have to watch. Dogs like to compete.

j) Frustration

The decoy agitates the dog to build up frustration (see page 100). At the right time he gives the dog a chance to grab the sleeve - by planned coincidence. After a very short fight the dog is allowed to obtain, "kill" (shake) and carry the sleeve, followed by some re-agitation. Do not repeat in the same training session.

k) Hit and Miss

The decoy agitates the dog, approaching him alternately from the right and the left side, teasing him to bite but keeping the sleeve just barely out of reach. The dog will be frustrated, but when the decoy sees a calm, calculated determination to jump and to get the prey for sure, he will get within range and allow the bite.

l) Victory

With the dog on leash, give him a chance for a bite. The decoy then lets his sleeve arm go limp and turns his back to the dog (the dog will most likely still "hang" on the sleeve). Keep the leash reasonably taut. After a while start pulling on it a little harder (steady!). The decoy now "revives" his sleeve arm, trying to slowly pull the prey away from his adversary. Most dogs will respond by shaking or yanking the sleeve. This should be rewarded instantaneously: the decoy surrenders / releases the sleeve. You can assist your dog by shouting at the decoy and chasing him off the field, and by lavishly praising your dog for the victory.

m) Suspension

Just before the dog's lunge to bite, the decoy holds the sleeve above his waist line and then clinched to his stomach or chest. This gives him better physical control over sleeve and dog, and it conditions the dog to jump up to get the sleeve. The dog's front feet will be off the ground, forcing him to take a full, hard bite (otherwise he would fall off). This position also discourages nibbling and bite repositioning.

n) Teasing

A dog that barely hangs on to the sleeve will usually firm up his grip if the decoy blows into the dog's face, or if he slides his stick along the dog's feet, chest or belly. This makes most dogs angry and they will fight more vigorously now, usually shaking or yanking the "prey". The decoy should release the sleeve immediately or after some more struggling, depending on the prior training.

o) Surprise

Carry the sleeve under your arm and heel your dog on lead. Suddenly, an unarmed and unprotected decoy jumps out of his nearby hiding place, grabs the sleeve from you, puts it on his arm and runs away. Release your dog and encourage him to get the "thief".

p) Leap # 1

Hold on to a tree or another anchor with your left arm stretched out (Fig.44). Hold your dog by the end of leash with an outstretched right arm. The decoy then agitates in order to determine how far out the dog can go. The training director observes and memorizes this spot. He now lines himself and the decoy up so that a straight line from the decoy to himself runs just barely within the dog's reach. Then the decoy moves in great leaps at not too fast a pace, but at a rhythmic and constant speed, toward the training director, holding his sleeve arm sideways, outward, at shoulder height. The bite bar, if the sleeve has one, should point at a slight angle downward (toward the ground, not up in the air). This may require some "arm-twisting". The decoy wearing a right arm sleeve must have the dog/handler team on his right side. With a left arm sleeve, the approach should be from the opposite direction (dog/handler team is on the left side of the decoy now, as in Figure 44).

While leaping toward the training director, he may want to count "leap - and - leap - and - leap (like the tick-tack of a grandfather clock). The decoy advances at a constant speed and in a straight line. The dog can now mentally prepare for the time of arrival and schedule his jump accordingly. Upon contact, the decoy moves closer into the dog's circle and stages a short fight. The dog wins, captures the sleeve, chases the decoy away and gets his praise from you. For a variation of this exercise, stake the dog. The handler can now concentrate on supporting his dog, the training director can evaluate as before.

q) Leap #2 ("airplane")
You, the handler, hold your dog by the collar for a modified version of the close-range escape.

The decoy runs away, holding the sleeve arm outstretched to the side like the wing of an airplane. Release your dog once he is about 20 ft away. The decoy continues running but takes smaller steps now to prepare for the impact. Follow your dog, encourage him to bite the sleeve but intercede if he goes for other parts of the decoy's body. As in "Leap #1", this exercise teaches the dog to take hold of escaping prey. The dog will only be successful if he jumps to take a full, hard bite.

r) Leap #3 ("ball players")
Two assistants, about 20 feet apart, "play ball", using the bite roll or a sleeve cover instead of the ball. They throw it at a low angle, and at a slow pace first, faster and a little higher later on. You and your dog are stationed in the middle, and you feed your dog enough lead (and encouragement) so that he can catch the prey. If he gets it, praise him and allow, even encourage, him to "kill" (shake) it.

s) Leap #4 ("catch")
Tie a bite roll or a sleeve cover to a short line. Swing it above your head, then let it fly past the dog. He will probably jump for it and try to catch it.

t) Pause
Not doing any protection work with a dog for several days, or even weeks, may revitalize him.
After being deprived of it for some time, he will give his best to enjoy it again and hopefully bite harder.

u) Changes
Avoid boredom. A new training field, a new decoy, visits to another club, a change in routines, new

exercises, games involving the protective or the prey instinct will often revive a lackluster dog. These changes may improve the bite as well, but they surely will make it more fun for you and for your dog - in training and in competition.

RELEASING THE BITE
The clean release after a fight is of concern to most Schutzhund trainers, but it seems to be of even more concern to the "non-Schutzhund" people. This, unfortunately, has caused some trainers to place too much emphasis on the "out" at too early a time in training. It is not necessary, because sensibly approached, any normal dog can be taught to release quickly on command.

Locking jaws on a man's arm (padded or not) is not a natural response, the dog has to be taught to do it. Letting go of it in due time, on the other hand, is the sensible and natural thing for a dog to do. Therefore, the desired unnatural response (biting) should first be firmly established BEFORE the natural response (out) is forcibly impressed upon the dog. Otherwise, a mediocre performance in protection work will be the result. A dog constantly worrying about "out" will pay more attention to his handler than to the decoy. His fighting spirit will be low, he will do the job half-heartedly only.

Excepting a few hard-headed dogs, it is, therefore, suggested not to bother with the "out" too much until the dog does spirited protection work. At that time the release can logically be dealt with, and quite effectively so.

To teach the "out" we suggest a gradual approach:
Introduce the command with the release of a favorite toy. Even a puppy can be taught to do that. Never rip the toy out of the dog's mouth, but work your way up from a soft to a firm command and demand compliance. Reward right away by throwing the toy, play again.

During the second phase play with the dog and compete with him for the prized possession. Get a hold on the toy and stand absolutely still. Wait for a few moments after the dog ceases to struggle, then command "out". Reward immediately. Tease him with a second toy, if needed, to get him to release the first one on "out".

In the next phase introduce the burlap bag or a soft sleeve and repeat the previous routine.

From there we can progress to actual protection exercises.

At first, ask the decoy to "freeze" after a very short fight, then to release the sleeve. Let the dog carry it off the field, but stay close (use the leash, if necessary) and observe your dog. Be patient. The moment he drops the sleeve voluntarily, say "out", hold him back a little and, with your foot, kick the sleeve out of reach.

Do this a couple of times, then command "out" just before the dog will drop the sleeve on his own. If it works, use the "out" still sooner. Give him a few seconds to obey. If he fails to release, step quickly on the sleeve with one foot and lift your dog off the sleeve with the leash. Then praise him.

Once the dog carries and drops the sleeve reliably, ask the decoy to hang on to his gear after the fight and to hold the sleeve horizontally, waist-high. He can use the free hand to steady the sleeve. With the dog in tow on the sleeve, the decoy moves into the blind and "freezes" (this is in preparation for the Search/Find/Bark exercise). Wait for a few seconds to let the dog calm down, then command "out". Walk up to your dog if he does not release. Don't say a word, grab him by the collar, lift and hold him suspended until he releases. At that point say "out" and praise him. A back-tie might help here (see page 99). In subsequent exercises skip the "lift". Just command "out", count quietly to ten, and enforce your command with threatening gestures, voice and a leash correction, as needed. In case of problems, consider the following options:

a) Distraction

Sensibly trained dogs do not develop the obsession for fighting which often leads to a refusal to release the bite. With them, praise and petting can, for a moment, divert the attention from decoy to handler. Casually approach the dog and reach for the collar. Praise him calmly with a steady stream of words, pat him on the shoulder, and lift him up by the collar. This will get nearly all dogs off the sleeve. Use the command "out" in a relaxed (not threatening) tone here. Then send the decoy off, rather than taking the dog away.

b) Switch the Command

After releasing, the dog must guard the decoy without taking another bite. Giving the "down" command then will nicely serve three purposes if the dog obeys it: "down", "out", "no afterbite".

In a trial this additional command is not allowed, but the dog does not really care which word you use. Some handlers say always "out" (not "down") when they want their dog to lay down. To obey this command, the dog has to release the bite first and then go down. Thus, a nice trial performance is within easy reach.

c) Supercharge / Overdrive

Excessive agitation and long fights, swinging the dog in a circle ("circus performance"), or use of the stick beyond reason cause advanced dogs to get so excited and angry at the decoy that they will not release. Moderation in the decoy's performance will take care of the problem.

d) Instant Freeze

The decoy can assist the dog in a clean "out" by making the transition from fighting to quitting not gradual but very abrupt, sudden. This is a "flash freeze". Then he stands absolutely still.

e) Mixed Signals

The decoy should stand motionless after the fight. If he moves, even if it is just to get more comfortable, then the dog will take it as a signal that the fight is still on.

f) Sleeve Position

The decoy can turn the sleeve abruptly from horizontal (fight) to vertical ("out"), pushing the far end of the sleeve toward the ground. He would do that at the end of the fight, just before standing absolutely still. The somewhat twisted head position will make the dog more responsive to the "out" command.

g) Elevation

Holding the sleeve horizontally in front of, and pressed against, the body, motionless, may discourage the dog from hanging on, and from taking another bite. If necessary, the decoy can lift up the sleeve still higher with the free hand (possibly below the chin), just before he stops fighting.

h) Instant Release ???

Giving the dog time to calm down insures better compliance with the "out" command. You should count at least to three (maybe up to ten), before giving the command.

Some trainers demand the "instant release". This can be taught by keeping the dog constantly in fear of punishment for disobeying an (unreasonable) "out" command. During the fight the dog will then pay more attention to you than to the "criminal", and he will lose much of his effectiveness. The "instant out" is a straight jacket for a dog's natural instincts. It does ruin his fighting spirit and should not be used.

I) Surprise, #1

Startling the dog will momentarily divert his attention and get him off the sleeve. This may require:

- threatening sounds (your angry command, a whistle blow, a gun shot, etc.)
- blowing (just puff air, or cigarette smoke) in his face

- a bottle with carbonated water squirted into his face
- a few pebbles or the throw chain thrown at him
- the use of the sling shot
- the use of an electronic training collar (use it to startle, not to punish the dog, meaning maximal two mild shocks. This can backfire, though: some dogs get mad and hang on harder.)

The dog learns faster and becomes more dependable when he can not quite determine who causes the disaster (who threw the chain etc.). The training director or an assistant on the field can be quite valuable; they are suspect to the dog even when they remain inactive, and even though the handler gives the correction.

k) Two Sleeves, #1
The decoy works with two sleeves, one on each arm. One sleeve is inconspicuously carried behind his back.

When the dog refuses to disengage after a fight, the decoy freezes and waits for a calm moment. Then he suddenly brings out the other arm and restarts the fight. If done right, the dog will let go of the (first) sleeve and aim for the "live" bait. At the very moment of release the handler gives the "out" command.

Repeat, use the first sleeve again. Make the fights short.

l) Two Sleeves, #2
The decoy wears one sleeve and has a second one laying on the ground nearby. When the dog refuses to disengage after a fight, the decoy surrenders the sleeve, quickly grabs and slips on the second one and restarts the fight. If done right, the dog will let go of the (first) sleeve and aim for the "live" bait. At the very moment of release the handler gives the out command. Repeat the procedure. Make the fights short.

m) Slam Bang
If the above suggestions do not work, then force must be used. Use prong (or choke) collar on your dog. Walk up to him, grab the leash close to the buckle, give a harsh "out" command and one quarter of a second later slam the end of the collar INTO the sleeve (not away from it !). Follow immediately with agitation / bite.

n) Two Leashes
Fasten chain "A" to a secure post in the ground, and hook the regular leash "B" to the live ring on the choke or prong collar. Both leashes are loose during the fight. When the decoy stops fighting (with "A" stretched out, fairly taut), reach for the the buckle on the regular leash "B" close to the dog's neck, command "out" and then slam it forcefully **into** the sleeve. The secured restraint "A" will double your force during the correction, it will also prevent afterbites. Your behavior at that time must clearly indicate that a major disaster will happen if the dog should decide to ignore the command. Follow immediately with agitation / bite.

o) Distance Control
In a variation of n) above, the decoy gives the correction.

The dog wears a prong collar with the dangle (short rope). During the fight, the decoy reaches inconspicuously for the dangle, feeds it under the sleeve and holds it loosely in his free hand. Then he stands absolutely still. The handler, at least 20 ft. away, waits for the dog to calm down, then he sternly commands "out". A fraction of a second later the decoy slams the dangle/collar into the sleeve, silently and without any obvious body movement - provided the dog has not released on his own. Follow immediately with agitation / bite.

p) Final Note
Mistreated, abused, or improperly trained dogs will require a sensible approach and a firm hand to release the bite, but even here success is possible if a meaningful dog/handler relationship exists, if you are determined to correct the situation, and if you give praise after the successful release.

AFTERBITES
Some dogs release the sleeve but come back for a second bite ("nibbling", "seconds", "dirty bites").

It usually involves an eager fighter who is not done yet. Re-train, use the "Find&Bark" exercise. Stage a short fight near the blind, after which the players can try one or more of the following options:

DECOY - quit struggling abruptly.
- before the bite, move the stick rapidly and forcefully over the sleeve right/left in quick succession (like a mad cellist - but sideways). This may discourage the dog from biting the sleeve.
- hold the sleeve in front of the chest (not lower), with both hands if needed.
- remain absolutely still ("instant freeze"), no body adjustments of any kind.
- drop the sleeve and walk away (handler standing by to prevent a "really dirty" bite !).

HANDLER - try to intercept the bite, by slicing the hand with a karate-chop between sleeve and snout just before the bite, saying "hey.. !" , or "no !", matter-of-factly.

- lift the dog calmly off the sleeve, if the dog has attached himself already.

- skip the decoy, work the dog yourself. With owner-agitation, the dog runs on half-throttle only and can be controlled more easily: take the sleeve, let him bite, teach him not to come back.

DOG - must learn that biting is allowed only after provocation, and that the sleeve bearer can be goaded into action by barking.

Practice the Find & Bark routine every day for 2-3 weeks, maybe longer. Do not tolerate even minor infractions. Only after barking for 5-10 seconds (or more) will the decoy (or the owner) move and fight. The dog must learn that biting a motionless person ends the fun - the decoy just walks away, no fight or bite forthcoming. Not dirty bites, but barking gets the dog another chance to fight.

Some handlers use electro-shock, but timing the shock is extremely important here (see pages 34, 116).

FALSE ALARM

Forcing a dog to instantly release the bite (page 107) causes as much psychological damage as sending him after an escaping decoy and then calling him back before a bite occurs. To avoid punishment, the dog will learn to be more concerned with the termination of the fight then with subduing the bad guy.

Such an association in the dog's mind is not well understood by many trainers, and the "dead run", also called "false alarm" or "protection recall", is quite popular with American Police K-9 handlers and some civilian trainers. Amateurs argue that the recall is necessary to prevent harm to a person who might turn out to be innocent. It's nonsense. These hoodwinked people trade in an effective weapon for a look-alike toy. A true professional will decide if his interference as Police Officer is justified before he pulls the trigger on his gun, and before he sends his dog, not after bullet and canine are on their way.

THE STICK

VDH Schutzhund Trial Regulations require that the dog's courage be tested using a stick, to see if the dog will stand his ground and protect his masters even when threatened or hit. Without this test the

Schutzhund title, a working dog title, has little value as a measure of the dog's worthiness for breeding purposes.

This requirement has caused considerable controversy and criticism, accusing Schutzhund trainers of cruelty and needlessly sacrificing the lives of their dogs by making them an easy target for the criminal. Neither is true. The use of the stick is more symbolic than painful. Granted, some decoys, with approval of the judge, beat the dogs severely, but such abuse is neither the intention of Schutzhund training, nor is it common. We suggest that you call your dog immediately and leave the field in such a case, accepting the (administrative) consequences that are sure to follow. If enough handlers have the courage to pull their dogs, these decoys and judges

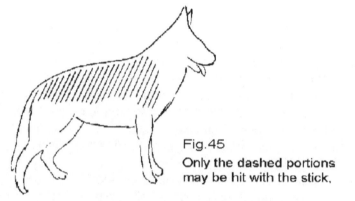

Fig.45
Only the dashed portions may be hit with the stick.

will be out of a job soon.   Secondly: Schutzhund dogs are not trained for active duty with law enforcement agencies. Unless employed by such groups, they will probably never face real life-or-death situations, therefore they will not be in jeopardy. Furthermore, if a criminal really slaughters the dog hanging on his arm, then this man must be very well prepared for it, he must be cruel, desperate, determined and skillful. The sacrifice of the dog buying the handler a chance to survive is then justifiable.

Training Phase I: The decoy raises, holds and shakes in a threatening manner above his head a twig with leaves, later on a ½ inch thick bamboo stick, or the whip (described in the equipment section). After a firm bite, quick blows from above onto the ground are used to condition the dog to the sound and the motion of a hit. Without ever touching the dog, this phase is continued for several days, weeks or months, as needed.

During **Phase II**, the decoy will hit the taut leash, his upper sleeve and the ground at random. He can also use the stick as a barrier in front of the sleeve (making it more difficult for the dog to get a bite), hold the stick across the dog's chest to push him back before the bite, or he can point the stick at the dog's chest and push him back gently. Sometimes he will just touch the dog's head and shoulders with his free hand.

During **Phase III** the decoy holds the stick only between thumb and index finger, touching the dog's back (simulating a hit), the leash, the ground and the sleeve in an irregular pattern. There are two training modes, used alternately: the "blow" and the "wipe". The blow is the commonly known hit, coming from above and landing on the dog's back. In the "wipe" the stick comes from above again but it is stopped short of the dog's body. The stick with the portion that just emerges from the hand (not the far end) is then gently laid on the dog's back and pulled across it, similar to the movement of a bow on a cello.

Phase IV is a repeat of Phase III but off lead, again with the stick held between two fingers.

In the final **Phase V** the stick is held in a normal grip and used at first gently, later with reasonable force on the dog, alternating fake hits and a few "blows" and "wipes" in an erratic sequence. The decoy is allowed to hit only back, withers and flanks (dashed in figure 45).

"Reasonable force" means that the decoy should use no more power than he would be willing to take when hit on his own bare arm. It can be practiced by holding taut a single page of a large newspaper and letting the decoy hit it to make a loud popping sound, but without breaking or tearing the paper. One should never overdo the hitting part, and one should never attempt to find the limit to which a dog would be able to stand hard blows.

Initial training is done on leash, then go to off-lead, then handler at a distance. The hit comes while the dog is biting the sleeve, and ¼ of a second later the decoy stops and surrenders the sleeve. The dog must emerge the winner. Encouragement, reassurance and praise from the handler are essential.

4. ADVANCED TRAINING

POWER MANAGEMENT

Seasoned Schutzhund dogs love protection work, often so much that they will forget you and do their own thing, like skipping blinds during quartering, biting the decoy in the blind, breaking away during the transport. The dog says "I love the fight, and I will talk to you later". Actually, he gives you a very important clue: Take away the opportunity to fight now and make him listen to you first. Make clear to him that he gets his bite AFTER he obeyed your command (see also pages 26, 30, 109, 115, 118).

In practical terms, just tell the decoy to freeze, or to drop the sleeve and to walk away. No command, no correction, no fight, no fun. Stay calm. Start over from the beginning, and repeat as often as necessary. Eventually the dog will realize that you are the boss, that following your instructions (like going to the empty blind first) will get him what he wants: the fight.

Try this: Secure your dog with a long line, allow for some slack and give the "down" command. Out of reach, the decoy moves about casually. As soon as the dog breaks the "down", the decoy drops the sleeve and walks away. The handler picks up the sleeve, approaches the decoy and hands it to him. Then he commands his dog to "down" again, in a matter-of-fact way, no compulsion, no correction, and the whole cycle begins anew. You may have to do this quite a few times, but eventually the dog will realize that he must obey your command before he is allowed to bite. Because now, after calmly waiting for the release, the decoy will let him fight.

Or try this: Play ball with our dog. A decoy does protection work with another dog some distance away. Most likely, your dog wants to get involved and runs over there. The decoy knows what to do: he drops the sleeve and casually walks away. Let your dog calm down, then invite him to play with you again. Do this a few times, and eventually your dog will learn that you are the center of the universe. At that time, get the decoy to work your dog.

You can also try this: Let your dog fight, then tell the decoy to drop the sleeve and to stand still. Now toss a ball a short distance and invite your dog to play with you. Tough decision, but the decoy plays dead and you are alive, so eventually he will come and play with you. Play, then stand still and send your dog after the fleeing decoy for a fight. Repeat this sequence a few times and your dog will realize that you call the shots.

ROUND ROBIN

The round robin offers a very efficient way of protection training for a group of at least 3 handlers (HI,H2,H3) with their dogs, provided a reasonably large training area is available.

Start by laying out a course with several well separated stations (SI, S2, etc.), each station

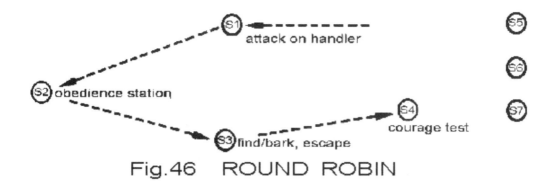

Fig. 46 ROUND ROBIN

For a group of three trainers, it might look like this (H = handler ; S = station) :
CYCLE 1: H1 ties his dog at S5 and decoys at S1
H2 ties his dog at S6 and decoys at S4
H3 takes his dog through the course. While doing obedience work at S2, H1 changes over to S3.
CYCLE 2: H3 ties his dog at S7 and decoys at S4
H1 takes his dog through the course as above
H2 ties his dog at S6 and decoys at S1/S3.
CYCLE 3: H2 takes his dog through the course as above
H3 ties his dog at S7 and decoys at S1/S3
H1 ties his dog at S5 and decoys at S4.

---

concentrating on one particular exercise. Then ask each handler to take his turn, and to play his part. Following this sequence, each handler has a chance to work his dog with two different decoys, and to gain experience as a decoy for the other two dogs. For larger groups, most people will be working in obedience at station S2, until their turn comes, or they could arrange for a course with a greater variety of stations.

MUZZLE AGITATION
Do muzzle agitation only with advanced, hard-biting dogs, and only when a German-made police muzzle is available (imitations are likely to cause injury to dog and decoy). The dog must first be conditioned to the muzzle, which is done independently of protection training. Let him wear the muzzle, initially a few minutes only, then longer for up to ten minutes. Do some **obedience** work with the **muzzled** dog in the following weeks. During that time conduct regular **protection** work with the **unmuzzled** dog. Give special attention to the three modified escapes listed below. They force the dog to speed up, to lunge with a powerful take-off, and to jump up high for a bite.
   a) "Leap # I" (see page 105),
   b) "Leap # 2" (see page 106), and the

c) "Straight-jacket" exercise:
The decoy runs away with the sleeve arm held across the back (like in a straight-jacket). The dog (no muzzle) will have to pursue, to speed up, and to jump up to get a bite. The bump in the back will cause the decoy to fall, but he will get up quickly and stage a short fight. After a week or so, this exercise is done with the muzzled dog. The preceding agitation and excitement will let the dog forget momentarily that he is muzzled. Responding as he was taught, he will still jump up, bump the decoy in the back and cause him to fall. If the bump was not forceful enough, the decoy must still fall - that is part of the training - and then lay still. The handler rushes up to his dog and praises him, holds him and removes the muzzle while the decoy gets up. The decoy agitates and escapes, giving the dog a chance to earn his reward: the bite (have the sleeve ready). Several training sessions later the decoy can run normally, keeping both arms in front of the body. He should maintain a rather fast speed. The muzzled dog has learned to bump into the back and will do so even when there is no sleeve as a target. The fall and the bite afterwards, however, are still important.

NIGHT EXERCISES

Night exercises provide an interesting change from the standard routines. They contribute greatly to building confidence, but only after a foundation in protection work has been laid already. Novice dogs should not participate. Even advanced dogs should not be entered "cold" in a night trial.

Start by taking your dog along for a stroll around the neighborhood when it is really dark. On another night, surprise him with a trash can left in the middle of your driveway. Continue your nightly excursions to the park, in the field, in the woods, to a busy section in town. Keep your dog on leash, or at least close to you. Teach him to alert you to hidden, suspicious strangers by barking or growling at them. If the dog ignores them, ask an assistant (w/sleeve) to hide and to sting your dog with a switch when passing.

Night trials will usually be sponsored by a club or an organization, since grounds, equipment and personnel must be secured. They will lay out a course with individual check points, spaced sufficiently apart. Each station provides a different attraction, which may be friendly or hostile, familiar or strange, startling or frightening.

The following suggestions are only starting points. Modify and expand them as desired.

a) **Friendly Encounters**
   - a friend standing still, asking for the time
   - a stranger with flashlight passing from the opposite direction, on foot or on bicycle
   - a guard posted near a gate or a door, asking for identification
   - a group of people, sitting, chatting, singing

b) **Startling Encounters**
   - a stranger sleeping and snoring in a large cardboard box
   - a parked car, suddenly turning on the headlights and blinding the team
   - a couple of garbage cans, oil drums or other large objects placed on the road
   - a hidden loudspeaker operated by remote control (voices, sounds, music)

c) **Frightening Encounters**
   - a large white bed sheet suspended from a tree and agitated by an assistant via an attached string
   - a scare crow dropped into the dog's path from above
   - a bag of tin cans suddenly emptied on a nearby hard surface

d) **Hostile Encounters**
   - a sudden and unexpected attack on the handler

- an escape of the decoy (illuminated by the headlights of a parked car - move in and out of the light beam)
- a courage test, lighting as above.

Cats are smarter than dogs.
Have you ever tried getting eight cats
to pull a sled through snow?

5. ROUTINES

** QUARTERING *******************

GENERAL

Quartering is the first part of the protection work in a Schutzhund trial, common to all classes. Logically, however, this exercise belongs into the obedience category. Natural hiding places (evergreens, dense shrubs) are seldom available on the training field. Artificial blinds can be constructed from a 4X8 sheet of plywood (Fig.47) for permanent installation.

A large tripod covered with cloth or plastic and secured with tent stakes makes a useful portable blind (Fig.48).

OBJECTIVE

The dog must investigate a series of hiding places in a systematic manner, as directed by his handler.

SUGGESTED COMMAND:

"search" or "find it"

PREREQUISITES:

It is helpful, although not necessary, when the dog already knows the go-out command.

PSYCHOLOGY

Quartering can be taught via two avenues, using either the hide-and-seek principle, or the systematic approach.

In the first case, the dog is directed to find a reward hidden in one of several blinds. To the dog, the essential part of the game is to locate the reward and to go to it as quickly as possible. If he senses the location of the reward before having quartered all empty blinds, it would be an insult to his intelligence to prevent him from going directly to it.

The second method concentrates not on finding WHERE the reward is, but on HOW to get there. The dog then realizes that to get the reward in the last blind, he must go around all the empty hiding places first. In a trial, this insures reliable quartering. With the first approach, the handler has to pray that his dog does not detect the decoy prematurely.

On the surface, the systematic approach seems to defeat the trial regulations. Yet even a police officer searching for suspects is better off with a dog trained according to the systematic method. He knows that the area behind him is clean. A dog that detects a suspect and goes directly for him could miss an accomplice hiding behind the officer.

TEACHING PROCEDURE

We can employ basic instincts / drives to develop a happy, enthusiastic performance:

the survival instinct (food)
the hunting instinct (ball/stick/toy - see also "Games / Olympics", page 42)
the fighting instinct (decoy).

For beginners, food is often used. Ball and decoy, however, are more powerful motivators for advanced dogs.

The procedure described in detail below uses rewards at the tent, on occasion also at the center line (A)-(H) every time after he has circled an empty blind. Select what suits your situation best.

Phase 1

Set up two blinds/tents about 30 ft. apart, blind (C) on the right, blind (E) on the left.

Run with him around (C), reward at (D). Repeat a few times. Then stand at (D), send him to(E), reward at (F). Repeat. Use food, then toy.

Phase 2

Use the two blinds from phase 1, blind (C) empty, blind (E) baited: treat, toy, or decoy. Food or toy work best at this stage. Show the dog where you place the bait, or let the decoy stand in front of the blind.

Start somewhere between point (A) and point (B). Send your dog ("search" or "find it" or "check it out") to circle blind (C). Initially you may have to run with him on leash. Then advance to (D) and call him to you. Say "good boy" without slowing him down and send him on ("find it") to blind (E) for the reward. Under no circumstances let him go to (E) directly, make him circle blind(C) first. Do this daily for a week, a month, or even longer, until the dog performs flawlessly off lead.

Phase 3

Let your dog see the decoy in front of (E) doing a little agitation and then disappearing in it. Hide with your dog in (A) while the decoy sneaks into (C). Send you dog to (C), but he might want to go to (E) directly. Tell him "no, over here". At this time, the decoy appears at (C), yelling, and hides there again. Stage a short fight near the blind, then repeat the sequence: decoy at (E), you hide in (A), etc. This time, however, let the decoy remain at (E). Then send your dog, first to (C), then to (E).

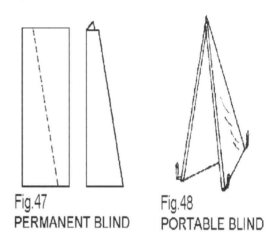

Fig.47
PERMANENT BLIND

Fig.48
PORTABLE BLIND

Phase 4

Now add a third blind (G), let the dog see the decoy disappearing in there, go into hiding at (A) while the decoy sneaks into one of the other blinds, send your dog -> (C), -> (E), -> (G). Correct if necessary. Repeat this over and over again, with the dog seeing the decoy go into one blind (*at random*) but then finding him in another one.

Phase 5

Use the three blinds as before, bait the third location and let the dog see where the reward can be found. Start just like in Phase 2, decoy remaining in full view

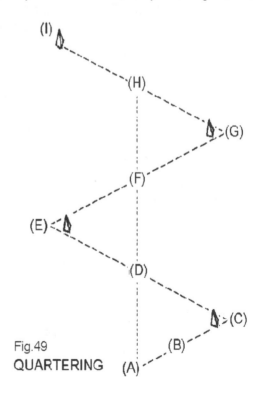

Fig.49
QUARTERING

throughout. Make the dog circle (C) and (E) before getting the reward at (G). Again, practice this daily until the dog performs flawlessly.

Phase 6: Repeat Phase 5, but this time with the decoy hidden in the blind.

Phase 7: - the real thing:

Set up the blinds fairly close together, maybe 30 ft. apart, and teach the quartering as follows:

- Sit your dog in front of (A) and proceed to (B).
- Excitedly call your dog and run toward (C).
- Once the dog passes you, command "search" and encourage him to continue toward (C) and to circle this blind. You may have to run with him toward (C), point to (C) with your outstretched arm, give him a little push from behind to get the message across. You may even have to run with him **around** (C).
- Now run toward (E) on the line C-E and call him from (D).
- Repeat that: send the dog to circle the blind (E), advance to (F), call your dog and run toward (G) etc.

Praise your dog ("good boy") when behind a blind and while approaching you, not when he is going away.

At the end of the exercise, praise and pet him lavishly, play his game (he played yours, you see !). In the beginning, you might have to run with him all the way, even around the blinds. Later on it will be sufficient for you to approach the blind and to let him continue to circle it.

At a still later time remove the tent at (A), then

a) Send your dog from point (A) towards the blind (C). Make sure that he approaches and circles (C).

b) At that time advance quickly to point (D). It is essential that you have reached location (D), the intersection of A-H and C-E, at the time the dog emerges from blind (C).

c) Call your dog excitedly ("here").

d) Don't let him slow down, send him on toward (E), running -if necessary- a few steps with him toward (E).

e) Make sure that you arrive at point (F) when your dog is behind blind (E).

f) Call him and send him on toward (G), then (I), just like above under d).

Once your dog is following the routine you will not have to leave the centerline A-H. Locations (D), (F) and (H), however, are still critical since these are the points from which you call and guide your dog in the search.

REFINING PROCEDURE

Gradually move the blinds farther apart, and occasionally bait one of the earlier blinds. Give praise and encouragement for good performance, correct him when needed. Make sure that the dog goes **around** all the empty blinds before approaching the target, and prevent every attempt of a short-cut. You can

- use sharp commands, use a throw chain or a sling shot, use a long leash (it's awkward and cumbersome)
- use an assistant, or use a physical barrier (like snow fencing) in critical spots
- run with the dog around the blinds, even grab the collar and drag the dog around the empty blind
- try to intercept when your dog runs directly to the wrong blind
- go back to the methods above, that is, standing at (B) and directing the dog from (A) to (C), etc.

Once in a while work the field from the other end, or start with blind (E) or (G), or practice on a strange training or trial field. This teaches the dog to quarter on your directions, it also eliminates boredom.

PROBLEMS

A) THE DOG SKIPS BLINDS

- Practice the go-out first.
- Train without the decoy for several weeks (see systematic approach, above).
- Grab the dog and make him go around all the empty blinds first (maybe on leash, with you running along).
- Quarter with the wind (air-scenting the decoy is more difficult then).
- Use several rewards in several blinds, at random.
- Use two decoys (#1 and #2) simultaneously. This may or may not work, since some dogs get confused, others may tire out easily. They will still try to air-scent the decoy.

Nevertheless, if you decide to use two decoys, proceed as follows:

Decoy #1 steps out of blind C, agitates briefly and steps back again. The dog is sent after him. Upon arrival the decoy moves, engages the dog in a fight and then stands absolutely still. At that time #2 steps out of blind E, yells, agitates and steps back again. The handler now sends his dog to blind E and the dog is allowed to bite as above. While the dog is fighting with #2, decoy #1 moves up to blind G and the whole cycle starts anew. Still later, one, two or three decoys are placed in the blinds at random. They are instructed not to reveal their where-about unless the dog wants to skip that particular blind.

B) THE DOG MOVES TOO SLOW
- Use only two or three blinds, for a while.
- Run along with your dog, get excited yourself, or run behind him, clap your hands.
- Don't do ANY protection work for a couple of weeks, after that let him bite only near the blind.
- Ask the decoy to make the fight more realistic, more to the liking of your dog.
- Get a different decoy.
- Have the decoy do some close-range agitation before quartering, without letting the dog bite.
- An assistant can reel in the lure (burlap bag on a long string) just like in dog races (see page 41).

C) THE DOG LEAVES THE FIELD
- Build up enthusiasm (as above).
- Practice the down (it is better to take the penalty for an improper command than to fail the trial since the judge must excuse your dog if he leaves the field).

** FIND AND BARK **********
GENERAL
"Find & Bark" has useful applications in Police work, in Search and Rescue work, for the private dog owner. The risk that a person gets bitten accidentally is greatly reduced if the dog masters this exercise.

It is not required, but the dog sitting while barking has an advantage: the dog must get up first before he can bite, he is more likely to watch the decoy, and there is less of a chance that the dog will leave the decoy.

Some trainers teach their dog to lie down instead of to sit. Try it, but it may not work: it is difficult to get the dog to go down, few dogs will bark in the down position, and if they bark it will not be the aggressive staccato we want to hear (have you ever tried to intimidate someone while laying on your belly ?).

OBJECTIVE
The dog alerts his master to a hiding or intruding person by constantly barking. He also guards the stranger until the handler arrives. Circling is undesirable but permissible if the dog continues to guard.

SUGGESTED COMMAND: none (for training only: "speak")
SUGGESTED RELEASE COMMAND: "OK"
PREREQUISITES: Speak on command, Protection work SchH I level

PSYCHOLOGY
We do not allow the dog to bite a person as long as that person stands motionless. It's called "Find & Bark", not "Find and Bite". We show him: Finding the decoy and barking = fight (the reward). Finding the decoy and biting = no fight (withholding the reward, the "punishment"). Finding the decoy and not barking = no fight either. Withhold the fight until the dog performs well. In a trial, the biting part is somewhat delayed, however. The Find & Bark should be taught independently of quartering.

TEACHING PROCEDURE
We use the protective instinct, the prey instinct (see "Tease", below), or an obedience command (page 92). In all instances, though, we do some close-range agitation first and then let the decoy run to the blind where he stands motionless in full view of the dog, later on hidden in the blind. Then send your dog, follow him, sit him in front of the decoy, and give the command "sit, speak".

Initially the decoy will offer the reward (short fight, then surrender the sleeve) at the very first sound, whine or bark, later he will ask for a longer bark. Even for advanced dogs we switch between shorter and longer barking before allowing a bite ("intermittent reinforcement"). To bark, some dogs need stimulation from the decoy: **very short** fearful/aggressive body expressions, hasty, jerky movements, brief hissing and snarling. Abruptly stopping this and "freezing" discourages biting. Watch a cornered cat that keeps a dog at bay !

Advanced dogs must indicate a "find" by barking, even when the decoy sits, kneels or lays down in the blind (with full protective gear).

The decoy can also "drive" the dog, pushing very slowly forward, making the dog back up - but still no bite. Or he can escape and invite a bite, but then he stops and freezes, and now the dog must bark and not bite. Always, however, should the decoy reward the dog with a short fight after a successful "find and bark".

TRAINING SUGGESTIONS:
A) TEASE #1
Hold the dog on leash, let the decoy in the blind agitate the dog, let the dog not bite until he barks.
If unsuccessful utilize the territorial instinct: work the dog at home or in the car.
B) TEASE #2
The dog is tied to a post with a chain. The decoy agitates and presents the sleeve but pulls it out of reach at the very last moment, just before the dog has a chance to bite. Frustration will make him bark.

C) TEASE #3

The sleeve, or the sleeve cover, is propped up high in the blind, the decoy stands next to it. Some decoys put the sleeve on their head, some hold it behind their back. This is risky with new, or unknown, or "unclean" dogs.

Send your dog from 20 feet away and command "sit, speak". The very moment the dog makes a sound he is rewarded with the prey: the sleeve is either just dropped to the ground and surrendered to the dog, or the decoy grabs it and runs away with it, giving the dog a chance to bite. Reassure your dog; this is essential.

D) TEASE #4

The decoy engages in a fight and then drags the biting dog to the blind. A triangular, sturdy blind is preferred. Having secured back cover, the decoy freezes and observes the dog's behavior. When he senses that the dog intends to release the bite on his own, he silently signals the handler to give the "out" command. As soon as the dog disengages, the decoy quickly swings his protected arm behind his back and makes the sleeve inaccessible. This, and maybe some hissing, causes the dog to jump up and - to bark, since he can not get to the sleeve. Once the dog barks, the decoy quickly brings the arm out and tries to escape, giving the dog a chance to bite, and to claim the sleeve in the end. After several repetitions in subsequent training sessions, the successful dog can be worked away from the blind, just as described here.

E) BARRIERS

Some decoys solicit barking and prevent biting by standing on a table (running away, then jumping on the table), sitting in a tree, standing in a barrel, or having a portable fence in front of the blind. Unfortunately, many dogs forget that they are not supposed to bite as soon as the decoy stands unprotected in the blind.

F) SURPRISE #1

Somewhat better results are obtained by burying a mattress just in front of the blind (cover it with an inch of soil). The unusual footing teaches the dog to keep distance, and to bark.

G) SURPRISE #2

Let an assistant hold your dog, hide unnoticed behind the blind or the decoy. Shout at and correct your (surprised) dog if he should go for a bite. Frustration than will make him bark - if not, the decoy must tease.

H) SURPRISE #3

Use two decoys. While one fights with your dog in the field, sneak into or behind the blind and let the second decoy stand in front of you. Then the first decoy stops fighting, drops the sleeve and stands motionless. The second decoy now steps out of the blind and agitates briefly, then moves back into the blind where he remains motionless. Shout at and correct your (surprised) dog if he should go for a bite.

I) LONG LINE   *(very popular but grossly overrated)*

Use a long, sturdy line (maybe 20 ft.), one end of it fastened to a secure anchor, the other end attached to the dog's collar or harness. Send the dog from the anchor to the decoy. A leash of proper length will stop him just short of his target.

Command "sit, speak" just before the correction occurs from the tightening leash. If timing and length of the leash are just right, then the dog may learn that obeying the command will save him from getting the leash correction the next time. You must, of course, run up to him, sit him and again tell him to speak - if needed. Make sure that there is some slack in the line, the dog can not bark with a compressed wind pipe.

The decoy displays suppressed aggression alternating with fear. He moves back and forth and presents the sleeve but never allows a bite. After a while he stands still. By that time the dog is so aggravated that he barks out of frustration, wanting to bite - which he gets.

K) SHOCK TREATMENT

An electronic shock collar or a rigged sleeve are used by some seasoned trainers (we prefer **NOT** to use these methods).

* The shock through the collar is given *after* the command "sit, speak", when the dog PREPARES to bite - but only if there is no doubt that he will bite. Timing is important. (Refer also to the equipment section)

* To make the rigged sleeve, a layer of metallized fabric (as worn by fencers - chicken wire or window screens will cause injuries to the dog) is wrapped

Fig.50   FIND & BARK #1

around the outside and covered with a layer of wet jute or burlap. Another piece of wire screen (chicken wire) is spread in front of, or around, the decoy, and covered with 1-2 inches of wet dirt. The two screens are wired to an electric fence charger, or to an induction-type generator (old-time army telephone). The dog punishes himself by receiving a mild shock whenever he contacts the sleeve (closed circuit). After the dog has barked for a while - with enthusiastic support from you, of course - the electric circuit is disconnected, the decoy runs away, and the dog is allowed to bite.

L) STICKS

An experienced, agile decoy can teach the Find & Bark with two sticks as his only tools (NO sleeve !!). One stick is used to keep the dog at a distance. Most often it is pointed at the dog's chest, sometimes it even makes contact to push the dog away. The other stick is held inconspicuously at the side but ready for a snappy hit across the dog's snout if he should decide to risk a bite. This hit comes from a flick of the wrist, with very little body or arm movement. This hit must be reserved for an emergency, to be given only after the dog is committed to bite (but before he actually bites!). Psychologically it is preferable to have the handler give the correction, with stick, throw chain, sling-shot or electronic collar. Nevertheless, the decoy must be allowed to use his second stick if needed. Have a sleeve ready to reward the dog with a bite, afterwards.

M) CHAIR

The following method is described in more detail since it has universal applications (Fig. 50-55). It involves a methodical, gradual learning process, and it is highly successful if done right.

Step 1: Hold your dog by the collar, about 30 ft. away from the blind. The decoy briefly agitates the dog and then stands completely still. Release the dog.

Step 2: Most likely, the dog will charge and bite, even though the decoy stands still and motionless. Do not say anything, just walk up and get your dog.

Step 3: Repeat steps 1) and 2).

Step 4: The decoy holds a light-weight aluminum lawn chair in his free hand and hides it behind his back.

Step 5: As in 1), lawn chair still hidden behind the decoy's back Step 6: When the dog has closed in to about six feet, the decoy suddenly brings the lawn chair up front and holds it between himself and the dog. He moves with the dog, always facing him. He uses the blind to cover his back, and the lawn chair to keep the dog at bay. He may growl, and shake the

Fig.51   FIND & BARK #2

Fig.52   FIND & BARK #3

Fig.53   FIND & BARK #4

Fig.54   FIND & BARK #5

chair lightly. Encourage your dog to speak.

Step 7: The decoy throws the chair aside (away from the dog) and tries to escape, giving the dog a chance to bite. Now rush to your dog's side and praise him.

Step 8: Repeat steps 4) through 7) as often as necessary.

Step 9: Similar to step 4), the decoy now holds a shovel, blade down, behind his back (not the lawn chair).

Step 10: As step 5), but using the shovel.

Step 11: As step 6), but using the shovel.

Step 12: As step 7), but using the shovel.

Step 13: Like steps 9-12, but shovel with the handle down.

Step 14: Similar to steps 9-12, but using the stick.

Repeat these steps as often as necessary. Usually the transition from chair to stick can be accomplished in 20-30 minutes total time. Some dogs, however, may need several of these sessions (e.g. day1: #1-8, day2: #1-12, day3: #1-14).

Cooperation between decoy and handler is important. While you encourage your dog to speak when prevented from biting, the decoy hisses, stamps the foot or makes other short, hasty movements to tease the dog. These minor movements must be distinctly different from the massive movements he makes after throwing the chair/shovel aside to let the dog bite the sleeve.

Since each section of this exercise ends with a fight, the dog will eventually realize that a motionless person is not to be touched but that angry, demanding, challenging barking gets the decoy to move and to fight.

PROBLEMS

A) NO BARK

- Practice "Speak on command" (obedience), often, and independently from protection work.
- Agitate longer before allowing the dog to bite.
- Let the dog watch another dog that does it right.
- Hope that the dog will bark better when he has matured (quit baby-sitting him).
- Some dogs will not bark after all. Often, they are marginal performers in protection work as well.

B) NO FIND OR NO GUARDING

Dogs who show no interest in finding or guarding may leave the decoy, investigate the surroundings, return to their handler etc. This is usually the result of improper conditioning.

In training, conclude every Search, Find and Bark exercise with an escape or a fight. This will keep the dog's interest focussed on the decoy. If the dog is still inattentive during guarding, then the decoy can

Fig.55   FIND & BARK #6

help by briefly moving a little, by growling, hissing, or (as a last resort) even stinging the dog with his stick. He can also escape in the direction opposite to where the dog is going. All this is not permitted in a trial, of course.

Some trainers teach their dog to automatically lay down in front of the decoy. This may cure the guarding problem (the dog can not leave), but many dogs are less willing to bark in this position.

C) BITING INSTEAD OF BARKING

- Tell the decoy to stand motionless, even to drop the sleeve. The dog wants to fight, but no motion = no fight, no fun. After a few times, the dog will most likely bark, challenging the decoy to move and to fight. Reward.
- Biting in the blind is a basic training problem (Refer to "Teaching Procedure", above. See also "Afterbites, Owner Agitation" page 108).
- For a Schutzhund 1 you may want to tolerate this undesired behavior, since discouraging the dog from biting in the blind may require harsh retraining which interferes with the development of the fighting drive.   For a young SchH I dog, many handlers accept the penalty of three points lost in a trial for biting in the blind, in favor of having an outgoing, courageous dog. They postpone enforcing the bark until a later time.

D) FAR SIT

A dog sitting too far away from the decoy is more likely to finish the exercise on his own and to walk away. Attach a 2 foot dangle to the choke collar (see page 33). The decoy then engages the dog in a short fight and unobtrusively reaches for the dangle, guiding it under the sleeve and holding it in his free hand. The dog will want to back off again after the fight, but a tug with the dangle, and the handler's command "sit, speak" will prevent that.

TRIAL DECOY

The decoy stands well hidden in the blind for this exercise, and he remains motionless throughout. He looks straight ahead and avoids direct eye contact with the dog. The sleeve on the right or left arm is held at an angle in front of the lower part of the body. The other arm hangs down naturally. The stick in this hand is an extension of the arm and points to the ground. Arm and stick are held with slight pressure against the side of the body.

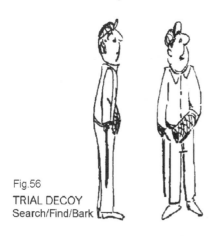

Fig.56
TRIAL DECOY
Search/Find/Bark

** ESCAPE *************************
GENERAL

The escape is one of the most basic, and also one of the most useful exercises in protection work. Some trainers even consider it a "cure all" for problems in man work.

By nature, dogs would not normally seek a fight with a human who is taller, who is smarter, and who uses tools to increase his chances of winning. However, if the dog is shown in training that his opponents - consistently - are weaker, give up, submit, run away, then an artificial response can be established.

OBJECTIVE

Acting on his own, the dog will seize the sleeve of a suddenly escaping decoy, and he will try to stop him by resisting forward movement.

SUGGESTED COMMAND: none (in training: "get him")

SUGGESTED RELEASE COMMAND: none (in training: "out")

PSYCHOLOGY

Retreating from a confrontation, escaping, is an obvious admission of weakness or defeat, and it tremendously

boosts the ego of the opponent. This psychological advantage is skillfully exploited in man work. We purposely deceive our dogs. We make them believe that they have an excellent chance to win over the "bad guy". Care must be taken, however, not to destroy this illusion - ever. One occasion where the dog is truly defeated, by an inconsiderate decoy, or by a real criminal, will require extensive retraining to at least partially repair the damage.

PREREQUISITES

While simplified versions of the escape can be practiced with beginning dogs, the complete, competition-style exercise requires a dog that will deliver a good fight and hold a firm bite after some close range agitation.

TEACHING PROCEDURE
A) START-UP:

Initial training is best done on a long leash. The decoy agitates the dog with hostile/fearful movements towards you and the dog, staying just out of reach for a bite. Your encouragement helps the dog to gain confidence and to strengthen his desire for combat with the bad guy.

B) CONTACT:

The decoy will approach the dog from an angle (not frontal!) and arrange the situation so that the dog has to follow him for a few paces before the bite occurs, with you holding the leash (Fig. 57).

At this time, give him enough freedom for the initial lunge onto the sleeve. Then pick up the slack in the leash and keep it reasonably taut (no pulls, no tugs).

C) STRUGGLE:

The decoy tries to continue on his escape route even after the dog has gotten a hold of the sleeve. He does not face or confront the dog, but he advances keeping a steady pull on the sleeve, dragging the dog along. Jolts, or trying to rip the sleeve out of the dog's mouth, or any other sudden fighting movements must be avoided.

The dog will eventually develop the technique to brace himself against the forward movement of the decoy, and to effectively slow down the decoy's escape.

D) TERMINATION:

In initial training, the decoy should release his grip on the sleeve, let it slide off and continue his escape. Get a hold of your dog's collar and praise him lavishly.

E) CONCLUSION:

Depending on your training philosophy, the dog is now either allowed to carry the sleeve (prey instinct), or diverted away from it and alerted to the fleeing criminal (fighting drive - have a second sleeve ready). Service dog oriented handlers prefer the second alternative, while many Schutzhund trainers

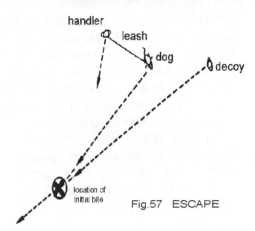

handler

leash

dog

decoy

location of initial bite

Fig.57 ESCAPE

favor the prey oriented approach. Repeat the exercise no more than once in the same training session.

REFINING PROCEDURE

Once the dog masters the basics, use the following training suggestions, one at a time:
- Surrender the sleeve less frequently.
- Introduce the "out".
- Introduce distractions (dogs, people, a cat, etc.).
- Change training locations, decoys, clothing, equipment, routines frequently.
- Increase the length of the pursuit.
- Work off leash.
- Practice the "out" from a distance.

PROBLEMS

A) NO PURSUIT

A dog might be reluctant to pursue
- if the decoy comes on too strong and intimidates
- if the decoy does not sufficiently excite the dog
- if you do not provide enough encouragement and support for him
- if another major distraction is present
- if he is exhausted or ill.

Such temporary conditions can be corrected by using common sense and some patience.

However, when a working dog consistently refuses to pursue the bad guy, then he is a poor candidate for the Schutzhund sport. Environmental problems (often originating with the owner/handler) or hereditary deficiencies (pet breeding) causing such behavior are very difficult or impossible to correct.

B) NO BITE

The dog pursues well, but then he just runs along. This is most likely the result of a very ambitious handler who pushed his dog too fast.
- Do several sessions with close range agitation.
- Make the pursuit much shorter.
- Check that the decoy is not too intimidating.

- Agitate the dog more, longer, before the escape.
- Eliminate delays between agitation and escape.
- Run along with your dog, encourage him.
- Use the leash properly (do not tug on it).
- Use the dangle at the start, then let go of it.
- Work off leash.

C) WEAK BITE / PREMATURE RELEASE / NO PULL

The dog barely holds on to the sleeve, does not pull to slow down the decoy, releases the bite hastily. Use the suggestions above, make the actual fight much shorter, check the chapter "Improving the Bite".

D) NO OUT

If your dog refuses to quit fighting after the escape, then see the chapter on "Releasing the Bite".

E) AFTERBITES (also called "nibbling" or "seconds")

Some dogs release the sleeve but come back for a second or third bite. Intercept immediately: a harsh command, a slap with the hand, a "karate chop" between sleeve and snout just before the bite, a leash correction etc. will work most of the time. The correction should not come from the decoy in this exercise, if possible at all. However, the decoy can assist by holding the sleeve in front of his chest (not lower) and by standing absolutely still. See also "Afterbites", page 108.

TRIAL DECOY

At the beginning, during guarding, and until the dog is biting, the decoy holds the sleeve steady on his side, in a horizontal position. He is not allowed to hold the sleeve in front of his body nor may he swing his arm unduly.

The handler positions his dog to guard the decoy. The decoy stands with a clear path of at least 15 paces in front of him. He is required to run straight ahead in the direction he is facing (Fig.57).

The exercise is done on instructions of the judge. The decoy runs forward. Once the dog is on the sleeve, the decoy keeps going for another ten paces. Then he stops abruptly and remains motionless.

There is no fighting in this exercise. Actually, the decoy pretends to not even concern himself with the dog.

Fig.58
TRIAL DECOY
Escape

** ATTACK ON HANDLER ********

GENERAL

A good performance in the "attack on the handler" is the true justification for training a personal protection dog. The exercise is also of great importance to handlers of police dogs and various other types of service dogs. The exercise is part of all three levels of Schutzhund testing. The assault can come from a hidden person (SchH I) or from the decoy being back-transported to the judge (SchH II and III).

OBJECTIVE

Acting on his own initiative, the dog will prevent a sudden attack on his handler by seizing the decoy's sleeve. He will bite hard in spite of being hit with the stick. Upon command, he will release the bite.

SUGGESTED COMMAND: none (in training: "get him")

SUGGESTED RELEASE COMMAND: "Out"

PSYCHOLOGY

The attack is sudden, and the dog is surprised by it, ideally. This requires a considerate approach in teaching.

PREREQUISITES

The attack on the handler should not be practiced with a novice dog, prerequisite is that the dog delivers a good fight and holds a firm bite after some close agitation.

TEACHING PROCEDURE

A) INTRODUCTION:

Almost all of the initial training for the attack on the handler should be done on leash. This includes the actual fight. Even the experienced dog is at times worked on lead.

Position the decoy in front of the hiding place, e.g. in full view of the dog. This helps to build confidence since it eliminates the surprise effect. Alert your dog while approaching the decoy: "watch that guy" (or the like). Speak with a low, subdued voice. Keep the leash short, bend down a little, point to the decoy, and pat the dog on the rump. The decoy makes himself noticed, moving and growling just a little.

B) HOSTILITY:

Hostility starts once you have come within about 15 feet of the decoy. Both you and the decoy should start shouting, getting ready to beat each other up. The decoy does not pay any attention to the dog, he just observes him out of the corner of his eye. The attack is directed toward you, not the dog!

C) CONTACT:

The decoy takes ONE step forward, threatens you, then retreats for several steps. This evokes the

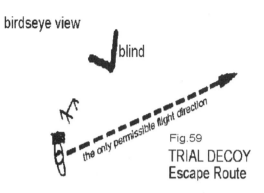

birdseye view

Fig.59
TRIAL DECOY
Escape Route

pursuit instinct in the dog and leads to a bite.

An inexperienced dog is not quite sure if the bite was the right thing to do. He, therefore, will let go of the sleeve, look at you and ask for approval. This is undesirable. Get involved from the very beginning, pursue the decoy, deal out a few punches. At the same time encourage and reassure your dog, both verbally ("good boy, get him") and physically, by patting him on the side. This will make it unnecessary for him to check with you, he does not have to let go of the sleeve.

During this and the following segments you should hold on to the end of the six foot leash, but make sure that the dog can move freely and that he does not get entangled in the leash.

D) FIGHT:

The fight should be realistic and may be noisy, but short. The hits (if any, as in SchH I) should be tempered (see page 109).

The decoy should move his arm gently all the time while the dog is biting. He can twist his arm inside the sleeve, and he can move the sleeve continuously with a slight give-and-take and a gradual, steady pull away from the dog. Sudden, jerky jolts are undesirable. The sleeve should never be ripped out of the dog's mouth, nor should it be yanked into it.

E) TERMINATION:

To terminate the fight, command the decoy to stand still, absolutely still: no adjustments of his position, no swinging arms, no body sway, no head movements - just perfect immobility.

This change from actively fighting to passively waiting for further directions must be sudden, abrupt, snappy. Most dogs are sufficiently impressed by this and they will automatically let go of the hold. You can assist by giving the "out" command in a firm, if necessary threatening manner. Shouting is unnecessary.

F) CONCLUSION:

Ask the decoy to run away after the completed attack

(hold your dog by the collar). This will strengthen your dog's self-confidence and relieve some of the tension that may have developed in the direct confrontation with the decoy. It will also encourage the dog to guard.

REFINING PROCEDURE

Advanced dogs should practice the attack on the handler under varying conditions, on and off lead, and in connection with the back and the side transport. Avoid rigid routines or doing the exercises always in the same order. The decoy can hide and stage an attack unexpectedly, use a stick to lightly tap the dog, and skip the retreat during and after the fight.

PROBLEMS

A) FORGING

The attack on the handler in a Schutzhund trial is supposed to come as a surprise to the dog. Past experience, however, has taught the dog the sequence of events, and hard dogs will forge in anticipation of the fight. That costs points, and in severe cases it may even interrupt trial proceedings.

- Avoid stimulating the dog's fighting drive while heeling, especially for hard dogs.
- Randomly do side and back transport with, or without, the attack on the handler.
- Change locations, hiding places, decoys, protective gear etc. as often as possible.
- Work with the (slip) leash more often than without it.
- Use the "look" command.
- Do a short heeling pattern with a forceful about turn in front of the "frozen" decoy. Reward with a bite.
- Use leash corrections with adequate force (maybe prong collar), followed by praise and reward.
- Use a 30 ft. leash dragging behind and handled by an assistant, if needed.

B) NO BITE

- Go back to basic protection training.
- Do close-range agitation followed by the attack.
- Ask the decoy to retreat right away.
- Encourage, support and praise your dog more.

C) PREMATURE RELEASE

- Make the fight short.
- Instruct the decoy to move his arm inside the sleeve, during the fight.
- The decoy can do an escape and let the dog bite again.
- See also "Maintaining the Bite".

D) RELEASE UPON HIT

Some dogs release the sleeve when hit. Try:

- Retrain your dog (see "Improve the Bite", "Stick").
- Use less force in the hit, temporarily.
- Give more encouragement and praise during the fight.

Fig.60
TRIAL DECOY
Attack on Handler

Fig.61
TRIAL DECOY
Positioning for the Hit

- The decoy surrenders the sleeve to the dog (let go of the handle) ¼ of a second after the hit, and runs away.

TRIAL DECOY

SCHH I:

The decoy hides behind a blind, a wall etc. and waits until the judge signals him to come out. At this time, dog and handler will be about five to ten paces away.

The decoy will move quickly, making threatening sounds and gestures in an effort to attack the handler. He raises the stick above his head, points it to the sky and moves it in a threatening manner back and forth in short strokes (shaking). To invite the dog to bite, the decoy moves back just a little bit. The sleeve he holds horizontally, chest high, somewhat away from his body to soften the impact. Now the dog should have a firm bite. The decoy moves the sleeve back toward his body and presses it against his lower chest. This gives him better control over his arm and over the dog. Pushing the dog sideways / backward, he maneuvers his adversary into the proper position for the hit.

A decoy wearing the sleeve on the left arm proceeds

as follows (Fig.62): Twist your body to the right and walk sideways to the left, in a side-stepping manner: left foot sideways / forward - move right foot next to left foot, then repeat side-stepping. This prevents stepping on the dog's toes and positions the dog for the hit.

Decoys with a right-arm sleeve move side-reversed. After two steps, the first hit is given. The decoy brings down the stick with reasonable force in one continuous motion from above his head onto the back of the dog.

Then he raises the stick again and follows it with another (double) side-step and another hit, just like above. The time between the two hits should be one to two seconds.

After the two hits, the decoy moves maybe another two or three steps sideways and then comes to an abrupt halt. He lowers the stick at this time and assumes

BASIC POSITION:

The decoy stands upright, facing the dog. The sleeve is carried in front of, and pressed against the body, held in a horizontal position. The other arm hangs down naturally. The stick is an extension of the arm and points to the ground (see Fig.63). The correct technique of hitting was discussed earlier (p.111).

SchH II and III:

At some time during the back transport the judge will signal the decoy to attack the handler. The decoy will then suddenly turn around and proceed just as above. There are, however, no hits scheduled in this exercise.

** DEFENSE ************************
GENERAL

The "Defense" (or "Re-attack") is practiced to teach the dog how to deal with a hostile person in the absence of his handler. Service Dog agencies will benefit the most from this training.

OBJECTIVE

While guarding, the dog is suddenly attacked by the decoy. The dog must seize the sleeve firmly and fight. He is required to release the bite when the suspect gives up struggling. Then guarding continues.

SUGGESTED COMMAND: none (in training: "get him")

SUGGESTED RELEASE COMMAND: none (in training: "out")

PREREQUISITES

Acceptable protection work, especially "attack on the handler" and "courage test".

PSYCHOLOGY

The re-attack is directed toward the dog, not the handler. The handler is either busy investigating the blind, or he is far away from his canine partner. The dog must be taught to take action on his own.

TEACHING PROCEDURE

Initial training should be done in the handler's presence. The procedures are identical to "attack on the handler", but the decoy pays attention to the dog, not the handler. Most dogs understand that quickly.

REFINING PROCEDURE

Advanced dogs can be left guarding the decoy, with you standing a few yards to the side. Verbal encouragement during the sudden attack of the decoy is needed only initially. Gradually, you can move farther and farther away, or hide in the blind.

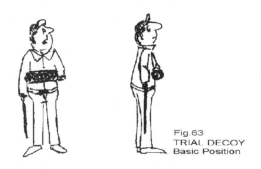

Fig.63
TRIAL DECOY
Basic Position

You may give the "out" command for the release.

PROBLEMS

See problem sections for "escape", "attack on handler" and "courage test".

TRIAL DECOY

In preparation for this exercise the decoy assumes BASIC POSITION (see "Defense; Trial Decoy").

He waits for the judge's signal to attack the dog and then proceeds just like it was described in "Defense; Trial Decoy SchH I", including the hits, but excluding the initial hiding part.

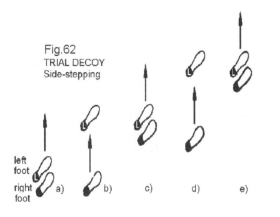

Fig.62
TRIAL DECOY
Side-stepping

left
foot

right
foot

a)   b)   c)   d)   e)

** COURAGE TEST ****************
GENERAL
This routine benefits mainly the handlers of canines on duty with law enforcement agencies. A civilian is rarely justified to send his dog after a distant person. The exercise is, however, an indicator of the dog's true talents in protection work, and Schutzhund fanciers utilize it as such.

OBJECTIVE
The dog is sent after a fleeing, distant "criminal" who turns around just before contact, wields a stick and threatens the dog. The dog accepts the challenge, bites the sleeve and fights the decoy. After a short struggle the decoy stops moving. The dog releases the bite, guards the suspect and waits for his handler.

SUGGESTED COMMAND: "get him"
SUGGESTED RELEASE COMMAND: "out"

PSYCHOLOGY
The dog works independently, far away from you. Without any support or reassurance, he has to make several decisions (to bite, to fight, maybe to take a hit, to release). It requires time, repetition and skill to prepare him for this task. Dogs not suited for Schutzhund training will fail the test, even with the best preparation.

PREREQUISITES   Acceptable protection work, in the "escape" and the "attack on the handler".

TEACHING PROCEDURE
Kneel on your left knee, next to the dog, holding him with the right hand by the collar. The decoy, about 30 feet away, agitates with threatening motions until the dog is ready for a bite, then he runs away.

Having encouraged your pal all the time - the kneeling position makes it easy -, you now release him and send him after the fleeing "criminal". The first few times you might want to run with your dog to catch the bad guy.

Once the dog has closed in to about 15 feet, the decoy turns around and comes back, lightly threatening the dog with gestures and the stick raised above his head. The dog must charge him and bite the sleeve. After some struggling the decoy suddenly "freezes", not moving at all. This is the signal for the dog to release his hold, which you can enforce with an "out" command, if necessary.

REFINING PROCEDURE
Dogs that do well in the exercise described above should be taught to
- pursue over a longer distance (up to about 100 paces)
- pursue with minimal prior agitation

- fight in spite of more severe threatening
- release the bite within one to five seconds after the decoy stops struggling
- release without a command
- guard well
- do the "Defense" after the courage test.

PROBLEMS
A) NO PURSUIT
If the dog refuses to pursue the decoy, try: shorter distances, more initial agitation, more encouragement from you, running with the dog, attacking the decoy yourself. If none of the these help, then the dog is either ill, not yet far enough advanced in protection work, or not suited for Schutzhund training.

B) EARLY DEPARTURE
The following suggestions can be tried if the dog has developed the habit of dashing out in pursuit of the decoy before the command was given:
- practice obedience while another dog does protection work
- do a short heeling pattern on the training field, including an about turn in front of the "frozen" decoy. Wait until the dog pays attention to you ("look" command) and reward it immediately with a bite
- use a slip leash (sliding the leash through the collar and holding on to both ends) to correct the dog; let one end of it go when sending the dog
- ask the decoy to walk up and down the narrow end of the field while you do the same at the other end of the field, heeling your dog. Exchange loud, hostile words with the decoy and make sure that the dog heels well. Send the dog after several passes, or walk up to the decoy, for variety.

C) NO BITE / WEAK BITE   See "Escape; Problems".
D) NO RELEASE   See "Training Techniques".
E) NO GUARDING
A dog leaving the decoy after the courage test considers the job done. Change his attitude by simply adding another exercise after the routine. The "escape" or the "defense" are suitable.

In a trial the dog will expect this added routine (which of course does not come) and guard nicely.

F) AFTERBITES See "Escape".

TRIAL DECOY
More than any other routine, the courage test requires special knowledge and skill of the decoy. Anybody can play steamroller and chase a dog off

the field, but few people can challenge and fight with the dog in a competitive, sportsman-like manner. Since the impact in the courage test can break a dog's neck if done improperly, the correct procedure is described in detail. We assume that the decoy wears the sleeve on the left arm (for right-arm sleeves, the directions have to be side-reversed).

- The decoy runs away, the dog is sent after him
- Once the dog has closed in to about 45 feet, the decoy turns around and comes back, threatening the dog.

The following steps, in sequence, each last for a tiny fraction of a second only (Fig.64):

a) - the decoy is holding the sleeve horizontally, chest-high but forward, away from his body by about 6-8"

b) - just before impact, the decoy stops his forward movement, actually he even backs up just a little bit. He also bends his knees somewhat, and he turns slightly to the right.

c,d) - the impact of the dog's bite will initially bring the sleeve arm closer to the decoy's body. However, the decoy deflects the dog's movement upward and sideways, to his right. To do so, he backs off somewhat more and straightens his knees, after the dog is on the sleeve already.

e,f) - at this time, the dog is airborne. The decoy continues to turn right. He bends his knees again slightly which will set the dog on the ground again. The dog is now facing the opposite direction.

Continue as described in "Defense; Decoy".

** TRANSPORT ***********************
GENERAL
The "Back Transport", or the "Side Transport", brings the apprehended suspect to the training director, or to the judge. This is a useful control exercise.
OBJECTIVE
The alert dog, remaining next to his handler in the heel position, assists in the transport of an apprehended suspect - mainly through his presence. He will not bother or bite the decoy.

SUGGESTED COMMAND: "heel "
SUGGESTED RELEASE COMMAND: "OK"
PREREQUISITES   Some prior obedience training, as well as some protection work is required.

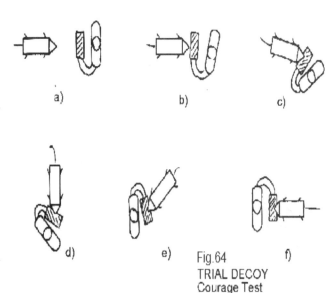

Fig.64
TRIAL DECOY
Courage Test

PSYCHOLOGY
Elements of obedience and of protection work are combined in the transport exercise. Some dogs will not remain at heel since they are anxious to bite the decoy. Other dogs are disinterested, they trot along dutifully. You must stimulate the dog's interest in the decoy, but you must also control your dog to keep him at heel.
TEACHING PROCEDURE
Do initial training on leash, give the "look" command. Observe your dog constantly, encourage and/or correct him as needed. Do not engage in any friendly conversation with the decoy.

The decoy decides how far to walk and when to turn, ignoring dog and handler. He will do a few left and right turns and round the corners, since the dog interprets sharp turns as an escape attempt. Correct your dog if necessary: make an about turn (away from the decoy) when he forges, let the decoy give you a push (side transport) and/or ask him to run away (back transport) when your dog is inattentive. A bite is the reward.

In the side transport, the dog walks between you and the suspect, the decoy wearing the sleeve on the arm next to the dog (it is all right to wear a left arm sleeve on the right arm for the transport).

In the back transport, you and your dog follow about five paces behind the decoy. The sleeve can be worn on either arm.

REFINING PROCEDURE
Advanced dogs should do the transport off lead. Slide a short piece of rope through the collar and

hold on to both ends of the rope to be prepared for a correction. For the re-attack, you just let go one end of it to quickly release your dog (a leash used in this fashion would get stuck during the release). The "slip lead" must be guided through the collar, not the ring.

PROBLEMS

A) FORGING

- Change locations, hiding places, decoys, protective gear etc. as often as possible.
- Work with the (slip) leash more often than without it.
- Use the "look" command.
- Do a short heeling pattern, including a forceful about turn in front of the "frozen" decoy. Reward immediately (bite).
- Use leash corrections with adequate force (maybe prong collar), followed by praise and a bite reward.
- Have a 30 ft. cord attached to the collar which is dragging behind and handled by an assistant, if needed.

B) BITING, NIBBLING

- Give a warning, and/or a quick, harsh correction (leash, nape grab, karate chop).

C) NO GUARDING DURING TRANSPORT

- The decoy should suddenly attack you.
- The decoy should escape.

TRIAL DECOY

The decoy walks in a normal manner, swinging both arms naturally. He behaves indifferent, neither hostile nor friendly.

I am telling you ...
on e v e r y tree !

Fig.65

An optimist and a pessimist go hunting. Mighty proud of his new dog, the optimist sends his dog to retrieve the duck he just shot. The dog walks on top of the water. The pessimist is unmoved.

After the third performance, the optimist can't stand it any longer: "What do you say to that?"

"It looks like your dog can't swim".

E. TRAINING TIMETABLES

Training must follow a logical sequence, a logical progression. Superior results can not be accomplished without having first laid the proper foundation at a young age. This is symbolized in the pyramid below.

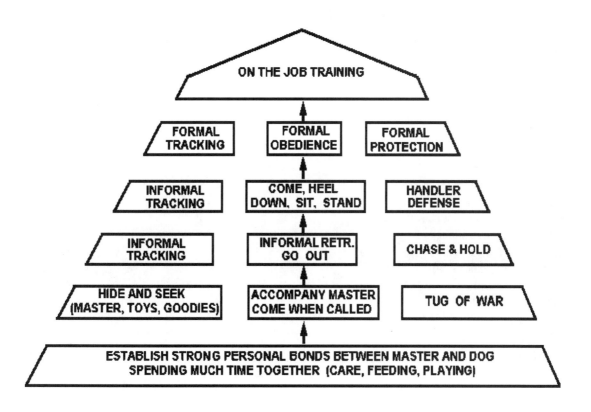

FIG. 66

Billy lives in a run-down neighborhood. He buys an expensive guard dog, but the dog does not do its job and lets thieves get away with three thousand dollars. Billy is furious and complains.
"The dog used to belong to rich people and does not bother with such small amounts of money" they tell him at the agency.

The timetables that follow are guidelines only. Each handler must use his discretion and determine the rate of progression for his own dog.

PUPPY TRAINING - PROGRESSION CHART

task / age (months)	1	2	3	4	5	6
family contacts, handling	X					
sound conditioning	X					
contact w. strangers (dogs/people)	X					
come when called (inductive)		X				
simple straight tracks		X				
fetch, gentle tug-of-war (inductive)		X				
collar/leash conditioning		X				
house breaking		X				
follow on lead (inductive)		X				
watch the club training sessions		X				
sit and down (inductive)			X			
holding the dumbbell			X			
heeling (inductive)			X			
longer straight tracks			X			
stand for grooming			X			
speak on command (inductive)				X		
single, distant gun shots				X		
indicating a handler's article				X		
"out" (for stick, ball, bone)				X		
go-out (inductive)					X	
carrying dumbbell					X	
longer, older tracks w/ one turn					X	
long down (inductive)					X	
chasing and "killing" the rag					X	

TRACKING SCHEDULE - PROGRESSION CHART

task / age (months)	7	8	9	10	11	12	13	14
distractions	X							
obtuse/acute angles	X							
various ground cover		X						
multiple turns		X						
var. weather cond.			X					
var. geographic areas, if possible				X				
simple cross track						X		
SchH I Trial								X

age(months) task	7	8	9	10	11	12	13	14
heel off lead (short)	X							
easy jumping	X							
quartering	X							
retrieve/flat	X							
long sit		X						
stand examination		X						
heel off lead		X						
sit out of motion			X					
down out of motion			X					
training in public places			X					
stand out of motion				X				
hurdle jumping				X				
obedience while another dog does protection work				X				
retrieve hurdle						X		
SchH I Trial							X	
scale/descend wall								X

age(months) task	7	8	9	10	11	12	13	14
Leap # 3 (B)	X							
line/circle agit.(R,SP)	X							
barking (R,SP)	X							
"rabbit chase" (B)	X							
stake agitation (B,SP)	X							
escape, close range (B,SP)		X						
prot. work near blind (B,SP)		X						
attack on handler (P,SP)		X						
defense (P,SP)		X						
line/circle agit.(H,SP)		X						
cour.test,close range (P,SP)			X					
find,bark,escape,bite (H,SP)			X					
quartering,escape,bite (H,SP)				X				
Leap #1 (H,SP)				X				
Leap #2 (H,SP)				X				
reg.courage test (H,SP)				X				
agit.,bite,hit (H,SH)					X			
cour.test, defense (H,SP)						X		
"out" (H,SH)						X		
SchH I Trial							X	

Explanation of codes:
R = rag   H = hard sleeve
B = bite roll   C = civilian sleeve
P = puppy sleeve or hard   SP = stick present
    sleeve w/very soft cover   SH = stick hit

*Two policemen stand on a street corner in Moscow. They cry bitterly. A sympathetic passer-by inquires and is told that their patrol dog ran away. "The dog surely will find its way back to the station" he consoles the cops. "Yeah, **HE** will ....."*

VI. THE RULES

A. VDH TRIAL REGULATIONS

More Schutzhund dogs are tested and certified according to the European VDH Trial Rules than on the basis of any other system. The following is a brief description of representative requirements.

The Schutzhund competitor is encouraged to obtain the most recent Rule Book from the organization that sponsors the trial in which he wants to show. Having trained a dog with "TOP WORKING DOGS", only minor and easily implemented adjustments will be needed to meet other specific regulations.

SCORING SYSTEM (POINTS)			
SchH A	SchH I,II,III	FH	Rating
0-72	0-109	0-35	Unsatisfactory
73-149	110-219	36-69	Insufficient
150-159	220-239	70-79	Satisfactory
160-179	240-269	80-89	Good
180-190	270-285	90-95	Very Good
191-200	286-300	96-100	Excellent

Max.points: Tr.100, Ob.100, Prot.100, FH 100   ☺   Pass: Tr.70, Ob.70, Prot.80, FH 70.

SCHUTZHUND A

This pre-Schutzhund degree is identical to SchH I, but without tracking.

SCHUTZHUND I

In **TRACKING**, the dog must follow an unmarked track of 300-400 yards laid by his own handler while on a 30 ft. lead. Track age is 20 minutes minimum. There are two turns, and two articles are dropped which must be located by the dog.

In **OBEDIENCE**, heeling is done on and off lead at normal, fast and slow pace, including walking through a group of people. A gun will be fired when the dog is off leash. If the dog should shy, he would fail the trial. There is one exercise in which the dog sits, and one in which he downs while heeling, the handler continuing on. On the sit, the handler will return to the dog, and on the down the dog will be called to the handler. There is a retrieve on the flat and a retrieve over a 40 inch hurdle. Also, the dog must on command leave the handler going ahead at least 25 paces, and he must drop on command. The handler will return to the dog. A long down is done while another dog goes through his paces, the handler some distance away and his back to the dog.

In **PROTECTION**, the dog must first locate the hiding decoy and just bark, not bite. Then, while heeling off lead, the decoy will come out of hiding and attack the handler. The dog will be hit with a stick and must not show fear, he must also stop his attack on command. The decoy will then run, acting in a belligerent manner, and the handler will send the dog after the man to attack and hold. After releasing the bite on command, there is a side transport to the judge.

SCHUTZHUND II

In **TRACKING**, the dog is on a 30 ft. lead. He must find two lost articles on a stranger's trail, with two turns, 400-500 yards long, aged at least 30 minutes.

OBEDIENCE includes all the exercises from the SchH I test, except there are three retrieve exercises: on the flat (1000 g dumbbell), over a 40 inch hurdle (650 g), and over a 71 inch inclined scaling wall (handler's article). Also, the "go away" is for 30 paces minimum.

In **PROTECTION**, the dog must first search several hiding places on command and just bark, not bite. The dog then guards the suspect while the handler investigates the hiding place. To stop the escaping decoy, the dog must seize the arm (sleeve), and he must release the hold when the suspect stops struggling. Then the decoy threatens the dog with a stick. The dog has to bite the suspect's arm firmly, and he will be hit twice. During the following back transport the handler will be attacked which the dog is to prevent. In the courage test, the dog is sent after the suspect 50 paces away, and he is to firmly seize the arm until called off by his handler. A side transport to the judge concludes this part.

SCHUTZHUND III

In **TRACKING**, the dog must search for three lost articles on a strangers trail 800-1000 yards long, with three turns, aged at least 50 minutes. The dog may be worked off leash or on a 30 ft. lead.

OBEDIENCE is identical to the SchH II test, with the following exceptions: no on-lead heeling, 2000 g dumbbell in the retrieve on the flat, stand-stay out of normal pace (handler returns) and running pace (handler calls dog), "go away" for 40 paces minimum, and long down with the handler out of sight.

PROTECTION is identical to the SchH II exercises, except that there is another "defense" after the courage test where the dog gets hit again.

FH (Adv. Tracking Degree)

Only dogs with at least a SchH I degree can compete in this test. The strangers track is 1000-1400 yards long, at least three hours old, has six turns and four articles. It also intersects with a misleading cross-track in three places, it leads through different ground covers, and it crosses a road way.

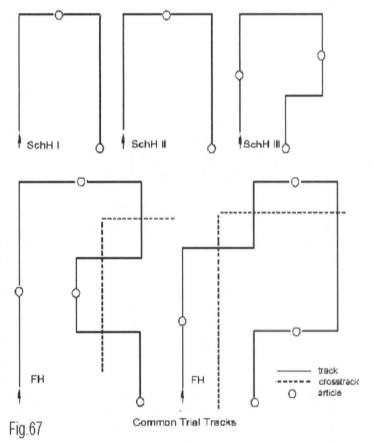

Fig.67

Common Trial Tracks

GENERAL

To allow for fair competition, Schutzhund trial regulations are structured and regulated to a great degree.

Officials of the AZG meet at regular intervals to evaluate field experiences, implement changes as needed, and enforce uniform interpretation of the official trial rules. Schutzhund competitors should therefore receive fair and uniform treatment from all judges, regardless of their affiliation with a particular dog sport organization. The judge expects that dog handlers are thoroughly familiar with the rules, and that they abide by them. It is wise to study these rules, the requirements, and their official interpretation.

In AKC obedience shows, an unexplained total score for each competitor is announced at the end of the trial. This is in contrast to Schutzhund competition: once a competitor has completed a segment, the judge openly comments on how well the participant did in the individual exercises. The judge has to account for, and explain, his decisions (an incompetent judge would not last very long), and the handler can learn from mistakes and do better the next time.

Here are a some of the facts of Schutzhund competition that every contestant would *benefit* from knowing, and some requirements that every one is *expected* to know:

TEMPERAMENT TEST

The judge is required to conduct an informal temperament test before the dog starts tracking. Overly shy or aggressive dogs will not be permitted to continue.

TRACKING

- SchH I and SchH II tracks are either U- or step-shaped, SchH III tracks are almost always R-shaped.
- The handler must inform the judge if his dog will "pick up" or "point out" the articles.
- The starting flag is always to the left of the starting scent pad, looking in the track direction.
- Articles are never placed close to a turn or close to a cross track.
- One article is always placed at the end of the track.
- Cross tracks will never be close to a turn or an article.
- When the dog has found an article, the handler must take it and hold it high over his head for the judge to see. The continuation of tracking proceeds like the initial start, the handler follows when the end of the 30 ft. line comes up.

PROTECTION

- SchH III dogs must come on the field off-lead.
- Commands in protection work do not have to be given instantaneously. Considerable leeway is given for timing the command (without penalty), and a slightly delayed command is often more effective.
- When quartering a dog, the handler should smoothly advance on the centerline of the field, adjusting his speed so that he can be at the proper location for calling and sending his dog. An erratic and discontinuous advance on the centerline indicates faulty training and costs points.
- If a handler must physically take his dog off the sleeve because he does not let go, the judge will fail that dog.
- A dog leaving the trial area while under test (be it in tracking, obedience or protection) will fail also.

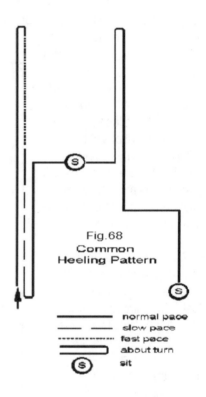

Fig.68
Common
Heeling Pattern

——— normal pace
— — slow pace
············ fast pace
▭ about turn
Ⓢ sit

OBEDIENCE

- The judge is looking for a spirited, happy, pleasant-to-watch demonstration of obedience work.
- A heeling pattern, while not specifically required according to the rules, can help the handler to remember which exercises must be shown here. The judge may insist that the pattern be followed.
- Every exercise starts and ends with the basic position.
- Using the dog's name in connection with a command will be faulted as a double command.
- The handler should swing his arms normally. This is a requirement!
- The dog must not be praised/rewarded during exercises; excessive praise between exercises is faulty.
- Many clubs provide a set of dumbbells for the trial. You can insist on using your own, but always bring your dog's favorite object for the retrieve over the wall.
- If the dumbbell has landed in an unfavorable location, the handler may ask the judge for permission to re-throw. There is no penalty if he gives his permission.

B. SCHUTZHUND JUDGES CHECK LIST

During the trial, the conscientious Schutzhund judge will take notes to record the performance of a dog under test. He may use a list similar to the one presented here. The aspiring or apprentice judge, as well as the dog handler in training, will benefit from such a check list also.

TEMPERAMENT TEST
- ❑ aggressive
- ❑ shy
- ❑ self-confident

TRACKING
- ❑ faulty / repetitive starts
- ❑ nose high
- ❑ turns incorrect
- ❑ short leash
- ❑ incorrect finding of articles
- ❑ excessive praise
- ❑ running
- ❑ handler assistance
- ❑ hunting
- ❑ circling / heavy circling
- ❑ eliminating

OBEDIENCE   Heeling
- ❑ starting position
- ❑ faulty sits
- ❑ lagging
- ❑ group problems
- ❑ forging
- ❑ sniffing
- ❑ going wide
- ❑ incorrect response to gun shots
- ❑ crowding
- ❑ handler assistance / error

Sit/motion
- ❑ slow response
- ❑ follows / moves
- ❑ downs or stands
- ❑ handler assistance / error

Down/motion and Recall
- ❑ slow response
- ❑ no/slow come
- ❑ sits or stands
- ❑ poor finish
- ❑ follows / moves
- ❑ handler assistance / error

Stand/motion (Recall)
- ❑ slow response
- ❑ no/slow come
- ❑ sits or downs
- ❑ poor finish
- ❑ follows / moves
- ❑ handler assistance / error

Retrieve/flat
- ❑ slow response
- ❑ no out
- ❑ no go-out
- ❑ drops / plays / chews
- ❑ no/slow return
- ❑ poor finish
- ❑ no retrieve
- ❑ handler assistance / error

Retrieve/jump
- ❑ slow response
- ❑ no out
- ❑ no jump (1) / (2)
- ❑ drops / plays / chews
- ❑ touches / steps on hurdle
- ❑ poor finish
- ❑ no retrieve
- ❑ handler assistance / error

Retrieve/wall
- ❑ slow response
- ❑ no out
- ❑ no scaling (1) / (2)
- ❑ drops / plays / chews
- ❑ jumps from top
- ❑ poor finish
- ❑ no retrieve
- ❑ handler assistance / error

Send away
- ❑ slow response
- ❑ anticipates down
- ❑ no go-out
- ❑ gets up prematurely
- ❑ too short
- ❑ poor finish
- ❑ no straight go-out
- ❑ handler assistance / error

Long down
- ❑ slow response
- ❑ incorrect response to gun shots
- ❑ leaves position / creeps
- ❑ poor finish
- ❑ restless
- ❑ handler assistance / error

PROTECTION   Search/Find
- ❑ disinterested
- ❑ eliminates
- ❑ too few blinds
- ❑ handler assistance / error
- ❑ one side only
- ❑ predominantly one side

Bark
- ❑ weak / no bark
- ❑ no guarding
- ❑ biting / nipping
- ❑ handler assistance / error
- ❑ afterbite

Attack/Handler
- ❑ uncontrollable
- ❑ afterbite
- ❑ no / weak bite
- ❑ no guarding

	❑ premature release	❑ handler assistance / error
	❑ no / poor out	
Escape	❑ no pursuit	❑ afterbite ❑ no / poor out
	❑ no / weak bite	❑ no guarding
	❑ premature release	❑ handler assistance / error
Defense	❑ afraid	❑ no / poor out
	❑ stick shy	❑ afterbite
	❑ no / weak bite	❑ no guarding
	❑ premature release	❑ handler assistance / error
Transport	❑ uncontrollable	❑ handler assistance / error
Courage Test	❑ no pursuit	❑ no / poor out
	❑ no / weak bite	❑ afterbite
	❑ afraid / stick shy	❑ no guarding
	❑ premature release	❑ handler assistance / error
Courage & Hardness	❑ shies	❑ no guarding
	❑ stick shy	❑ returns to handler
	❑ no / weak bite	❑ leaves field
	❑ premature release	❑ eliminates

C. HANDLER ERRORS

Small mistakes can add up to a big disappointment. In a Schutzhund trial, many handlers give away points while they could easily have competed for top placement.

Listed here are some of the more common problems as well as some suggestions to earn higher scores:

GENERAL

- Know the rules by heart, abide by them.
- Practice in mock trials, fun matches, participate in AKC trials.
- Don't arrive at the last minute. Come early and relax.
- Give your dog a chance to explore and to sniff out the trial fields, if possible at all.
- Familiarize yourself with the grounds and the procedures.
- Don't be nervous, calm down. Your dog will be more relaxed that way too.
- Act normal, just like in training. Don't change your voice (pitch, loudness) or your behavior now.
- Listen to the judges' critique of earlier dogs, learn from it.
- Report to the judge before and after each trial section.

TRACKING

- Don't round the corners too much when laying the track.
- Don't drag your feet too much when laying the track.
- Untangle the long line before you start.
- Let the line run out to the full length before you follow your dog on the track.
- Avoid jerking the line when starting on the track.
- Keep the line reasonably taut at all times, maintain a reasonable speed.
- Let your dog do his job, don't try to steer him.
- Read your dog, and communicate with him. You are allowed to give calm reassurance/praise (when he is on the track), or low-key disapproval when he goofs.
- Keep your dog long enough at the article, to convincingly indicate a find.
- Hold the article up high for the judge to see.
- Don't make your dog come back if he over-runs an article but is still going strong on the track. If you call him back, you may ruin his performance for the rest of the track, and the points for the article are lost already anyway.
- When re-starting the track after finding an article, do not give a hand signal (do not point).
- If your dog runs into problems, think. Take the most logical step to continue (re-start, cast your dog, praise or scold him, help him even if it costs a few points). Don't quit on your own, keep trying until the judge blows the whistle.

OBEDIENCE

- Carry on as usual, maintain your attitude, your posture, your voice. Consider the trial as another routine training session. If, for instance, you bellow your commands now, your dog gets confused.
- Have enough slack in the leash so that you do not inadvertently give a correction.
- Don't stop or make sudden changes in pace, your dog can not follow that quickly (no penalty unless you overdo it).
- For off-lead work, get rid of the leash, hang it over your shoulder, or stash it away securely. Keep your hands free.
- Praise your dog only between exercises, unobtrusively.
- Avoid "body language".
- Don't use the dog's name (double command).
- With a SchH III dog, enter the field off leash.
- Heeling: Show all parts of the pattern. Go for the required distances.
- Sit/motion: Don't give the command too forcefully (or your dog will lay down). Don't turn your head to observe the dog.
- Down/motion: Don't turn your head to observe the dog. When you call your dog, wait until he pays attention to you.
- Stand/motion: Don't give the command too forcefully(your dog may lay down),don't turn your head to observe the dog.
- Retrieve: Throw the dumbbell so that it lands in the right place. Request a re-throw, if needed (no points are deducted if the judge gives permission). Don't change your position, stay put. Don't send your dog from too close to, or too far away from, the obstacle.
- Send away: Lower your arm either right after the go-out command, or after the dog went down (otherwise it will be a double command).
- Long down: Don't touch your dog when giving the "down" command. Get him to sit at heel before you leave the field.

PROTECTION

- Be authoritative when guiding your dog through the quartering routine.
- Be also authoritative when heeling your dog (transports, SchH I attack on the handler, etc.).
- Excite your dog, gear him up for the courage test. Talk to him, touch him, kneel next to him.
- Place your dog in an advantageous position for the defense exercise (see that chapter).
- Wait for the judge to tell you to give the "out" command.
- Give your "out" command loud and threatening (you only have one chance).

D. SIMPLE ARITHMETIC

Competing in a Schutzhund trial is in a way like gambling: know the rules of the game and use them to your advantage, like taking a temporary loss in order to increase chances for a big gain in the end.

For instance: you may want to give a second command - and take the penalty - if you can be reasonably sure that your dog will do better for the rest of the trial. This has nothing to do with cheating or with dishonesty, it is just using simple arithmetic to increase the odds in your favor.

Another example: The protection work in Schutzhund I competition starts with the Search / Find / Bark exercise. The rules require that the dog does not bite at this time. Novice handlers stress that point, but let us look at the *whole* picture. There are three possibilities:

1. The dog rushes to the decoy, barks excitedly, challenges the decoy to move, guards him - but he does not touch the guy. This is a rare sight in SchH I, it earns full points. Dog, handler and trainer should be congratulated.

2. The dog barks briefly and dutifully, or not at all. He will not bite, but he will not stay with the decoy either - no guarding. He considers the job done at this point. Remembering that he was punished for biting in the past, he wants to stay out of trouble now, so he just wanders off.

   This behavior pattern usually carries over into the other protection exercises as well and it will be heavily penalized, here and in the rating for the dog's courage and hardness. These penalties will make a passing score unlikely.

3. The dog eagerly searches for the decoy, barks once or twice, then hits the sleeve. He may or may not release the hold without handler interference, but then he will focus all his attention on the bad guy. Afterbites here and there are likely also. In a trial, the judge will deduct three points for biting (SchH I) and a few more points later on for possible afterbites. There will, however, be no loss in the rating of courage and hardness.

A handler can train his dog to end up in either one of the three groups, at will, but the novice trainer with an unexperienced dog should always aim for group three. Usually he does not spend the necessary time and he does not have the knowledge and experience to make group one. His only alternative would be group two, the losers. See the summary here:

SEARCH / FIND / BARK OPTIONS

	GROUP 1	GROUP 2	GROUP 3
overall behavior	committed, dedicated, controlled	disinterested	committed, dedicated, uncontrolled
typical behavior	ideal (barks, guards)	weak bark, no guarding, leaves decoy	bites, guards
point deductions for this exercise	none	one or more	three
anticipated point deductions for other exercises	none	ten or more	four or more
negative effect on courage/hardness	none	severe	none
chances for a passing score	very high	slim	high

E. THE SCHUTZHUND TRIAL

A well planned and organized trial that runs smoothly can make or break the reputation of your club.

1. Pick a trial date and an alternate date. Try to coordinate the event with other nearby clubs.
2. Appoint a Trial Chairman and a Trial Secretary.
3. Notify the Parent Organization of your club and obtain approval for the trial. Also request a copy of their Schutzhund Trial Regulations.
4. Contact the judge, either directly, or through your club's Parent Organization.
5. Secure grounds for the trial: a large tracking area, and fields for the obedience and protection work. Draw a rough map for the judge's approval.
6. Prepare for inclement weather: shades, heaters, a tent, hot coffee, umbrella for the judge, etc.
7. Consider buying/renting a public address system (loudspeakers, or a bullhorn)
8. Check the equipment:
   tracking - flags, articles, 2 tracklayers
   obedience - jump, wall, dumbbells, blank pistol, blanks (32 cal. preferred), 4-6 people for group
   protection - 8 blinds, sleeves and covers, leather pants, stick, first aid kit, 2 decoys.
9. Contact motels that will accept trained dogs.
10. Consider buying insurance for the trial.
11. Consider purchasing trophies for the winning entries.
12. Send out trial advertising at least 2 months before the trial (magazines, flyers, etc.).
13. Send out entry forms with deadline, list of motels, map of the trial location, banquet information. Request that prior score cards, current rabies certificates, and signed injury waivers be submitted.
14. Contact the judge for detail arrangements on travel and accommodations.
15. Make banquet arrangements, reserve early. Consider also a Sunday lunch.
16. Decide on refreshments / food.
17. Contact a photographer for trial coverage.
18. Invite the local press as well as radio and TV reporters.
19. Secure adequate rest room facilities on the trial grounds.
20. Prepare a catalog, offer paid advertising. Include an explanation of the Schutzhund sport, what is required for each degree. List club officers, judge, decoys, entries.
21. Set up a practice trial about one month before the real event, to uncover potential problems and weak spots, and to give dogs and handlers a chance to prepare for the big day.

22. Send out final notices to all entrants, with information and instructions. Include location, day, date, time, and place to report. Also include starting numbers for entrants.
23. Make arrangements to meet the judge at the airport, and act as his chauffeur during the entire trial.
24. Make time for the judge to inspect the grounds, and to evaluate the decoys.
25. Assist the judge during the trial at all times, and eliminate delays by having handlers, dogs, helpers and equipment ready when needed.
26. Help the judge with all paperwork.
27. Consider a post-trial lunch on Sunday afternoon, for awarding the trophies.
28. Take the judge to the airport.
29. Write down what went well, what went wrong, suggest changes for the next trial.
30. Relax and write a short article about the trial for publication in your favorite newsletter/paper.

Some of these tasks can be assigned to responsible individuals or committees, but it is the trial chairman who will have to answer to the judge if any of these items are omitted. Early planning, good participation from all club members and thorough follow-through and check-up is the guarantee for a successful Schutzhund trial.

F. EASTERN EUROPEAN TRIAL REQUIREMENTS

Eastern European (Communist) countries used to generously support the training of working dogs by private citizens, to secure suitable canines for their military and law enforcement agencies. As a result, the training was more rigorous and more praxis related than in Western countries. The former East German Trial Regulations are listed here.

SCHUTZHUND I (SchH I)

Tracking (100) - owners track, 30 minutes age
- 600 m, 2 ninety degree turns, 2 articles

Protection(100)- search/find/bark, guarding (20 sec.)
- search and transport of decoy
- courage test (60 m), guarding (20 sec.)
- transport / attack on handler

Obed. (100) - on/off lead, R,L,about turns,
slow/normal/fast pace, group
- down / recall from 20 m
- retrieve/flat and over 1 m hurdle
- long down/distractions (50 m)
- 2 gun shots

SCHUTZHUND II (SchH II)

Tracking (100) - strangers track, 45 minutes age
- 1000 m, 2 ninety degree turns,
- 1 acute angle, 2 articles

Protection (100) - search/find/bark, guarding (40 sec.)
- search and transport of decoy
- courage test (75 m), guarding (40 sec.)
- transp/ attack on handler/ guarding (40s)

Obed. (100) - heeling off lead like SchH I
- down / recall from 50 m
- sit/down/stand /normal/fast pace
- retrieve/flat and over 1 m hurdle
- retrieve over 1.50 m upright wall
- walk over a suspended plank
- long down/distractions (70 m)
- 2 gun shots

SCHUTZHUND III (SchH III)

Tracking (100) - strangers track , 60 minutes age
- 1500 m, 4 ninety degree turns,,
- 1 acute angle, 1 cross track, 3 articles

Protection (100) - search/find/bark, guarding (60 sec.)
- search and transport of decoy
- pursuit (90 m) of decoy out of sight,
- courage test, guarding (60 sec)
- transport, attack on handler

Obed. (100) - heeling off lead like SchH I
- go-out (50 m), handler hidden
for 60 sec., signal for recall
- sit/down/stand /normal/fast pace,
DH continues and returns
- retrieve/flat and over 1 m hurdle
- retrieve over 1.80 m upright wall
- crawling for 10 m, 3 gun shots
- long down/distractions (70 m)

FAEHRTENHUND I (FH I)

Tracking (100) - strangers track, 90 minutes age
- 1500 m, 6 ninety degree turns,
- 4 articles, 1 acute angle, 1 cross track

Protection (100) - attack on handler, escape
- search and transport of decoy

Obed. (100) - heeling on/off lead like SchH I
- down, recall from 20 m
- one-way jump over a 1 m hurdle
- long down/distractions (50 m)
- 2 gun shots

FAEHRTENHUND II (FH II)

Tracking (100)   - strangers track, 120 minutes age
- 2000m, 8 turns 90degree, 5articles
- 2 acute angles, 4 cross tracks

Protection (100) - attack on handler, escape
- search and transport of decoy

FAEHRTENHUND III (FH III)

Tracking (100)   - strangers track, 90 minutes age
- 3000m, 12turns 90degree, 6 articles
- 4 acute angles, 8 cross tracks

Protection (100) - attack on handler, escape
- search and transport of decoy

Obed. (100)   - heeling on/off lead like SchH I
- down, recall from 50 m
- one-way climb over 1.50m wall
- walk over a suspended plank
- long down/distractions (70 m)
- 2 gun shots

Obed. (100)   - heeling on/off lead like SchH I
- down out of motion
- recall on signal
- one-way climb over 1.80m wall
- long down/distractions (50 m)
- 3 gun shots

*People call their dog "Rover" or "Boy", I named mine "Sex".
Last night he ran off, again. I spent hours looking for him, and
then this cop comes over and asks me "What are you doing
in that street at three o'clock in the morning?" I told him I was
looking for Sex.*   *My case comes up Friday.*

VII. AUXILIARIES

A. DOG FIGHTS

There are many reasons why dogs would fight, yet all are related to a natural instinct: pack, territorial, protective, or survival instinct. Find the cause and deal with it early on.

NOVICE FIGHTERS

In the original phase of a fight it is fairly easy to separate the two combatants. Someone - not necessarily the handler - must step in fearlessly and energetically. Use the surprise effect, do something the dogs do not expect, like jumping with both feet (not barefoot!) between, or next to, the two dogs and scream as loud as you can. This impresses most dogs sufficiently so that they forget to fight - for a moment. Determine which one of the two dogs is the most likely to start anew. He will be the more dominant animal, he will advance and assume a confident, aggressive, maybe even fearless, posture. Try to intimidate him with shouts and gestures, chase him away using any tools that are handy (stick, umbrella, briefcase, book).

In rare instances the strange dog will then direct his aggression towards you. Stand still and keep all your limbs close to your body. Avoid any continued movement, stand like a statue. Use your foot to kick him, or any available tool to hit him, with lightening speed if he gets too close, but don't hold your foot or your arm out like bait. Short, sharp shouts may help. Try to inch toward something that provides rear cover, like a wall, a car, a tree. Wait for the dog to

move away or to be called off. Then leave the scene slowly - don't run.

SEASONED FIGHTERS

Real problems develop once the two dogs are locked unto each other at the height of a fight.

- It is impossible to intimidate the two dogs sufficiently, or to command them to cease fighting. The first dog to comply with the request would still feel the bite of the adversary, and out of self-preservation he must bite back.
- Kicking or hitting two fighting dogs will only intensify the battle, even if both release their grip at the same time.
- Throwing a blanket or a bucket of water, sand or pebbles on the dogs impresses them very little, as long as the fight is in full force. To shove sand in their mouths holds very little promise either. Besides, you risk losing a couple of fingers.
- Reaching for the collar, even if it is a prong collar, will only aggravate the fighters. In addition, the hand comes in close proximity to the teeth while searching for the collar. Even your own dog may bite you in such an instance - not because he wants to, but your hands are between his teeth when he closes his fangs.
- Remote-controlled electronic collars accomplish the same as beating: the fight intensifies.
- In professional dog fights, handlers use short wooden dowels to pry the fighters' fangs open.

However, their dogs "work" according to certain rules (lock grip), which are unfamiliar to the occasional fighter. It is therefore very risky for non-professionals to use theses dowels, aside from the fact that they are usually not available when needed.

SEPARATING FIGHTERS

We have perfected the following procedure over the years. It carries minimal risks.

- One person is needed for each dog, preferably the two dog owners. Each handler tries to get a hold of that part of his dog's body that is removed the farthest from the teeth: the tail (for docked dogs, one hind foot).
- After securely holding the tail (do not pull!), grab one of the hind legs (more precisely: the metatarsus) with the other hand.
- Now let go of the tail and transfer that grip to the other hind leg. Both handlers must securely hold both hind feet of their dog before they can proceed with the next step.
- Both handlers stand upright and lift - at the same time - the hind feet of their dogs off the ground (about one yard). This makes the dogs insecure and deprives them of their mobility and balance.
- Both handlers yell at their dogs and try to separate them by pulling on their hind legs at the same time. If necessary, they may bang on the fangs with their feet (shoes!).
- As soon as the dogs release the grip they must be pulled back / separated, and kept separated !
- The dogs must be punished only when they try to resume the fight - one sharp hit with lighteningspeed for every attempt. Punishment must not be administered if the dog just stays alert!

CURING FIGHTERS

Seasoned fighters can only be cured by applying drastic measures (out you go, Dr. Spock !!!, see page 26). However, the forces must be goal oriented, and the dog must be able to connect it to the undesirable deed.

Some trainers still recommend "hanging" (suspending the dog on collar/leash over your shoulder) as an appropriate remedy. Even the editor of a well-known American obedience training magazine supports it publicly in his periodical. We believe that hanging is despicable, senseless cruelty. It could best be compared to the "expert" who wants to extinguish a small fire in the frying pan with the blast from a load of dynamite - the side effects are devastating in both cases.

We suggest that after a fight the two dogs be fitted with prong collars and short leads. The dog/handler teams then walk in opposite directions past each other, dog next to dog, but at first the teams are separated by at least 20 feet. At the slightest sign of aggression, for instance raised hackles, snarling, curled lips, pulling toward the other dog, readiness to jump forward etc., the handler must interfere. Using the feedback principle, the handler should silently and rapidly count to three and do the following on each count (½ seconds each), to correct aggressive behavior:

1) Give a sharp, short command ("NO").
2) Observe the reaction of your dog.
3) a) If your dog did quit the hostilities on (2) and gives you his attention, then praise him ("good boy").
   b) If your dog continues to be hostile, quickly correct him with the collar and give him ONE sharp blow across the snout with a 2 ft. piece of rubber hose (3/8" diameter, soft, pliable, couplers removed - don't hit the eyes !).
   Command: "NO", punish **ONLY** the offending dog, then praise lightly.

Repeat, but decrease the distance between teams. Continue walking past each other until both dogs are under complete control when separated by only 12 inches. Practice on a loose lead, a longer leash, and finally off lead, under constant control of the two handlers. Repeat for days, weeks, months - as needed.

Dr. Spock fanatics recommend goodies to cure fighters, to offer the treat when a fight becomes imminent. Praying would help more than that.

Think:

Fighting is an innate response, eating a cookie is a simple pleasure. Would you go for a candy that your girlfriend offers you - when someone comes at you with a knife?

ROOM MATES

Fighting dogs belonging to the same household often end up in separate homes, or in the pound. The owner usually favors one of the combatants and then chooses the easy way out since he can not bring himself to apply the necessary force (and patience) to correct the quarreling canines. It does not have to be that way.

These dogs (usually two males or two females) vie for their master's attention. They have not been allowed to settle their place in the ranking order, and the keeper has not established his preeminent dominance either.   Often these dogs are kept confined or isolated, they are not well socialized, they may have been neglected in one way or another, they may have been removed from the mother/pack too early, they may not have had any supervision (or the wrong kind), or they may have had improper upbringing, care or training.

If you are the primary caretaker of two such dogs, you have several choices:

a) Give one away - that is the easy way out

b) Let them fight it out - it will get bloody. They are not going to kill each other, but you may not want to risk the injuries.

c) Rehabilitation. There are seven equally important parts to it, and they must be done in sequence:

1. Dominance: Keep them separate, for the time being. Establish you role as the pack leader.

2. Care: Personally provide physical and mental stimulation (exercise, walks, play, training .....), and personally care for them (feeding, grooming, nail trimming .....). Treat them alike, one at a time.

3. Socialization: ONE AT A TIME, socialize them. Take them with you whenever possible, meeting strange people, dogs, places. Keep them on a leash. If hostility should ever erupt, act quickly, angry, forcefully.

4. Counterconditioning: Train. Teach "down". Demand instant, unconditional compliance, no matter what the distractions are. Enforce it, use meaningful corrections, drastic measures if needed. Practice on and off lead, short and long down (up to 30 minutes !).

5. Conditioning: Solicit volunteers (people, dogs), seek out tempting, unfriendly encounters, then command "down". Make sure that you are in complete control and that nobody gets hurt.

6. Homeland Security: Once steps 1-4 are mastered, let the two dogs meet on neutral territory. Initially you may want to have one handler for each dog and follow the suggestions from above ("Curing Fighters"). Then tolerate minor quarrels. Yell "down" when things escalate. Enforce an instant "down", then calmly say "OK" (release). Watch like a hawk. Scream "down", use drastic measures if they go after each other again.

7. Emergency Procedures
Separating fighting dogs is a risky business - most likely you will get bitten. Refer to "Separating Fighters", above. Never use physical punishment **during** a fight, it will only aggravate the situation.

d) Some moron will undoubtedly suggest castration/neutering, pulling out the teeth, or to "hang" the dog. Ask if you could practice these three options on him, because you want to see which one works best.

"Does your dog like children?"
"Yes he does. But I usually buy him beef, it is cheaper."

B. BOARDING OR TRAVELING ?

If you board your dog, or get a dog sitter, or take the dog along, always make sure that your dog is in good health: veterinary check-up; treatment for parasites if necessary; rabies shots and other indicated vaccinations; cleaning the ears; clipping the toe nails; and grooming and bathing.

BOARDING

Find the best boarding facility available: research, check, visit. Look for:

◆ escape-proof, solid construction, complete enclosures, double fencing

◆ clean concrete floors, and individual, temperature-controlled runs (minimum 3x10 ft.)

◆ a friendly, competent operator who follows established emergency procedures (vet, police, fire...)

◆ opportunities to exercise your dog (play, walks, road work etc.)

A friend's home may provide individual attention but is more risky (non-professional care, escape, risky interaction with other pets).

DOG CHECKING (Pet "Sitting" is a misnomer, they spend only minutes each day with your dog)

An (expensive) alternative to boarding is keeping the dog at home and hiring an attendant, usually a total stranger. Left alone more than 23 hours each day, your dog may devise some kind of (destructive) entertainment, and he may manage to escape searching for you. If you still want to go that route, require at least two 30 min. visits each day, and that the sitter is familiar with your dog, your home and any essential routines.

TRAVEL

A dog will restrict your freedom considerably.
Buy a wide leather collar, keep it on him all the time, and attach license tag, rabies tag and a tag offering a reward (your address, area code and phone number). Make sure that the dog is welcome at the destination and at intermediate stops.
Take along: doggie dishes, food, water, leash, tie-out chain, crate, towel, blanket, medication and grooming supplies.

CAR TRAVEL

Use a wire screen barrier in your car, a trunk lid extension, or a small trailer custom made for the transport of dogs. If you have a well-behaved dog, let him ride in the passenger compartment. The dog must not bother you nor stick his head out of the window. Collisions or eye injuries do happen.
Some dogs may dislike cars, but tranquilizers are not needed. Condition your pet by feeding the regular meal inside the stationary, then the moving car for a few days. Go to exciting places. Do not offer food in between.
During travel, ration food and water somewhat. Come summer, fill a plastic milk jar with water and freeze it - in time it will become a cool drink. Schedule rest stops frequently but keep him on leash. If he runs away, stay on the spot as long as possible. Finding his way back may take days.
For your dog's safety, always park in the shade, turn off the engine, remove the ignition key and engage the brakes. Lock the doors and roll up the windows but leave a gap open.

AIR TRAVEL

Except for Seeing Eye Dogs and toy breeds, dogs must travel in an airline-approved containers in the cargo hold. Make your reservations far in advance. Accustom your dog to the crate beforehand: coax, praise, reward him, take your time.
A large sign on top and side of the crate should read: **LIVE ANIMAL**, showing also the dogs name, your name, address and phone, departure and destination airports. Update it for the return trip. Secure the doggie door to the kennel frame with a plastic tie (police handcuff-type) to prevent tampering and possible escapes facilitated by well-meaning airline personnel.
Before departure let your pet exercise, eliminate, drink a little bit. Do not leave any food with him. They may let you take your dog to the gate, in the crate. Usually, though, you must drop him off as luggage (and that can get lost).

MAKE EVERY EFFORT TO ACTUALLY OBSERVE THE LOADING AND UNLOADING OF YOUR DOG AT BOTH ENDS OF THE TRIP.

Once, porters deliberately tumbled the crate with my dog in it down the stairs. I demanded to see the airport manager, and the apology I got from him in writing was very useful in all of my subsequent journeys.

INTERNATIONAL TRAVEL

Traveling with a dog to Canada or Mexico is a fairly simple matter, if a recent health certificate and a rabies vaccination document can be presented to the border guard. Regulations change, however, so check with a customs office.

For travel to other countries write in advance a letter to their Government Department of Health / Agriculture. Take this correspondence with you. Don't rely on travel agencies, they may have outdated information.

Some countries demand a quarantine which is longer than the average vacation. Other countries require special vaccinations and/or special documents. Upon re-entry, US authorities also insist on certain formalities (vaccinations, proof of ownership etc.). All these conditions can usually be met for a well-kept dog, at some expense, and at some inconvenience. However, usually it is best to leave the dog at home.

C. SCHUTZHUND SPORT IN NORTH AMERICA

EUROPE

The Schutzhund concept evolved in Europe at around 1900. Envisioning a training and testing program for privately owned canines of the working group, dog fanciers wanted to collect information on improving their respective breeds. Early efforts were highly individualistic. Today, though, dog/handler teams throughout the world compete according to the "VDH Trial Regulations" (or slight modifications of it) which offer the SchH A, SchH I, SchH II, SchH III titles, the international Schutzhund titles INT I, INT II, INT III, an advanced tracking degree (FH), a watchdog degree (WH), a traffic-steady companion dog degree (VB) and others.

NORTH AMERICA

In North America, Schutzhund had a late start, because traditionally, dog sport meant conformation and obedience only. Tracking was added later on, and protection training still faces rejection by many. Furthermore:

- Unfavorable publicity and slanted press reports have branded the Schutzhund as a killer dog. Inept and unfit "attack dog trainers" exploited the Schutzhund idea, contributing to the molding of such a false image.
- Pending, or enacted, legislation in many states classifies the Schutzhund as an attack dog.
- Some breeders resist the rigors of this type of test, fearing perhaps they have lost the true "working dog" character in their quest for conformation titles.
- The AKC's negative attitude towards Schutzhund, even today, is endorsed by many loyal AKC exhibitors. Sporadic attempts to promote Schutzhund training during the 1950's and 1960's failed. At that time small, usually two or three man groups worked their dogs individually, independently and often unnoticed by the rest of the world. The Peninsula Police Canine Corps (PPCC) with Gernot Riedel in the San Francisco area was the most prominent club. Henry Friehs' group operated near Los Angeles, Hombach's group near Chicago. Southern Canada was active, and Lauren Myers organized training on the East Coast. All these groups were German Shepherd Dog oriented and supported German SV (Shepherd Club) trial regulations and breed standards.

NSA

In January 1969, Dr. Herbert Preiser founded the "National Schutzhund Association (NSA), the first national Schutzhund organization in the US. In 1970 it was renamed NASA, "North American Schutzhund Association", after other West Coast and Canada based groups had joined. The founding members agreed to train and test their dogs according to the German Dog Sport Model. This organization collapsed in less than a year because of personality conflicts, however three of its leaders continued the mission: Dr. Herbert Preiser, Mr. Alfons Ertelt and Mr. Kurt Marti.

ASCA

Preiser reorganized the club and named it "Affiliated Schutzhund Clubs of America (ASCA)". Under his guidance, and with a team of advisers, ASCA pioneered non-commercial Schutzhund Trainer Schools with European staff members, and published a national periodical "The Schutzhunder". It held the first combined SchH Trial and Breed Survey in the US (June 1970), conducted the first American SchH Judges Apprentice Training Program (1974), and established contacts with the AKC through personal visits at their office in New York City (Oct.1972).

NASA

Ertelt and Marti founded the "North American Working Dog Association (NASA)" in 1971 and severed the umbilical cord to German Schutzhund counterparts in an effort to win the approval of the AKC (which did not pay off). The goal was to become a member of the FCI and thereby gain international recognition of its Schutzhund degrees. The mere existence of the AKC, however, made that impossible.

WDA

Working Dogs of America, Inc. (W D A) was formally established on April 2, 1975 through efforts of Dr. Dietmar Schellenberg, the first licensed, FCI accredited German Schutzhund Judge to reside in North America. It is not accountable to, and not controlled by, professional breeders, trainers, importers, businesses or breed clubs.

To offer world-wide accepted, FCI recognized Schutzhund titles, WDA's strategy was to affiliate with an already recognized Schutzhund organization. This goal was realized in October of 1975, when WDA

Reprint from the catalog of the
12. Weltmeisterschaft der WUSV
(12th World Championship of the WUSV),
honoring the 100th Anniversary of the SV
September 30 - October 3, 1999

100 Jahre SV
1899 - 1999

XXII. WUSV-WELTMEISTERSCHAFT
BAUNATAL/DEUTSCHLAND
VOM 30.SEPTEMBER BIS 3.OKTOBER 1999

United Schutzhund Clubs of America
1975 - 1999

Nearly 25 years ago a group of men led by a cigar smoking visionary, schutzhunder and sports friend named Gernot Riedel, and including such pioneers as Phil Hoelcher, our first Administrator Luke McFarland, and Dr. Schellenberg, met in front of a restaurant near San Francisco, California. From that meeting sprang the United Schutzhund Clubs of America. Feeling a need to form an organization to administer and encourage the sport of Schutzhund in the United States, these men, along with others, put together what started as less than 10 clubs, but has become a way of life in well over 200 local clubs and 11 regions making up USA (United Schutzhund Clubs of America).

In March of 1967, under Editor Mike KcKowan, the first issue of Schutzhund USA was printed. From humble beginnings, this magazine is now sent throughout the world by the thousand. This magazine and the efforts of the teams USA has sent to the WUSV-Weltmeisterschaft have gained international recognition for USA as a top Schutzhund organization as well as a German Shepherd Dog breed club.

From our third place showing in the first WUSV-Weltmeisterschaft, to our eventual achievement of first place on the podium, we have always tried to do the best we can and to be true sport friends and ambassadors of our sport and our chosen breed.

We are extremely proud to be in the WUSV and we wish all the teams the best of luck and much fun in this, the 100th Anniversary of the greatest breed of dog in the history of the world, the German Shepherd Dog!

John Oliver, USA Team Captain
Mike Hamilton, USA President

merged with the German DVG and became "Division America", with Dr. Schellenberg as its Managing Director. In May 1976 this Division was converted to a DVG Landesgruppe, named "Working Dogs of America, DVG Division USA, Canada, Mexico, Member VDH, Member FCI". **The acceptance of WDA as an FCI Member Club was a milestone in the history of the American Schutzhund sport** since for the very first time competitors and their dogs could earn a world-wide recognized FCI Schutzhund title right here in America. Realizing the significance of this development, all ASCA Member Clubs decided unanimously to join WDA. Other groups and individuals did likewise.

WDA incorporated in the State of New York as a not-for-profit organization, and the US Government classified it as an educational institution with tax-exempt status (no other dog sport organization in the US was ever granted such an exclusive recognition). Dr. Schellenberg was elected President and Director for Trials and Judges. WDA's quarterly publication "WDA TRAINER" gained the reputation of the best Schutzhund periodical anywhere in the world.

Lack of organizational, financial and ideological support, repeated breaches of the affiliation contract by the DVG, and finally the DVG's attempt to force new, crippling rules upon WDA, led to an emergency meeting of the seven-member WDA Board of Directors in Detroit (April 1979). There it was decided to sever all ties to the DVG and to seek affiliation with another FCI organization. In March 1980, WDA joined the German BHV - VLDG but during the one year interim period it had lost many individual members and clubs to other organizations, and it never regained its earlier status.

USA

During the summer of 1975, the American Kennel Club declared all Schutzhund activities a violation of its regulations. Member clubs were threatened with expulsion in case of continued involvement in this sport. In response, the German Shepherd Dog Club of America (GSDCA) terminated all its Schutzhund activities (8/1975) and abandoned in the process several formerly sanctioned Schutzhund clubs (they regretted this decision later on, see GSDCA below).

Gernot Riedel and his Peninsula Police Canine Corps (PPCC, San Francisco), a very active and influential SchH club, had received weighty support from the German SV (Shepherd Club) and from the GSDCA. Facing the AKC challenge, Riedel invited interested parties to a meeting. Ten delegates (Flawson, Hansen, Liedtke, McArdle, McFarland, Memming, Schellenberg, Strasser, Stuermer and Tackett) representing 15 Schutzhund clubs and organizations, and many guests, met on November 21, 1975 in Palo Alto, CA. The delegates declined an invitation to join the recently established DVG - FCI Division North America, even though that decision wiped out any hope for international recognition of its SchH degrees. They voted to form instead an independent Schutzhund and Breed Association for German Shepherd Dogs under SV guidance and VDH Trial Regulations. The organization was named "United Schutzhund Clubs of America (USA)", and Luke McFarland was elected its first chairman.

The organization went through a very turbulent growing stage, and its controversial issues were given widespread publicity. Nevertheless, USA has expanded to become the largest Schutzhund organization in the United States with more than 200 local clubs. Dogs of many breeds can participate in USA Schutzhund trials, however participation in international (WUSV) competitions and breed surveys are open to German Shepherd Dogs only. While close contacts to the SV do exist, USA is independent and not affiliated with it or with any other national or international organization.

The USA operate their own judges' program and license the successful graduates. A loose arrangement exists with the SV for recognition of USA-Judges and of titles awarded by them, yet USA Schutzhund titles are not SV degrees, and their international recognition is still in limbo.

GSDCA

Regretting earlier decisions (see USA, above), the GSDCA re-established Schutzhund activities in 1983. The GSDCA / Working Dog Association now has many clubs throughout the United States who operate under the guidance of, and with assistance from, the German SV.

DVG America

Having lost a prime position in the Schutzhund sport in North America through disputes with WDA (see WDA), the DVG re-entered the scene in 1979. At that time, personality conflicts within the leadership of the United Schutzhund Clubs (see USA) led to an expulsion of several key members. They were immediately recruited by the struggling DVG which now operates local Schutzhund Clubs in the US and Canada.

AWDF

The American Working Dog Federation is the other national all-breed organization that was formed in the wake of USA's internal problems. It offers a Schutzhund program besides other dog sport activities, and member clubs are spread throughout North America. Like NASA it strives to become an FCI member, but the mere existence of the AKC makes this a futile endeavor.

NSC

Because of common interests in the sport, the various Schutzhund organizations in North America would benefit from a coordination of their activities. Early documented efforts date back to 1974, when Dr. Schellenberg suggested to form a council ("North American Schutzhund Council (NSC)"). With support from the WDA Board of Directors, the proposal was renewed in 1978, inviting the presidents of NASA, USA and WDA to an organizational meeting in New York City. USA refused to participate, and for the benefit of the movement in general, NASA and WDA agreed to postpone a decision of jointly forming the NSC.   The need for such a body is still apparent, to promote the sport, to present an undistorted image of the Schutzhund dog to the public, to coordinate publicity via the News media, and to deal intelligently and successfully with detrimental Schutzhund legislation.

D. FEDERATION CYNOLOGICQUE INTERNATIONALE (FCI)

The FCI, the World Dog Federation, is an umbrella organization for national dog club associations throughout the world. Its operation could be compared to the United Nations, but the FCI has *real* power.

Founded in 1911 by Germany, Austria, Belgium, France, Netherlands, it represents about 70 countries today. The largest member is the VDH of West Germany with more than 350 000 individuals. Neither Canada nor the USA are FCI affiliated. If they wanted to be represented, it would have to be through their national canine organizations CKC and AKC, respectively. Since the FCI regulates all phases of the dog sport of which Schutzhund is just a small part, no other American organization would qualify for direct membership in the FCI, now or in the foreseeable future.

The FCI has no performance or conformation registry. The FCI has no breed registry or stud book, it does not have judges as such or even member clubs, but it registers kennel names. The *FCI Assembly* is made up of one representative per country regardless of size, each one having one vote. The VDH delegate speaking for 350 000 members has the same rights as the delegate from Monaco representing about 100.

General business is entrusted to a nine-member *Board of Directors*, chaired by a President.

Special committees, including a scientific committee, advance the work in particular areas. Schutzhund affairs are controlled by the Commission for Working Dogs, staffed predominantly by Swiss representatives. FCI titles are: **CACIB** (conformation), **CACIT** (performance), **INT SchH DEGREE I,II,III**. Awarded by local judges and recorded with the national organizations, CACIB and CACIT trials require FCI permission.

Rules for the International Schutzhund Degrees I, II, III are very much like those for the corresponding VDH degrees, and, of course, they are the same for all FCI member countries.

E. AMERICAN SCHUTZHUND ORGANIZATIONS

.*(check the Internet for the latest information on these clubs)*

American Working Dog Federation (AWDF)
4282 Illinois Hwy ,   Alpha, IL 61413

DVG America
17 7543 Gartner Rd. , Evergreen, CO 80439

German Shepherd Dog Club of America /Working Dog Association
732 Lindley Blvd. , DeLand, FL 32724

United Schutzhund Clubs of America (USA)
3810 Paule Ave.,   St. Louis, MO 63125

Working Dogs of America, Inc. (WDA)
3910 Wesley Chapel Rd NE,   Marietta, GA 30062

F. SCHUTZHUND ABBREVIATIONS

Many abbreviations are of German origin since this is the country where the sport originated.

A St.	"A Stempel"	= OFA Certification normal
AD	"Ausdauer Test"	= Endurance Degree
ADRK	"Allgemeiner Deutscher Rottweiler Klub"	= General German Rottweiler Club.
AZG	"AG Zucht-/Gebrauchshundverbaende"	= Affiliation of Breed and Working Dog Organizations.
BVH	"Berliner Verband Hundesportvereine,e.V."	= Berlin Association for Dog Sport Clubs, Inc.
BC	"Boxer Klub"	= Boxer Club.
BLH	"Blindenhund"	= Seeing Eye Dog
BpDH	"Bahnpolizei Diensthund"	= Railroad Police Dog
CACIB	"Certificat d'aptitude au championat conformation, international de beaute"	= Certificate of internat. championship achievement in FCI governed conformation championship trials/titles.
CACIT	"Certificat d'aptitude au championat international de travail"	= Certificate of internat. championship achievement in performance, FCI governed working dog championship trials/titles.
DBC	"Deutscher Bouvier Club v. 1911, e.V.	= German Bouvier Club.
DH	"Diensthund"	= Service Dog (police, railroad police or customs)
DHV	"Deutscher Hundesportverband"	= German Dogsport Ass., founded 5/21/1977, over 70,000 members
DV	"Dobermann Verein"	= Doberman Club.
DVG	"Deutscher Verb.Gebrauchshundsportvereine"	= German Association for Working Dog Sport, founded 1902.
FCI	"Federation Cynologique Internationale"	= Association for Cynology International, founded 1911, 40+ countries.
FH	"Fährtenhund"	= Tracking Dog. Advanced training degree by VDH Trial Rules
G	"Gut"	= good (Show / Performance Rating)
GHK	"Gebrauchshundklasse"	= Utility Dog Class
HGH	"Herdengebrauchshund"	= Herding Dog
IPO	"Internationale Prüfungsordnung"	= International Trial Regulations (SchH)
KFT	"Klub für Terrier"	= Club for Terriers (Airedales are served by this club)
KK 1	"Körklasse 1"	= Breed Survey Degree 1 (excellent)
LH	"Lawinenhund"	= Avalanche Dog
M	"mangelhaft"	= lacking (Show / Performance Rating)
PH	"Polizeihund "	= Police Dog
PSK	"Pinscher-Schnauzer Klub"	= Pinscher-Schnauzer Club (Giant Schnauzers belong to it)
RGH	"Rauschgifthund"	= Narcotics Detection Dog
RH	"Rettungshund"	= Disaster Dog
RZVHH	"Rassezuchtverein für Hovawart-Hunde"	= Breed Club for Hovawart dogs.
SchH	"Schutzhund"	= protection dog.
SG	"Sehr Gut"	= very good (Show / Performance Rating)
SV	"Verein für Deutsche Schäferhunde (SV) e.V."	= Germ.Sheph.Dog Club,founded 1899 by von Stephanitz.
U	"ungenügend"	= insufficient (Show / Performance Rating)
V	"vorzüglich"	= excellent (Show / Performance Rating)
VB	"Verkehrssicherer Begleithund"	= Traffic-Steady Companion Dog
VDH	"Verband für das Deutsche Hundewesen"	= Association for German Dog Affairs, founded 1878, then 1949
VLDG	"Vereinigung der Landesverbände für das Deutsche Gebrauchshundewesen"	= Dog Club Ass.of all regions. Parent Club for Schutzhund and Police Dog Clubs, mainly in Southern Germany.
WH	"Wachhund"	= Watch Dog (degree)
ZB	"Zuchtbuch"	= Stud Book
ZB	"Zuchtbewertung"	= Conformation Show Rating
ZH	"Zollhund"	= Customs Dog

G. RELEASE FORM

To minimize potential problems it is suggested that Schutzhund Clubs and training groups incorporate, that they buy insurance coverage, and that they have all members, participants and guests sign a release form. The form suggested below may require some modification for your group, it may not provide all the legal protection you are seeking, it may not even be recognized by some courts of law. It will prove, however, that a person who signed it understood, and accepted, the risks involved in this sport.

WAIVER, ASSUMPTION OF RISK AND AGREEMENT TO HOLD HARMLESS

I understand that attendance of a dog training program is not without risk to myself, members of my family or guests who may attend, or my dog, because some of the dogs to which I will be exposed, as well as my own dog, may be difficult to control and may be the cause of injury even when handled with the greatest amount of care.

In consideration of, and as inducement to, the acceptance of my application for training, I hereby waive and release

XXXXXXXXX YYYYYYY (the club),

its employees, officers, members and agents from any and all liability of any nature, for injury or damage which I or my dog may suffer, including specifically, but without limitation, any injury or damage resulting from the action of any dog, and I expressly assume the risk of such damage or injury while attending any training session, or any other function, of X.Y., or while on the training grounds or the surrounding area thereto.

I also agree to indemnify and to hold harmless X.Y., its employees, officers, members and agents from any and all claims, or claims by any member of my family, or any other person accompanying me to any training session or function of X.Y., or while on the grounds or the surrounding area thereto, as a result of any action by any dog, including my own. I shall personally assume all responsibilities and liabilities for any loss or injury which may be alleged to have been caused directly or indirectly to any person or thing by the act of my dog while participating in an X.Y. dog training program or while on the training grounds or the surrounding area thereto.

(My dog in the above statements means any dog in my custody upon approaching the training grounds or adjacent areas)

SIGNATURE .... DATE ....

STREET .... CITY .... ZIP ....

H. ILLNESS

We all have seen our club's most consistent worker fail in one way or another on a certain day, in training or in a trial performance. The dog's basic temperament has not changed from one day to the next, but was he ill?

TRACKING can be influenced by respiratory infections, sinus problems, allergies, increased body temperature and certain medications.

OBEDIENCE can be influenced by soft tissue injuries (sprains and bruises), bone injuries, arthritis, ocular defects, ear infections, parasites (internal and external), shoulder, elbow and hip dysplasia, diarrhea, and other medical problems.

PROTECTION work can be influenced by mouth, gum, and teeth problems, fractures of the small bones in the throat where the collar presses, neck injury, ocular defects, ear infections and structural defects.

Dogs can not tell us where it hurts. YOU must make sure that he is in good health before you correct him.

I. FIRST AID

1. Prepare a list of emergency phone numbers and keep it with the First Aid kit.
2. Have a First Aid kit available at all club functions. A list of items it should contain is suggested below.
3. Invite a Red Cross team or a physician to your next club meeting. Ask questions, learn from them.
4. Know the basic First Aid procedures. However, do not do more than necessary until professional help arrives, and call a physician as soon as possible.

POISON IVY
Repeatedly wash exposed area with soap and water.

STINGS / BITES
from snakes, scorpions, black widow spider, brown recluse spider, bees: make victim lie down, tourniquet on limb between wound and heart but don't stop blood stream completely.

FOREIGN MATERIAL IN EYE
Immediately hold eye lid open and wash for at least 15 minutes in a gentle stream of water.

BRUISES
Apply cold compresses.

BITES, CUTS, ABRASIONS
Prevent infections. Cleanse with soap and warm water, then stop bleeding with sterile pad.

HEAVY BLEEDING
Immediately try to stop bleeding by pressing a pad against the wound. Offer(don't force) liquids, like water, coffee, tea.

SPINE, NECK, HEAD INJURIES
Don't move the victim. Call physician immediately.

FRACTURES
Prevent further injuries by applying splints.
Stop bleeding.

DISLOCATIONS
Treat like fractures.

SPRAINS & STRAINS
If necessary treat like fractures. Apply cold compresses.

SHOCK
Has many causes. Make victim lie down, head lower than feet. Keep air passages open.

UNCONSCIOUSNESS
If uncertain, treat like head injuries.

BREATHING STOPPED
Start artificial respiration immediately (manual or mouth-to-mouth), keep air passages open.

FIRST AID KIT SUGGESTIONS

sterile dressing (sealed)	scissors with blunt tips	splints	band aids
(var.)roller,triang.+ adhes. bandages	tourniquet	tweezers	tongue blades
alcohol preparation pads	short stick	flashlight	eye cup, eye pad
burn ointment	ammonia inhalant	safety pins	First Aid instructions
adhesive tape	Anacin (etc.) tablets	large bath towel	CELL PHONE

CAUTION:
If a tourniquet should be required, use only a strong, wide piece of cloth, never any narrow material. Mark the letters "TK" and the time on the victims forehead with crayon, pencil, soot, etc. Do not cover the tourniquet.
Apply the tourniquet just tight enough to stop bleeding. If there is delay in getting to a doctor, cautiously loosen the tourniquet after 20 to 30 minutes. If bleeding has stopped, leave tourniquet loosely in place and keep it under continuous observation.

EMERGENCY TELEPHONE NUMBERS

Physician - day / night .... Ambulance ....

Police Department .... Hospital ....

Fire Department .... Pharmacist ....

J. LOST & FOUND

In the US, more than 15 million dogs are euthanized each year, and quite a few of them are run-aways. Dog thieves, dog nappers, blackmailers, suppliers to animal laboratories contribute to this bleak picture. Don't let your dog become a part of those statistics.

TAKE PRECAUTIONS
No matter how careful you are, your dog may still get away. To prepare for that possibility, you may want to
- teach him to "come when called". When he approaches you on his own free will, you must never connect anything unpleasant with it.
- condition him to a signal (blow a whistle, ring a bell, or bang the metal food bowl before you feed him)
- make sure that your pet is properly vaccinated and wears his tag.
- have a second tag on his collar, with your phone number and the word "REWARD" inscribed.
- have him tattooed with your SS#, fitted with a microchip implant, listed with respective national registries.
- keep a current color photograph and a detailed description of him on file. You will need that to prepare flyers when he wanders off.

USE COMMON SENSE
- While at home, make sure that your dog does not run away.
- Install a 6-foot high, escape-proof fence around your property, one that preferably includes your home. Secure the fence at ground level to prevent digging under it. This is not cheap but well worth the money.
- An "Invisible Fence" will cost you even more money, but it only works for a few dogs some of the time. Just ask the sales people for a reasonable guarantee, like money back if it does not work ALL THE TIME. Stage an irresistible temptation for your dog, then try it out. Even if you could get such a guarantee, you would never be able to collect on it.
- Outside your home, even on your daily walks, use collar and leash. Let him run free at the training field, a fenced-in doggy park, an open field in the country side, etc.
- Letting your dog roam in the neighborhood is, of course, a very bad idea.

SEARCH
- Don't waste any time if he does run away. Try to find him as soon as you are aware of his departure.
- Search the area around your home.
- Check places where he could hide or where he may have been trapped.
- Use the whistle, bell, food pan (see above).
- Enlist the help of others, coordinate efforts, stay in touch with each other via radios or cell phones.
If unsuccessful, repeat the search on the following days.

LET THE WORLD KNOW
- Call or visit friends, neighbors, shops, gas stations, businesses and other public places in your area and tell them about your dog.
- Get about 1000 fliers printed with the photograph and a description of your dog, say when and where he got lost, offer a reward, and include your phone number (not your address). Distribute them to everybody you can think of. Include the mailman, the meter reader, gas station attendants, joggers, hunters, etc. Within a radius of 2 to 5 miles, post fliers on bulletin boards, at intersections, and on posts, poles and trees.
- Newspaper, radio and TV ads are expensive but they might be helpful.
- Personally visit animal shelters, veterinarians, and kennels in your area, on a daily basis. Many municipalities keep stray animals without identification for forty-eight hours only, then they destroy them. Ask to see every animal in holding, do not rely on phone calls. Too many times a pet was euthanized because of mis-understanding or misinformation.

SHOW GRATITUDE
Be grateful to all those who help you to find your dog. A small gift, or a reward, are always appreciated.
Any caller claiming the reward you offered should first describe your dog. If all he has to do is to say "yes" to your description, he will. Meet for the exchange in a public place rather than in your own home, or at least have someone with you at the time. And hand over the reward money only after you have taken possession of your dog.

K. SCHUTZHUNDING

(From a letter by Tony to Billy:)

Billy, good thing it's me telling you this and not some forked-tongue stranger because you're going to be boggled. Grab your Dog Person notebook and pens -, no better make that pencils. You're going to hear stuff you'll swear is from a Monthy Python skid and you'll scribble 'Balderdash' and 'utter nonsense' all over the margins and you'll have to go back and erase because it's all true.

Let me warn you: Schutzhunding is not for the average pick-up-the- poop-every- fortnight-or-so Dog Person. Schutzhunding is to normal dog business like scaling Mount Everest is to stepping up a curb. It requires more bodies than a Michael Jackson tour, and heaps of advanced planning. You just can't wander out some morning and schutzhund. Nosirree. Here's what you'll need in the way of basic equipment:

First, find a large, flat area. A polo field is dandy. If you're going to be schutzhunding soon after the last chuckker, remember the First Rule of Dog Personing and don't step in anything. Polo ponies don't take time out to find a loo. Got the field lined up? Now get a wheelbarrow.

The next items on the list are two small-to-medium storage sheds. One may be a rough lean-to, a shabby structure to provide a minimal shelter, but the other must be of good quality (Sears Roebuck galvanized Urban Estate Model #269 with the mansard roof and Pennsylvania hex sign decals is an excellent choice). You want something weather-tight. Put the two sheds in one corner of the field.

Begin to assemble your team. Schutzhunding is terribly personnel-intensive. Acquire two foreign judges. Schutzhunding judges are always foreign, usually German or from the Netherlands. I've never seen a Pakistani Schutzhund judge. You cannot get by with a southerner in bib overalls, a John Deere cap, and a chow of Redman. I mean a real foreign judge. Besides, a Yank will laugh himself silly when you explain what you're about to do.   Get a clipboard too. I'm not quite sure why this is necessary, but one of the judges (usually the shorter one) has to carry a clipboard.

About a week to ten days before you're ready to schutz, put the two judges and the clipboard in the tackier of the two sheds. You probably should include some saltines, a jug of water and a transistor radio or a concertina. No telling how long they're going to be in there. Don't worry about locking them in; they won't run away. Especially if you remember the concertina. They may frisk and make a gladsome yowlp, but they'll hang around 'til you need them.

This next part's tougher. Go out and locate an aggressor (sometimes called an agitator, instigator, or inciter). In German, the technical name is Der Weirdnutty Domkoffninny. However, in English-speaking climes, the preferred title is the Darned Fool, or simply, the DF.

You're going to waste a lot of time because an experienced Darned Fool isn't going to be schlepping around the mall waiting for you to show up. What you're looking for is a dedicated masochist who has no real reason to live. Go over to the adult bookstore and check out the bunch simpering over the leather manuals. When you spot one wearing a Northwestern Football Booster button, nab him. Oh, and try to get one a bit taller than a glandular Watusi. With a short nose. The London-based Centre for the Study of Statistics and Stuff estimates that there are only twenty-seven perfectly suited DF's in the whole world, so chances are you'll have to settle for less than the ideal.   When you've selected your DF take him out and put him in the shed with the judges. Unlike the judges, you'd be wise to shackle your DF to a post or something. When he finds out what he's let himself in for, he's likely to flee if unrestrained.

Now for the dog. Again, not just any old shambling flea hotel will cut it. Your true schutzhunding dog has a glazed, homicidal stare as if he's been lunching on hashish kibbles, incisors the length of a longshoreman's hook, and the panache of a dum-dum bullet. Got one? Ok, put him in a maximum-security crate with a copy of Winning Through Intimidation. Set so far? You're almost ready. Almost but not quite. Schutzhunding is the ne plus ultra of the fritter-away-a-whole-bunch-of-money dog business.

Get your wheelbarrow. Mortgage your house, borrow on your life insurance, tap the kids' piggy bank, hit uncle Lee for a loan. Take all the money you can lay your hands on and put it in the wheelbarrow. Push the wheelbarrow to the nearest tent and awning shop and start dickering. You're going to wind up with enough canvas to rig the Cutty Sark. You need:

- A really sturdy set of canvas waders. Stout enough to repel a lance or a thunderbolt. Have the salesman stitch three or four extra layers of six-ply canvas over the crotch. That's in case your Schutzhund doggie can't jump very high.
- A canvas sleeve. Don't go for the dinky Little League model. My stars, no. You'll know you've got the right one if it looks like a jai lai mitt for Arnold Schwarzenegger.
- Now - are you ready for this? - buy three single-occupant wigwams. You may call them tepees. In any case, you need three. Think that's odd? Well, this will amaze you: chop them in half, top to bottom, chop them in half. If you've paid careful attention, you will now have six semi-wigwams (or semi-tepees). Count them. If there are five or seven, better start all over.
- Stop by the lumber yard and buy a gross of supple sticks. One-half inch dowels will do nicely.

Put all these supplies in the good shed. This is expensive stuff, so you don't want the weather to damage it. Then wait for a hot, steamy day. Midsummer high noon in Uganda is about right.

We're ready to Schutzhund. Put the little semi-tents around the field with the open sides facing away from the center. Put the judges near one end of the field. Hand one of the judges the clipboard. If he holds it upside down or keeps dropping it, give it to the other one. Leave the DF chained in the shed for now.

Schutzhunding is not pass-fail like a heavy petting session at the drive-in with Shirley Grasorifaikis. Each event is carefully scored (I suspect that accounts for the clipboard). The whole thing is divided into 2 parts.

Part 1 : A sort of warm-up. Ask the dog to do quite a few tricks. Maybe scale a six foot wall, run fifty yards then drop flat in the grass like an Apache scout - the normal, everyday stuff any Rottweiler should know. For each of these tricks give him ten or twenty points. It doesn't make much difference because this is just the prelims, something to get him stoked up for.

Part 2 : This is what schutzhunding is really about. Get the Darned Fool and put him in one of the little tents where the dog can't see him. Stroll casually down the middle of the field with the dog and suddenly point to one of the empty tents. In a clear, authoritative voice, order: "Schutzhund Dog! Go look in that empty tent and tell me what you find!"

A properly trained dog should dash pell-mell to the empty tent, sniff around, wet on the side to mark it, and then race back to you. If he does this, give him 15 points. If you have to go over and piddle for him, give yourself 10 points and the dog a Styrofoam cookie. Do this three or four times.

Now send the dog to the tent with the DF. The DF must stand absolutely still and not even tremble although heaven knows how he can avoid it. I know if I was in a skimpy half of a tent and a hundred-odd pounds of Rottweiler suddenly lurched around the corner with malicious intent, I'd at least quiver.

As soon as the dog sees the DF, he will immediately make an unbelievable racket, leap into the air and clack his jaws a millimeter (or less) from the DF's face. See why the poor devil should be tall with a short nose? You get a squat Darned Fool with an oversize schnoz and it's instant rhinoplasty.

Call the dog. If he comes to you, give him 15 points. If he comes to you bearing vital parts of the DF, say "Bad Dog!", penalize him 3 points, and call it quits for the day.

Peek inside the tent and inspect the DF. If his hair has turned white and he has soiled his canvas waders, give the dog a 10-point bonus.

Go back to the middle of the field. Pet the dog affectionately, telling him he's a wow. This is to distract him while the DF sneaks into another tent.

Order the dog to reconnoiter the tent in which the DF is lurking. This time the DF should wrinkle his nose and wave his stick in a threatening manner and pretend to beat the dog. The properly trained Schutzhund dog will take immediate and insane umbrage at this. The dog should snarl, "You ugly Darned Fool, you. I'm going to shred your arm into itsy-bitsy pieces!" and then should turn the threat into suitable action. Meanwhile, the DF should continue to wave his stick like a maniac orchestra leader. If I were Leonard Bernstein or George Solti, I would not rehearse in the same county as a Schutzhund dog.

Look at the judges. If they are drooling ecstatically, jumping up and down in a frenzy and screaming "Bite! Bite! Bite!" everything is going correctly.

Here it gets tricky and we separate the true schutzhunding dog from a demented carnivore.

When the DF stops waving his stick and stands immobile, the dog should stop biting

and put a goodly distance between himself and the DF's arm and body, reverting to Plan A (with the barking, the leaping and the jaw-clacking). Look at the judges. Do they look disappointed? Then we're on schedule. Call the dog.

At this point the DF is supposed to take off like a turpentined tabby across the field, running just as fast as ever he can in his canvas bloomers (assuming, of course, the dog has left him enough legs to scamper with). If the DF runs all the way to the bus station and hops a Greyhound for Oaxaca, Mexico, give the DF -I points for cowardice, 82 points for smarts, and knock off until you trap a replacement.

What is supposed to happen (and here's where he warrants The Darned Fool appellation) is just when he's getting up a good head of steam, he has to stop, whirl around, and waggle his stick again. Thereupon the dog

Fig.70

will go nuts and try to destroy him.

Walk over, take away the DF's stick, and stroll back to the judges. At this point, the judges will bob their heads, grin, and mark all over the clipboard. Then all of you (except the DF who crawls into an ambulance for a trip to the emergency room) go to the nearest saloon for a celebration drink.

That, nutshelled, is schutzhunding. See you there.

Tony Stockanes, via A.S.A.

"Do you know that your dog barked all night?"
"Yes, but don't worry. He sleeps all day."

K. LIST OF ILLUSTRATIONS

L. BIBLIOGRAPHY

Ames,F.;Manual of Dog Care;Signet 1968
Anderson,B.; Cognitive Psychology; Academic Press 1975
Anochin,P.K.; Physiologische Architektur d.Verhaltensaktes
Barbaresi,S.; German Shepherd; TFH 1957
Barnett,S.A.; Modern Ethology; Oxford Univ. Press 1981
Bartlett,M; Puppy Aptitude Testing/AKC Gazette 3/1979
Barwig/Hilliard; Schutzhund Theory/Methods; Howell 1991
Bechthold,W.; Ausbildung zum Schutzhund; 1982
Beckman,E.; Praise and Reward; Putnam 1979
Benjamin,C.; Dog Problems; Doubleday 1981
Benjamin,C.; Mother Knows Best; Doubleday 1985
Bennett,J.; Command-train your Dog; Spec. 1979
Bergmann,G.; Why does your dog do that; Howell 1971
Bodingbauer,J.; Wesensanalyse; 1973
Born,Moller,Disselhorst;Pferdekunde; Parey 1928
Bosshard,M.; In Freiheit erzogen; 1979
Braund,K.; Obedience Training Manual; Denlingers 1982
Brehm,P.; Schäferhunde;
Brown; Bring Your Nose over here; 1982
Brunner,F.; Der unverstandene Hund; 1961
Bryson, S.; Search Dog Training; Boxwood 1983
Burke,L.; Dog Training; TFH 1976
Burnham,P.G.; Play Training; St.Martin 1980
Burtzik,P.; Dienst- and Gebrauchshunde; Meissner 1967
Burtzik,P.; Erziehung/Ausbildung d.Hundes; Meissner 1965
Busack,W.; Der Deutsche Schäferhund; Falken
Busack,W.; Hundebuch; Falken 1970
Button,L.; Practical Scent; Alpine Publ. 1990
Buytendijk,F.J.; The Mind of the Dog; Aver 1936
Campbell,W.E.; Behavior Problems in Dogs; Am.Vet.
Campbell,W.E.; Owner's Guide Better Behavior in Dogs; 1989
Carras,R.;Pet Book; Holt,Rinehart; Winston 1976
Chance,P.; Learning and Behavior; Wadsworth 1988
Cleveland,R.; Your German Shepherd: Hawthorn 1966
Cree,J.; Training the Alsatian; Merrimack 1978
Cross/Saunders; Dog Care and Training; Greystone 1962
Daniels,J.; Enjoying Dog Agility; Doral Publ. 1991
Davis,H.; New Dog Encyclopedia; Galahad 1970
Davis,W.; Go Find; Howell 1974
Denlinger,M.; German Shepherd; Howell 1961
Dildei,G.; Schutzhund Obedience/Training and Drive; 1992
Dobberstein,Koch; Anatomie d.Haustiere; Hirzel 1953
Dobson,J.A.; 14 Day Method; Winchester 1981
Dunbar,I.; Dog Rehavior; THF 1979
Eden,R.S.; Dog Training Law Enforcement; Detselig Ent. 1985
Eisenmann,C.; Stop,Sit,Think; 1968
Elton,C.; Animal Ecology; Methuen & Co.; 1966
Fatio,A.; Prakt. Handb. Erziehung/Ausbildung des Hundes
Fischel,W.; Seele des Hundes; Parey 1961
Fischel,W.; Tierpsychologie/Hundeforschung; 1941
Fischer,W.; Koennen Tiere denken?; Leipzig, 1970
Foerster,U.; Der Deutsche Schäferhund; 1980
Fox,M.; Understanding Your Dog; Coward,McCann 1972
Fox,M.; Behavior of Wolves/Canids, Harper&Row 1971
Fryer/Henry/Sparks; Gen. Psychology; Barnes & Noble 1954
Fuller,W.;Strength/Aggress.Factors/ Dobermann Temperament
Gibbs,M.; Leader Dogs for the Blind; Denlingers 1982
Goldbecker/Hart; German Shepherd; TFH 1967
Granderath,F.; Hundeabrichtung; 1981
Grewe,J.; Schutzhund Training; Quality Press 1981
Haberhauffe/Albrecht; Schutz/Diensthunde; Neumann 1980
Hacker,A.; Deutscher Schäferhund; Falken 1969
Haggerty/Benjamin; Dog Tricks; Howell 1982
Harmar,H.; Train/Show; David & Charles 1983
Hart, E.; Train your Dog; TFH
Hartmann,W.; Übungsleiter; W-B Dressurverband 1960
Hegendorf/Reetz; Gebrauchshund; Parey 1980
Hilgard/Atkinson; Psychology; Harcourt 1975
Hillgemann,M.; Private Conversations

Hillmann,W.; Train Retrievers; Seattle Pub. 1979
Hirschhorn,H.; Guard Dogs; TFH 1976
Hollinghaas/Capps; Trained Dog; Barnes 1979
Holmes,J.; Training and Care; ARCO 1981
Holmes,J.; The Obedient Dog; David/Charles Publ. 1985
Hulse/Egeth/Deese; Psychology of Learning; McGraw-Hill1980
Humpal,N.; Rassehunde; Landwirtschaftsverlag 1982
Humphrey/Warner; Working Dogs; John Hopkins 1934
Johnson,G.; Tracking Dog; Arner 1975
Johnson,G.; Tracking Trainers Handbook; Arner 1975
Jones,R.; Guard Dog Training; David/Charles Publ.
Kasco,N, Dog Owners Guide; Toledo 1950
Kee,R.; Obedience Champion; Condor 1981
Kenworthy,J.; Dog Training Guide; Pet Library 1969
Kerr,D.; Training your Dog; David & Charles 1978
Kessopulos,G.; Dog Obedience Training; Wilshire 1975
Klever,U.; Dein Hund, das unverstandene Wesen
Klinkenberg,T.; Hundeerziehung ohne Zwang
Klix,F.; Entwicklungsgeschichte menschl Intelligenz; VDW 1980
Knorr/Seupel; Aufz.von Hunden; Landwirtschaftsverlag 1973
Koch-Kostersitz; 400 Ratschläge; Neumann 1973
Koehler,W.; Dog Training; Howell 1962
Koehler,W.; Guard Dog Training; Howell 1973
Koehler,W.; Tracking Dog Training; Howell
Kolb,E.; Verhalten d. Haustiere; Hirzel 1986
Konorski,J.; Journal General Psychology 1968
Kotljarewski,L.; Hoehere Nerventätigkeit (Pavlov); 1954
Kramer,C.L.; Agility Dog Training; Cascade Press
Krech/Crutchfield/Livson; Psychology; Knopf 1969
Lamprecht,J.; Verhalten; Herder 1972
Lembke,B.; Der Polizeihund; Lehrmeister 1972
Levorsen,B.; Mush; Arner 1976
Loeb,J.; Supertraining; PH 1980
Loeb,J.; Complete Dog Training; PB 1977
Lorenz,K.; Vergleichende Verhaltensforschung; 1978
Lorenz,K.; Tierisches/Menschliches Verhalten; 1965
Lorenz,K.; Man Meets Dog; Penguin 1953
Loring,M.; Your Dog and the Law; Alpine Publ.
Luce,G.G.; Biological Rhythms; Dover 1971
Lucky,M.; Trick Training; Denlingers 1981
Luedicke, H.; Polizei/Schutzhunde; Stern 1957
MacInnes/Badyk; Schutzhund Annotated; 1988
MacInnes/Badyk; Through Judges Eyes (Schutzhund); 1988
Maller/Feinman; 21 Days; S&S 1979
McMains,J.M.; Dog Logic, Companion Obed.; Howell 1992
Mech,D.; The Wolf; NHP 1967
Meiners,J; Zucht, Haltung, Ausb. SchH; Reutlingen 1976
Menzel,R.; Hundeausbildung; Falken 1974
Messent,P.; Hunde - Verhalten/Sprache; Piper 1980
Miller,F.; World of Dogs; Chronicle 1972
Mooney,H.J.; How to train your own dog; B&B 1908
Morsell,C.; Win Obedience Titles; Howell 1976
Most,K.; Training Dogs; Popular Dogs 1972
Mueller,M.; Spezialausbildung des SchH; Reutlingen 1980
Mueller,M.; Vom Welpen zum idealen SchH; Reutlingen 1961
Mueller,M.; Der erfolgreiche Hundeführer, Reutlingen 1979
Mueller,M.; Leistungsstarker Fährtenhund; Reutlingen 1982
Muir,J.; Passion for Nature; 1838-1914
Mulvany,M.; Obedience Training; Merrimack 1983
Mundis,J.; Guard Dog; McKay 1970
National Geographic; Man's Best Friend; NGS 1971
New Skete; Dogs Best Friend; Little/Brown 1978
Nicholas,A.; Dog Judging; Howell 1970
Oberlaender,G.; Dressur/Führung d. Gebrauchshundes; 1983
Ochsenbein,U.; Hundeausbildung Dienst-/Rettungshund; 1979
Oese,E.; Pferdesport; Sportverlag 1979
Patterson,G.; Schutzhund Protection Training; Sirius 1989
Patterson,G.; Tracking, From the Beginning; Sirius 1992
Pavlov,I.P.; Conditioned Reflexes, Lectures; 1927

Pawlow,I.P.; Gesammelte Werke; AV 1953/54
Pearsall/Leedham; Dog Obedience Tr.; Scribner 1956
Pearsall/Verbruggen; Scent; Alpine Publ. 1982
Pfaffenberger,C.; Dog Behavior; Howell 1974
Philipp,W.; Das Alpha Tier; Safari
Pickup,M.; German Shepherd Guide; Pet Library 1969
Pinkwater,J/M; Superpuppy; Seabury
Pittendrigh,C.S.;Behavior and Evolution 1958
Pryor,K.; Don't Shoot the Dog; 1984
Radakovic,R.; Psyche of the Dog
Raiser,H.; Der Schutzhund; Parey Verlag 1979
Rapp,J.; Rappid Obedience/Watchdog Training; Denlingers
Reiter,F.; So erzieht man seinen Hund zum Hausgenossen
Research Machines; Psychology Today; Delmar 1970
Rheenen,J.; Hundefreunde Lexikon; Safari 1969
Restle,F.; Learning; McGraw-Hill 1975
Rolfs,K.; Abrichten des Jagdhundes; Landwirtschaftsv. 1982
Rose/Patterson; Training Comp. Working Dog; Giblaut 1985
Rossi,B.; About Dogs; Banner 1973
Sauer,H.; Mensch-Tierbeziehungen, Diss. Giessen
Saunders,B.; Obedience Training Courses; Howell 1976
Schellenberg, D.; Top Working Dogs; 2012
Schmidt/Koch; Grundausbildung Gebr.Hunde; Falken 1993
Schnabel,E.: Unser Hund wird gut erzogen; 1981
Schnabel,E.; Hundekindheit; SV-Zeitung 1977-1979
Schneider,E.; Train your dog; Pet Library 1975
Schoenherr; Erziehung und Ausbildung
Scott/Fuller; Dog Behavior; U of Chicago Press 1965
Scott,T.; Obedience/Security Train. Dogs; Traf.Sq. 1987
Seiferle,E.; Grundlagen/Wesensprüfung
Sessions,B.; Watchdog; TAB 1975
Seupel,I.; Hunde; Landwirtschaftsverlag 1974
Seupel,I.; Rassehunde; Landwirtschaftsverlag 1976

Sinz,R.; Lernen und Gedächtnis; VVG 1980
Sir,J.; Wie richte ich meinen Hund ab; Bauernverlag 1953
Skinner,B.F.; Technology of Teaching; Appleton 1968
v.Stephanitz,H.; Der Deutsche Schaeferhund; Lehrmeister
v.Stephanitz/Foerster; Zuechten, Aufzucht, Haltung DSH
Stern,H.; Bemerkungen ueber Hunde
Strickland,W.; Expert Obedience Training; Macmillan 1970
Strickland,W.; Obedience Class Instruction; Macmillan 1972
Sundberg,N.; Assessment; Prentice Hall 1972
Syrotuck,W.; Scent & Scenting Dog; Arner 1972
Tembrock,G.; Grundr. Verhaltenswissenschaften; Jena 1968
Tembrock,C.; Grundl. Tierpsychologie; Berlin 1971
Thomas; Dogs for Police Service; 1963
Thorne,M.; Handling your dog; Doubleday 1979
Tortora,D.; Schwieriger Hand, was tun? 1979
Trayford/Hall; Puppy and Dog Care; McCall 1970
Trumler,E.; Ratgeber fuer den Hundefreund; Piper 1980
Trumler,E.; Hunde ernst genommen; 1970
Trumler,E.; Mit dem Hund auf Du; 1971
Trumler,E.; Hunde kennen and lieben; 1980
Trumler,E.; Your Dog and You; Seabury 1973
Tuerk,F.; Der Deutsche Schaeferhund; Cosmos 1978
Ullrich,W.; Tiere - recht verstanden; Leipzig 1969
Verband Deutsches Hundewesen; Pruefungsordnung
Vine,L.; Total Dog Book; CBS Publications 1977
Vine,L.; Behavior and Training; ARCO 1977
Volhard/Fisher; Step by Step; Howell 1983
Watson,M.; Basic Dog Training; TFH 1979
Weiss/Rose; Protection Dogs for You/Family; Denlingers 1992
Whitney,L.; Dog Psychology; Howell 1975
Working Dogs of America, Inc.; WDA TRAINER, 1976-1981

I got indoor plumbing !

Epilogue

In our high-tech society, people push the buttons on their iPhone day to night, instead of interacting face-to-face with their fellow men. Pets may be our connection to a more normal life-style, and Schutzhund is definitely one of the more engaging ways to accomplish that.

Some readers might not want to actively participate in our sport. To them I highly recommend to at least watch a Schutzhund trial on the national or international level, of which the WUSV-Weltmeisterschaft in Germany is the ultimate experience. **"TOP WORKING DOGS"** will have prepared you for it.

Dietmar Schellenberg

ABOUT THE AUTHOR

Dietmar Schellenberg, author of "Top Working Dogs", is one of those few individuals who through a life-long love for, and association with, domestic animals have come to really understand and truly communicate with pets, and dogs in particular. As a practicing Animal Behavior Specialist he saw the plight of the working breeds whose owners kept and treated them as overgrown lap dogs. He knew that *Schutzhund* training was the cure, but Americans had never heard of it, and hardly anybody had ever seen it. There were no books to teach it.

"Top Working Dogs, A Training Manual"
was an idea who's time had come.

That Dr. Schellenberg would write it was no coincidence: very few people are equally well qualified to do it, judging by his credentials and by the success the past editions of the book have achieved.

Dr. Schellenberg gathered a wealth of knowledge and experience in canine matters, from various breed and training clubs as well as such prestigious institutions as the German Police Dog Academy and the German Railroad Police Dog School, and through his many associations with cynological authorities. He personally trained and supervised the training of more than twelve thousand dog/handler teams. He is an acclaimed Animal Behavior Specialist, and he designed, built and operated dog training and boarding facilities in New York, Georgia and Alabama. With more than 60 years of experience in the field, he is well known as an internationally licensed Police Dog / Schutzhund Judge, author of the predominant, world-wide recognized training manual for working dogs, editor of a dog training magazine, writer, lecturer, consultant, Canine Specialist for the Technical Advisory Service for Attorneys (US/CANADA), President of Working Dogs of America, Inc., Founding Member and Officer of the North American Schutzhund Association, Inc., and Honorary Member of many Schutzhund Clubs. He is also the President of a large Ballroom Dance Club in Pensacola, Florida, and he has appeared on a variety of radio and TV shows.

Dr. Schellenberg is a native German. An academic teacher and scientist by training, he holds two Pd.D.'s (Nature Science, and Psychology/Education) and several patents in chemistry. His varied interests, aside from canine training, include teaching, writing, graphic arts, men's exquisite jewelry design, ballroom dancing, classical music, sailing, traveling and energy conservation. Other books published by him are

HUMOROUS MAGNIFICUS - SURVIVAL GUIDE FOR PET OWNERS - TAURUS, MOSTLY - BALLROOM DANCING.

NORTH AMERICAN SCHUTZHUND COUNCIL

SCHELLENBERG :   "TOP WORKING DOGS"

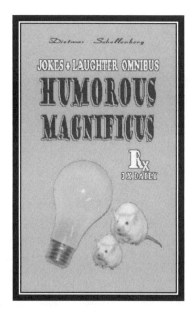